£9.95

D0521905

# Through the
# BIBLE
## EVERY DAY IN ONE YEAR

# Through the
# BIBLE
## EVERY DAY IN ONE YEAR

## SELWYN HUGHES
## TREVOR J. PARTRIDGE

**CWR, Waverley Abbey House, Waverley Lane, Farnham, Surrey GU9 8EP**

## National Distributors

**AUSTRALIA**
Christian Marketing Pty Ltd.,
PO Box 519, Belmont, Victoria 3216
Tel: (052) 413 288

**CANADA**
CMC Distribution Ltd.,
PO Box 7000, Niagara on the Lake,
Ontario LOS 1JO
Tel: 1-800-325-1297

**MALAYSIA**
Salvation Book Centre (M),
23 Jalan SS2/64, Sea Park,
47300 Petaling Jaya, Selangor
Tel: (3) 7766411

**NEW ZEALAND**
Christian Marketing NZ Ltd.,
Private Bag,
Havelock North
Tel: 0508 535659 (toll free)

**NIGERIA**
FBFM (Every Day with Jesus), Prince's Court,
37, Ahmed Onibudo Street, PO Box 70952, Victoria Island
Tel: 01-2617721, 616832

**REPUBLIC OF IRELAND**
Scripture Union,
40 Talbot Street, Dublin 1
Tel: (01) 8363764

**SINGAPORE**
Campus Crusade Asia Ltd.,
315 Outram Road,
06-08 Tan Boon Liat Building, Singapore 169074
Tel: (65) 222 3640

**SOUTH AFRICA**
Struik Christian Books (Pty Ltd)
PO Box 193, Maitland 7405
Cape Town, South Africa
Tel: (021) 551 5900

**U.S.A.**
CMC Distribution, P.O. Box 644,
Lewiston, New York 14092-0644
Tel: 1-800-325-1297

The order of chronology in this book is based on the Chronological Bible edited by Edward Reese.
We are grateful to Robert Backhouse who supplied many of the background articles.
Design: Harold King
Illustrations Vic Mitchell.
Cover photograph: Pictor International - London.
Typeset by Watermark, Norfolk.
Printed in Great Britain by The Bath Press.
ISBN 1-85345-010-3
First Published in 1984 as a bi-monthly six-part work and reprinted 1985, 1986, 1990.
Revised, single volume edition first published 1990. Reprinted 1992, 1993, 1994, 1995 and 1996.

# Introduction

Six inch cracks between bristling brambles. Tracks luring you through quagmire paths to barred gates and *Private: No Entry* placards. Stiles dropping into fields the size of a continent with no other traceable exit. The casual rambler who braves the world beyond the garden quickly discovers the hazards of the countryside.

This, as any boy scout will tell you, is where maps and compasses come into their own. They may not rescue you from the horns of a territory-proud bull, but at least they give you an idea of where you might meet him! And with their help, a whole world of uncharted territory opens up.

What maps and compasses can do for the rambler, this book has been designed to do for the Bible reader. Not that Scripture is littered with hazards, of course, but there are places where we can launch in and find the going hard. Or we lose our bearings and don't understand where events have come from, or in which direction they are going.

*Through the Bible Every Day in One Year* has been written to be a friend and guide through all the pages of Scripture. It is organised so that you can follow the events in the order in which they happened and see the interplay between different Bible books, people and events and the fulfilment of God's promises. It will help you watch the unfolding of God's promises over the centuries and see how all of His Word fits together.

The programme of daily readings is designed not only to bring you face to face with God's Word day by day, but to draw out from it a personal challenge, so that in addition to the new perspective on Scripture, this year will give you a fresh glimpse of God and a new closeness to Him.

We have been privileged and thrilled to see over a hundred thousand people who have already used this course in its previous booklet form. It is now our prayer that many more will find it valuable in this revised, more permanent format.

May the Lord unfold to you throughout every day of this year the wonder of His Word!

**Selwyn Hughes** and **Trevor J. Partridge**

# THE WAY IN

God has spoken. In the Bible He has given us His thoughts in print. In Jesus He has given us His thoughts in flesh. That second Word, the Lord Jesus Christ, saw His entire life and direction predicted and guided by the Old Testament. The Scriptures, He said, were as vital as food and drink for our systems. They offer salvation, guidance and equipping "for every good work".

The comments and background material in this course will help you to understand and apply something from each day's reading in the Scriptures. But space is limited — God will also draw many other things to your attention to grasp and put into practice. To help you in your approach to these, there are some important guidelines to follow:

### Trust it

The Bible was inspired or "breathed out" by God (2 Tim. 3:16). He used the personalities of human writers but so guided their minds that their words were His words too. Treat them as Jesus did: as authoritative and entirely trustworthy. Jesus built His own life and ministry upon God's commands and promises, obeying them even to the cross (Luke 24:27, 45–47).

### Know the author

The Bible's human authors were "borne along" by the Holy Spirit to give us God's Word (2 Peter 1:21). So we need the Holy Spirit to be its interpreter. Knowing God personally as the Lord of our lives and Christ as our Saviour is the essential key to a proper understanding of the Bible.

### See the lasting principle

For most of us daily life is very different from the days of Israel's tent cities in the wilderness; far, too, from life under the Roman Empire. Where these differences exist, look to see the lasting principles below the instruction or event — what do they teach in general about God or about serving Him? Jesus' example and exhortation about footwashing, for instance, ought to lead us to other 20th century forms of service and care for one another (John 13:14).

### See the background

Statements taken out of context can be misleading, to say the least — ask any public figure who is quoted in the press! Aim to understand the meaning and purpose of a passage as a whole. This will put into perspective the point of any verse or phrase within it.

### See the whole picture

The Bible has one author and is a harmonious whole. This means we should interpret individual passages in the light of what we know generally from Scripture and from other sections on the same subject. Some of James' statements, for example, could imply that our works help to save us (James 2:20, 24). The entire force of Scripture contradicts this, however, and shows that this understanding cannot be right (e.g. Eph. 2:8, 9; Rom. 3:23–24). Realising this, a careful rereading of James reveals that he is not answering the question about how we are saved; his message is that genuine faith in Christ must result in good works.

### Live it out

Always remember that your aim in reading the Scriptures is to draw closer to the Lord and live a life that brings praise to Him. Reading the whole sweep of Scripture is stimulating, but God's Word is to be obeyed! As you search God's Word, ask for His Spirit's empowering to put it into practice. Take it in and live it out!

### Value expert help

This year your aim is to read through the Bible — you won't have time to study all of it in detail. Even so, there may be particular passages you will want to dig deeper into, to apply in your own Christian living or to get to grips with difficult issues. Help in understanding harder passages can be found by using a good commentary by scholars who know the Bible and love its author. A further reading section is given at the end for your help.

## Further Reading

**Straightforward**

*The Lion Handbook to the Bible* — David and Pat Alexander (Editors), Lion

*30 Days to Understanding the Bible* — Max E Anders, Kingsway

*Pocket Guide to the Bible* — Cyril Bridgland and Francis Foulkes, IVP

*Uncage the Lion* — Becky Totterdell (Editor), Scripture Union/Spring Harvest

**More detailed**

*New Bible Commentary* — D Guthrie, J A Motyer, A M Stibbs and D J Wiseman (Editors), IVP

*Matthew Henry's Commentary on the Whole Bible* — Matthew Henry, Marshall Pickering

Individual commentaries in *The Bible Speaks Today* and *Tyndale commentary series*, IVP

# GETTING STARTED

As you begin this year of discovering the Bible, you will naturally want to get the very best out of these studies. With that aim in mind, here are our suggestions:

1. Make sure that you have a good translation of the Bible.
2. Find a place and establish a specific time to follow these daily studies.
3. Pray before commencing to seek God's help and guidance as you study His Word.
4. Read the passages through to understand the general meaning.
5. Ponder upon the main truths the Holy Spirit is bringing to your attention.
6. Have a notebook and jot down the main thoughts and how they apply to you. Four helpful words to remember are:

    Observation — what does it say?

    Interpretation — what does it mean?

    Application — how does it apply to me?

    Communication — how can I relate it to others?

7. If you miss a day, don't give up, remind yourself of the 4 d's of achievement — desire, dedication, determination and discipline.
8. After reading, spend a few moments in thanking God for what you have learned and asking Him for strength to put it into practice.

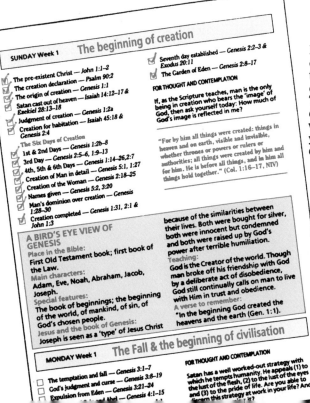

Follow the readings in the order given, working first down the left-hand column, and then down the right-hand column. Tick the box as you complete each section of reading. This will enable you to keep track of your reading and avoid duplication.

# TIME CHART

A specially prepared guide to help you chart your progress in reading 'Through the Bible in One Year'.

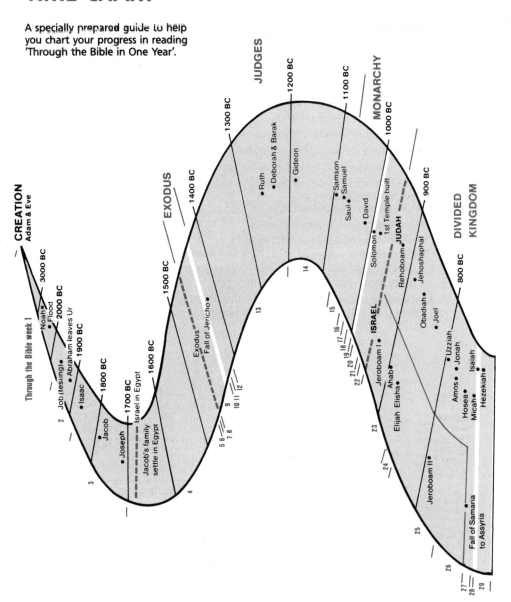

CREATION
Adam & Eve

Through the Bible week 1

3000 BC

Noah
Flood
2000 BC

Job (testing)
Abraham leaves Ur
1900 BC

Isaac

1800 BC

Jacob

Joseph

1700 BC
Israel in Egypt

Jacob's family settle in Egypt

1600 BC

1500 BC

EXODUS

1400 BC

Exodus
Fall of Jericho

1300 BC

JUDGES

Ruth
Deborah & Barak

Gideon

1200 BC

1100 BC

Samson
Saul Samuel

David

MONARCHY

1000 BC

Solomon
1st Temple built

Rehoboam JUDAH
Jeroboam I ISRAEL

Ahab
Elijah Elisha

900 BC

Jehoshaphat
Obadiah
Joel

DIVIDED
KINGDOM

800 BC

Uzziah
Amos Jonah
Hosea Isaiah
Micah
Hezekiah

Jeroboam II

Fall of Samaria
to Assyria

We recognise that the dating of early events depends on Scriptural interpretation.
This time chart is based on the Chronological Bible edited by Edward Reese

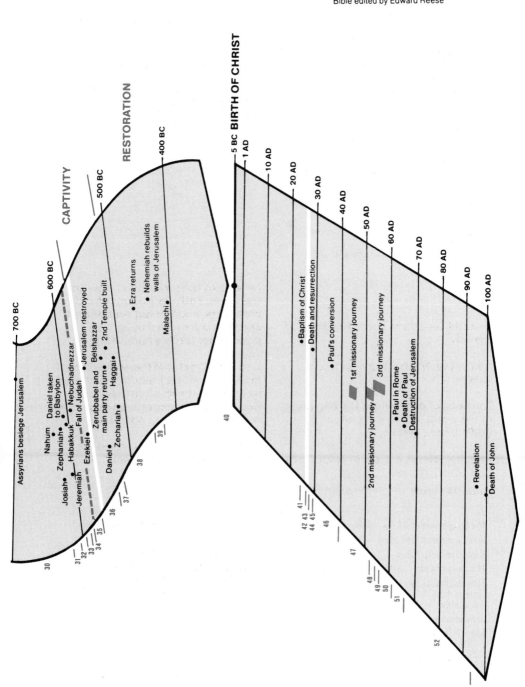

RESTORATION

CAPTIVITY

BIRTH OF CHRIST

700 BC
600 BC
500 BC
400 BC

5 BC
1 AD
10 AD
20 AD
30 AD
40 AD
50 AD
60 AD
70 AD
80 AD
90 AD
100 AD

Assyrians besiege Jerusalem
Nahum
Daniel taken to Babylon
Nebuchadnezzar
Jerusalem restroyed
2nd Temple built
Zerubbabel and main party return
Haggai
Zechariah
Daniel
Ezekiel
Fall of Judah
Habakkuk
Zephaniah
Josiah
Jeremiah
Belshazzar

Ezra returns
Nehemiah rebuilds walls of Jerusalem
Malachi

Baptism of Christ
Death and resurrection
Paul's conversion
1st missionary journey
3rd missionary journey
2nd missionary journey
Paul in Rome
Death of Paul
Destruction of Jerusalem
Revelation
Death of John

30
31
32
33
34
35
36
37
38
39
40
41
42
43
44
45
46
47
48
49
50
51
52

19.01.13

# The beginning of creation

- ☑ The pre-existent Christ — *John 1:1–2*
- ☑ The creation declaration — *Psalm 90:2*
- ☑ The origin of creation — *Genesis 1:1*
- ☑ Satan cast out of heaven — *Isaiah 14:12–17 & Ezekiel 28:13–18*
- ☑ Judgment of creation — *Genesis 1:2a*
- ☑ Creation for habitation — *Isaiah 45:18 & Genesis 2:4*

  The Six Days of Creation
- ☑ 1st & 2nd Days — *Genesis 1:2b–8*
- ☑ 3rd Day — *Genesis 2:5–6, 1:9–13*
- ☑ 4th, 5th & 6th Days — *Genesis 1:14–26,2:7*
- ☑ Creation of Man in detail — *Genesis 5:1, 1:27*
- ☑ Creation of the Woman — *Genesis 2:18–25*
- ☑ Names given — *Genesis 5:2, 3:20*
- ☑ Man's dominion over creation — *Genesis 1:28–30*
- ☑ Creation completed — *Genesis 1:31, 2:1 & John 1:3*

- ☑ Seventh day established — *Genesis 2:2–3 & Exodus 20:11*
- ☑ The Garden of Eden — *Genesis 2:8–17*

FOR THOUGHT AND CONTEMPLATION

If, as the Scripture teaches, man is the only being in creation who bears the 'image' of God, then ask yourself today: How much of God's image is reflected in me?

---

"For by him all things were created: things in heaven and on earth, visible and invisible, whether thrones or powers or rulers or authorities; all things were created by him and for him. He is before all things, and in him all things hold together." (Col. 1:16–17, NIV)

---

## A BIRD'S EYE VIEW OF GENESIS

Place in the Bible:
First Old Testament book; first book of the Law.
Main characters:
Adam, Eve, Noah, Abraham, Jacob, Joseph.
Special features:
The book of beginnings; the beginning of the world, of mankind, of sin, of God's chosen people.
Jesus and the book of Genesis:
Joseph is seen as a 'type' of Jesus Christ

because of the similarities between their lives. Both were bought for silver, both were innocent but condemned and both were raised up by God's power after terrible humiliation.
Teaching:
God is the Creator of the world. Though man broke off his friendship with God by a deliberate act of disobedience, God still continually calls on man to live with Him in trust and obedience.
A verse to remember:
"In the beginning God created the heavens and the earth (Gen. 1:1).

---

MONDAY Week 1 # The Fall & the beginning of civilisation

20. 01. 13

- ☑ The temptation and fall — *Genesis 3:1–7* ✓
- ☑ God's judgment and curse — *Genesis 3:8–19*
- ☑ Expulsion from Eden — *Genesis 3:21–24*
- ☑ The story of Cain and Abel — *Genesis 4:1–15*
- ☑ Seth and his descendants — *1 Chronicles 1:1, Genesis 4:25, 5:3, 4:26, 5:6 & 9, 1 Chronicles 1:2, Genesis 5:12, 15 & 18*
- ☑ Cain and his descendants — *Genesis 4:16–24*
- ☑ Adam's descendants continued — *1 Chronicles 1:3, Genesis 5:21 & 25, 5:4–5, 5:22–24, 5:7–8, 5:28–29, 5:10–11, 5:13–14, 5:16–17, 5:19–20*

20 · 02 · 14

FOR THOUGHT AND CONTEMPLATION

Satan has a well worked-out strategy with which he tempts humanity. He appeals (1) to the lust of the flesh, (2) to the lust of the eyes and (3) to the pride of life. Are you able to discern this strategy at work in your life? And are you overcoming it?

---

"For since death came through a man, the resurrection of the dead comes also through a man." (1 Cor. 15:21, NIV)

*22 · 01 · 13*

# The story of the Flood

☑ Corrupt civilisation — *Genesis 6:1–7, 11–12*
☑ Instructions for building the ark — *Genesis 6:8, 13–21*
☑ Birth of Noah's sons — *Genesis 5:32, 6:9–10, 1 Chronicles 1:4*
☑ Death of Lamech — *Genesis 5:30–31*
☑ Death of Methuselah — *Genesis 5:26–27*
☑ Entering the ark — *Genesis 6:22, 7:1–9*
☑ The Flood: rain falls — *Genesis 7:10–24*
   The Flood approx. 2319 BC
☑ The Flood: rain stops — *Genesis 8:1–19*
☑ God's rainbow covenant — *Genesis 8:20–22, 9:8–17, 9:1–7*

FOR THOUGHT AND CONTEMPLATION

God took Noah into the Flood — *and He also brought him out of it.* Similarly, He has not brought you to this point in your life to abandon you. Whatever the problems you face at this moment — *God will bring you through.*

"For in the days before the flood, people were eating and drinking, marrying and giving in marriage, up to the day Noah entered the ark; and they knew nothing about what would happen until the flood came and took them all away. That is how it will be at the coming of the Son of Man." (Matt. 24:38–39, NIV)

## JOB'S FOUR COMFORTERS

ELIPHAZ
Chs. 4,5,15—22
BILDAD
Chs. 8,18,25
You don't know God 18:21

ZOPHAR
Chs. 11,20
You are deceitful 11:11
ELIHU
Chs. 32—37
You rebel against God 34:37

Their speeches  Their accusations
Their conclusion: "You are suffering because of your sin."
Job's conclusion: "I have heard many things like these; miserable comforters are you all!" 16:2
God's restoration: "After Job had prayed for his friends, the Lord made him prosperous again and gave him twice as much as he had before." 42:10

*23 · 01 · 13*

# From the Flood to the Patriarchs

☑ Noah's descendants — *Genesis 9:18–19, 10:32, 10:1*
☑ Sons of Japheth — *Genesis 10:2–5, 1 Chronicles 1:5–7*
☑ Sons of Ham — *Genesis 10:6–20, 1 Chronicles 1:8–16*
☑ Sons of Shem — *Genesis 10:31, 10:21–23, 1 Chronicles 1:17 & 24, Genesis 11:10*
☑ Noah's vineyard and drunkenness — *Genesis 9:20–21*
☑ Curse of Ham — *Genesis 9:22–27*
☑ Birth of Salah — *Genesis 11:12, 10:24, 1 Chronicles 1:18*
☑ Birth of Eber — *Genesis 11:14*
☑ The history of Joktan & Peleg — *Genesis 10:25, 1 Chronicles 1:19 & 25, Genesis 11:16*

☑ Lineage of Joktan — *Genesis 10:26–30, 1 Chronicles 1:20–23*
☑ Lineage of Peleg — *Genesis 11:18 & 20*
☑ The Tower of Babel — *Genesis 11:1–9*
☑ Noah's descendants continued: Nahor — *1 Chronicles 1:26, Genesis 11:22*
☑ Terah — *Genesis 11:24*
☑ Birth of Terah's sons — *Genesis 11:26*
☑ Death of Peleg — *Genesis 11:19*
☑ Death of Nahor — *Genesis 11:25*
☑ Death of Noah — *Genesis 9:28–29*
   Birth of Abraham approx. 1967BC
☑ Birth of Abraham — *1 Chronicles 1:27*
☑ Birth of Lot, Haran's son — *Genesis 11:27*

Some regard the genealogies here as dull and uninteresting, but it is a lesson in how God pays attention to details. He is concerned not only about the general features of your life, but every detail of it. Remember that the next time you feel God doesn't care.

*24/01/13*

---

## THURSDAY Week 1 ✔ Job's affliction

☑ Early history of Job — *Job 1:1–5*

   Birth of Job approx. 1967 BC

☑ Satan discusses Job's character — *Job 1:6–12*

☑ God gives him permission to test Job — *Job 1:13–2:10*

☑ Job complains to his three friends — *Job 2:11–13, 3:1–26*

   The First Round of Speeches:

☑ Eliphaz reproves Job — *Job 4:1–11*

☑ The vision of Eliphaz — *Job 4:12–21*

☑ The sin of sinners is their ruin — *Job 5:1–7*

☑ God to be regarded with affection — *Job 5:8–16*

☑ The happy result of God's correction — *Job 5:17–27*

☑ Job justifies his complaints — *Job 6:1–7*

☑ He wishes for death — *Job 6:8–13*

☑ Job reproves his friends — *Job 6:14–30*

*25. 01. 13* ✔

Sometimes the greatest thing you can do for a person who is going through a difficult trial is to sit down with them, saying nothing, but show by your actions that you really care. This is usually far better than a round of speeches.

---

"When you pass through the waters, I will be with you; and when you pass through the rivers, they will not sweep over you. When you walk through the fire, you will not be burned; the flames will not set you ablaze. For I am the Lord, your God ..." (Isa. 43:2–3, NIV)

---

## FRIDAY Week 1 ✔ Job's friends

☑ Job's troubles — *Job 7:1–6*

☑ Job expostulates with God and begs release — *Job 7:7–21*

☑ Bildad reproves Job — *Job 8:1–7*

☑ Hypocrites will be destroyed — *Job 8:8–19*

☑ Bildad applies God's just dealing to Job — *Job 8:20–22*

☑ Job acknowledges God's justice — *Job 9:1–13*

☑ He is not able to contend with God — *Job 9:14–21*

☑ Job complains of troubles and hardships — *Job 9:22–35 & 10:1–7*

☑ Job pleads with God as his Maker — *Job 10:8–13*

☑ He complains of God's severity — *Job 10:14–22*

☑ Zophar reproves Job — *Job 11:1–6*

☑ God's perfections and almighty power — *Job 11:7–12*

☑ Zophar assures Job of blessings if he repents — *Job 11:13–20*

☑ Job reproves his friends — *Job 12:1–5*

☑ The wicked often prosper — *Job 12:6–11*

☑ Job recognises the wisdom and power of God — *Job 12:12–25*

It is not sinful or 'unspiritual' to acknowledge one's confusion in the presence of sickness, distress or suffering. *Emotions that are not faced cause trouble.* You don't have to agree with them, but you do have to face them in God's strength.

---

"A man of many companions may come to ruin, but there is a friend who sticks closer than a brother." (Prov. 18:24, NIV)

## A BIRD'S EYE VIEW OF JOB

**Place in the Bible:**
Eighteenth Old Testament book; first book of poetry and wisdom.
**Main characters:**
God, Satan, Job, Eliphaz, Bildad, Zophar, Elihu.
**Special feature:**
Discussion about undeserved suffering.
**Jesus and the book of Job:**
Bildad cries out, "How can a man be righteous before God?" (Job 25:4). The question is answered in Jesus who gave Himself "to be sin for us, so that in him we might become the righteousness of God" (2 Cor. 5:21). Jesus Christ is the Redeemer whom Job trusted to vindicate him (see Job 19:25).
**Teaching:**
No simple solution is given to the problem of suffering. Job's four counsellors receive no thanks from Job or commendation from God for their advice, which was largely faulty and unhelpful. The key comes in the last five chapters of the book, and especially in chapter forty-two. There Job sees God's greatness and that he is not to question but to trust and accept the perfect will of his Lord.
**A verse to remember:**
"I know that my Redeemer lives, and that in the end he will stand upon the earth" (Job 19:25).

---

## SATURDAY Week 1 — The story of Job continues   26-01-'13

- ☑ Job reproves his friends — *Job 13:1–12*
- ☑ He professes his confidence in God and entreats to know his sins — *Job 13:13–28*
- ☑ Job speaks of man's life and death — *Job 14:1–15*
- ☑ By sin man is subject to corruption — *Job 14:16–22*

The Second Round of Speeches:
- ☑ Eliphaz reproves Job — *Job 15:1–16*
- ☑ The unease of wicked men — *Job 15:17–35*
- ☑ Job reproves his friends — *Job 16:1–5*
- ☑ He represents his case as deplorable and maintains his innocence — *Job 16:6–22*
- ☑ Job appeals to God — *Job 17:1–9*
- ☑ His hope is in death — *Job 17:10–16*

- ☑ Bildad reproves Job — *Job 18:1–4*
- ☑ Ruin awaits the wicked — *Job 18:5–10*
- ☑ The ruin of the wicked — *Job 18:11–21*

FOR THOUGHT AND CONTEMPLATION

Many in today's Church follow the pattern of Job's counsellors — giving advice before making sure they understand the problem. Never try to win a person to your point of view until you are sure you understand theirs.

"A man finds joy in giving an apt reply — and how good is a timely word!" (Prov. 15:23, NIV)

---

## SUNDAY Week 2 — Job stands accused

- ☐ Job complains of unkind treatment — *Job 19:1–7*
- ☐ God was the author of his afflictions — *Job 19:8–22*
- ☐ Job's belief in the resurrection — *Job 19:23–29*
- ☐ Zophar speaks of the short-lived joy of the wicked — *Job 20:1–9*
- ☐ The ruin and the portion of the wicked — *Job 20:10–29*
- ☐ Job entreats attention — *Job 21:1–6*
- ☐ The prosperity of the wicked — *Job 21:7–16*
- ☐ The dealings of God's providence — *Job 21:17–26*
- ☐ The judgment of the wicked — *Job 21:27–34*

The Third Round of Speeches:
- ☐ Eliphaz shows that man's goodness does not profit God — *Job 22:1–4*
- ☐ Job accused of oppression — *Job 22:5–14*
- ☐ The world before the flood — *Job 22:15–20*

- ☐ Eliphaz exhorts Job to repentance — *Job 22:21–30*
- ☐ Job complains that God has withdrawn — *Job 23:1–7*
- ☐ He asserts his own integrity — *Job 23:8–12*
- ☐ The divine terrors — *Job 23:13–17*

FOR THOUGHT AND CONTEMPLATION

Life makes sense only when we learn to see it from God's point of view. This is what turned the tide for Job, and this is what will turn the tide for you. Is life unfair to you? Then look at it from God's perspective. Now what do you see?

"... keeping a clear conscience, so that those who speak maliciously against your good behaviour in Christ may be ashamed of their slander." (1 Pet. 3:16, NIV)

## MONDAY Week 2 — Job defends himself

- Wickedness often unpunished — *Job 24:1–12*
- The wicked shun the light — *Job 24:13–17*
- Judgments for the wicked — *Job 24:18–25*
- Bildad shows that man cannot be justified before God — *Job Ch. 25*
- Job reproves Bildad — *Job 26:1–4*
- Job acknowledges the power of God — *Job 26:5–14*
- Job protests his sincerity — *Job 27:1–6*
- The hypocrite is without hope — *Job 27:7–10*
- The miserable end of the wicked — *Job 27:11–23*
- Concerning worldly wealth — *Job 28:1–11*
- Wisdom is of inestimable value — *Job 28:12–19*
- Wisdom is the gift of God — *Job 28:20–28*
- Job's former comforts — *Job 29:1–6*

- The honour paid to Job: his usefulness — *Job 29:7–17*
- His prospect of prosperity — *Job 29:18–25*
- Job's honour is turned into contempt — *Job 30:1–14*
- Job a burden to himself — *Job 30:15–31*

FOR THOUGHT AND CONTEMPLATION

**Why do bad things happen to good people? If you have often pondered that problem you are not alone. There is only one answer: God allows bad things to happen to His people only if He sees a way of turning the bad into a greater good.**

"… For God is greater than our hearts, and he knows everything." (1 Jn. 3:20, NIV)

## TUESDAY Week 2 — Elihu's perspective

- Job declares his uprightness, integrity and mercy — *Job 31:1–23*
- Job not guilty of covetousness, idolatry or hypocrisy — *Job 31:24–40*
- Elihu is displeased at the dispute — *Job 32:1–5*
- He reproves Job and his friends — *Job 32:6–14*
- He speaks without partiality — *Job 32:15–22*
- Elihu offers to reason with Job and entreats his attention — *Job Ch. 33*
- Elihu accuses Job of charging God with injustice and reproves him — *Job Ch. 34*
- Elihu speaks of man's conduct and reproves Job's impatience — *Job Ch. 35*
- Elihu desires Job's attention and counsels him — *Job Ch. 36*

FOR THOUGHT AND CONTEMPLATION

**The best time to learn the art of navigation is not when you are *in* a storm, but *prior* to it. How would you cope with a Job-sized problem? Have you a strategy for dealing with issues *before* they arise? If not perhaps now is the time to start working on it.**

"Blessed are you when people insult you, persecute you and falsely say all kinds of evil against you because of me." (Matt. 5:11)

## WEDNESDAY Week 2 — God answers Job

- Elihu observes the power of God — *Job 37:1–13*
- Job required to explain the works of nature — *Job 37:14–20*
- God is great, and is to be feared — *Job 37:21–24*
- Discourse with Jehovah: God calls upon Job to answer — *Job 38:1–3*
- God questions Job — *Job 38:4–41*

- God inquires of Job concerning several birds and animals — *Job Ch. 39*
- Job humbles himself before God — *Job 40:1–5*
- The Lord reasons with Job — *Job 40:6–14*
- God's power shown — *Job 40:15–24 & Ch. 41*
- Discourse with Jehovah continued: Job humbly submits to God — *Job 42:1–6*
- He intercedes for his friends — *Job 42:7–10a*
- His renewed prosperity — *Job 42:10b–15*

God often deals with our problems and difficulties, not by removing them, but by giving us a greater vision of Himself. This may not remove the irritating circumstances, but it deepens our conviction that God knows what He is doing.

"'For my thoughts are not your thoughts, neither are your ways my ways,' declares the Lord." (Isa. 55:8, NIV)

## THURSDAY Week 2 — God calls Abram

- [✓] Death of Reu — *Genesis 11:21*
- [✓] Marriage to Sarai — *Genesis 11:29–30*
- [✓] Death of Serug — *Genesis 11:23*
- [✓] Death of Haran — *Genesis 11:28*
- [✓] Travels from Ur to Haran — *Genesis 12:1–3, 11:31*
- [✓] Chedorlaomer in power — *Genesis 14:1–4*
- [✓] Death of Terah — *Genesis 11:32*
- [✓] On to Canaan — *Genesis 12:4–9*
- [ ] Trip to Egypt: journeys — *Genesis 12:10*
- [✓] Lies about wife — *Genesis 12:11–20*
- [✓] Abram leaves Egypt wealthy — *Genesis 13:1–2*
- [✓] Arrives back in Bethel — *Genesis 13:3–4*
- [✓] Abram and Lot separate — *Genesis 13:5–13*
- [✓] Covenant renewed — *Genesis 13:14–17*
- [✓] Abram goes to Hebron — *Genesis 13:18*

FOR THOUGHT AND CONTEMPLATION

The life of faith, though intriguing and exciting, is never without its periods of testing. Are you in such a period at this moment? Then take heart — God tests in order to entrust.

"By faith Abraham, when called to go to a place ... obeyed ..." (Heb. 11.8, NIV)

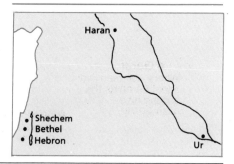

## FRIDAY Week 2 — The Abrahamic covenant

- [✓] Lot taken captive — *Genesis 14:5–13*
- [✓] Abram delivers Lot — *Genesis 14:14–16*
- [✓] Abram with the king of Sodom — *Genesis 14:17, 21–24*
- [✓] Abram with Melchizedek — *Genesis 14:18–20*
- [✓] God's covenant with Abram — *Genesis 15:1–21*
- [✓] Ishmael — Sarai gives Hagar to Abram — *Genesis 16:1–14*
- [✓] Birth of Ishmael — *Genesis 16:15–16*
- [✓] Death of Arphaxad — *Genesis 11:13*
- [✓] Abram becomes Abraham — *Genesis 17:1–8*
- [✓] Circumcision a sign — *Genesis 17:9–14*
- [✓] Son promised and Sarai becomes Sarah — *Genesis 17:15–19*
- [✓] Ishmael's destiny foretold — *Genesis 17:20–27*

FOR THOUGHT AND CONTEMPLATION

When God wants to turn a situation from despair to delight, all He has to do is breathe into it. The aspirate (the letter 'h') is inserted in Abram's and Sarai's names, thus indicating that the breath of God was at work. He does the same with the word 'impossible'. He breathes into it and it becomes 'Him-possible".

"For this reason Christ is the mediator of a new covenant, that those who are called may receive the promised eternal inheritance — now that he has died as a ransom to set them free from the sins committed under the first covenant." (Heb. 9:15, NIV)

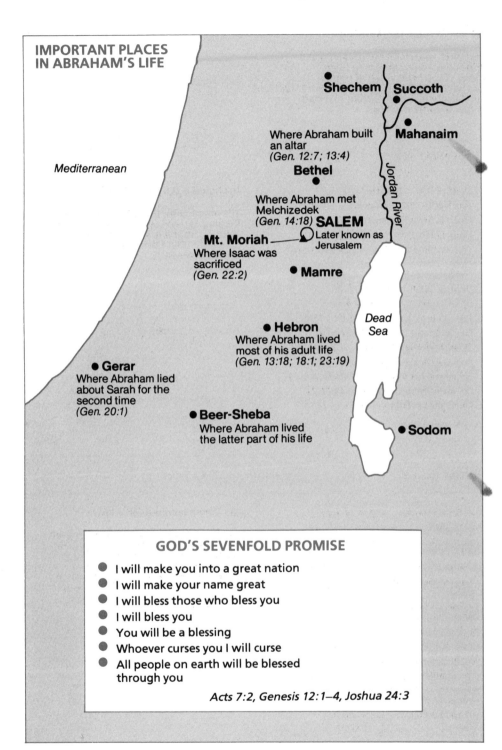

# IMPORTANT PLACES IN ABRAHAM'S LIFE

**Shechem**

**Succoth**

**Mahanaim**

Where Abraham built an altar
*(Gen. 12:7; 13:4)*

**Bethel**

*Mediterranean*

*Jordan River*

Where Abraham met Melchizedek
*(Gen. 14:18)* **SALEM**

Later known as Jerusalem

**Mt. Moriah**

Where Isaac was sacrificed
*(Gen. 22:2)*

**Mamre**

*Dead Sea*

**Hebron**

Where Abraham lived most of his adult life
*(Gen. 13:18; 18:1; 23:19)*

**Gerar**

Where Abraham lied about Sarah for the second time
*(Gen. 20:1)*

**Beer-Sheba**

Where Abraham lived the latter part of his life

**Sodom**

## GOD'S SEVENFOLD PROMISE

- I will make you into a great nation
- I will make your name great
- I will bless those who bless you
- I will bless you
- You will be a blessing
- Whoever curses you I will curse
- All people on earth will be blessed through you

*Acts 7:2, Genesis 12:1–4, Joshua 24:3*

## SATURDAY Week 2    The birth of a nation

- ☑ The Lord appears to Abraham and Sarah is promised a son — *Genesis 18:1–10*
- ☑ Sarah's unbelief reproved — *Genesis 18:11–15*
- ☑ God reveals to Abraham the impending destruction of Sodom — *Genesis 18:16–22*
- ☑ Abraham's intercession for Sodom — *Genesis 18:23–33*
- ☑ Angels warn Lot — *Genesis 19:1–23*
- ☑ Dead Sea formed — *Genesis 19:24–29*
- ☐ Abraham's later years: lies to Abimelech — *Genesis 20:1–18*
- ☑ Birth of Isaac — *Genesis 21:1–7, 1 Chronicles 1:34*

FOR THOUGHT AND CONTEMPLATION

How do God's true servants react in times of emergency or great crisis? They react, as did Abraham, by turning to God in fervent, believing prayer. Life's best outlook is a prayerful uplook!

"This is the assurance we have in approaching God: that if we ask anything according to his will, he hears us. And if we know that he hears us — whatever we ask — we know that we have what we asked of him." (1 Jn. 5:14–15, NIV)

## SUNDAY Week 3    Incidents in Abraham's life

- ☑ Lot's daughters give birth to sons — *Genesis 19:30–38*
- ☑ Conflict of Isaac and Ishmael — *Genesis 21:8–13*
- ☑ Hagar and Ishmael cast out — *Genesis 21:14–21*
- ☑ Death of Salah — *Genesis 11:15*
- ☑ Ishmael's children — *Genesis 25:12–16, 1 Chronicles 1:29–31*
- ☑ Abimelech's covenant with Abraham — *Genesis 21:22–34*
- ☐ Abraham's sacrifice of Isaac — *Genesis 22:1–19*
- ☐ Abraham learns of Nahor's family — *Genesis 22:20–24*
- ☑ Death of Sarah — *Genesis 23:1–20*

Death of Job — *Job 42:16–17*

FOR THOUGHT AND CONTEMPLATION

Faith never quibbles at God's demands, even though those demands sometimes go against reason. But what is faith? No greater definition of faith has ever been given than that contained in the simple acrostic:

**Forsaking All I Trust Him**

"Now faith is being sure of what we hope for and certain of what we do not see." (Heb. 11:1, NIV)

## MONDAY Week 3    The death of Abraham

- ☐ Isaac marries Rebekah — *Genesis 24:1–67, 25:20*
- ☐ Abraham's marriage to Keturah — *Genesis 25:1*
- ☐ Abraham's children — *Genesis 25:2–4, 1 Chronicles 1:32–33*
- ☐ Death of Shem — *Genesis 11:11*
- ☐ Birth of Esau and Jacob — *Genesis 25:19, 21–26*
- ☐ Isaac heir of all things — *Genesis 25:5–6*
- ☐ Death of Abraham — *Genesis 25:7–10*
- ☐ Abraham's survivors — 1 Chronicles 1:28, Genesis 25:11

- ☐ Death of Eber — *Genesis 11:17*

FOR THOUGHT AND CONTEMPLATION

No matter how effective and important a man may be, his time and work on this earth are limited. How gratifying, therefore, to know that though God buries His workman, He always carries on His work.

"… before Abraham was born, I am!" (Jn. 8:58, NIV)

# Incidents in Isaac's life

- Sale of birthright — *Genesis 25:27–34*
- Esau marries two Canaanite women — *Genesis 26:34–35*
- Death of Ishmael — *Genesis 25:17–18*
- Famine and covenant renewal — *Genesis 26:1–5*
- Isaac lies about Rebekah — *Genesis 26:6–10*
- Isaac's success at Gerar — *Genesis 26:11–16*
- Isaac the well-digger — *Genesis 26:17–22*
- Isaac makes altar at Beersheba — *Genesis 26:23–25*
- Isaac's truce with Abimelech — *Genesis 26:26–33*
- Jacob obtains Esau's blessing — *Genesis 27:1–46*

## FOR THOUGHT AND CONTEMPLATION

When we lean upon our own reason rather than on God's clear commands, we run counter to the design of the universe. The theory that the end justifies the means may be part of man's order, but it is not part of the eternal scheme.

---

"Trust in the Lord with all your heart and lean not on your own understanding; in all your ways acknowledge him, and he will make your paths straight." (Prov. 3:5–6, NIV)

---

## IMPORTANT PLACES IN THE LIVES OF JACOB, ISAAC AND JOSEPH

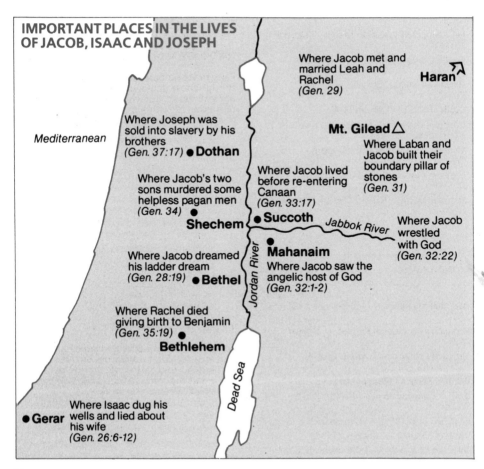

Where Jacob met and married Leah and Rachel *(Gen. 29)*

Haran

Mediterranean

Where Joseph was sold into slavery by his brothers *(Gen. 37:17)* ● **Dothan**

**Mt. Gilead** △

Where Laban and Jacob built their boundary pillar of stones *(Gen. 31)*

Where Jacob lived before re-entering Canaan *(Gen. 33:17)*

Where Jacob's two sons murdered some helpless pagan men *(Gen. 34)* ●

**Shechem**

● **Succoth**

*Jabbok River*

Where Jacob wrestled with God *(Gen. 32:22)*

●
**Mahanaim**
Where Jacob saw the angelic host of God *(Gen. 32:1-2)*

Where Jacob dreamed his ladder dream *(Gen. 28:19)* ● **Bethel**

*Jordan River*

Where Rachel died giving birth to Benjamin *(Gen. 35:19)* ●

**Bethlehem**

*Dead Sea*

● **Gerar** Where Isaac dug his wells and lied about his wife *(Gen. 26:6-12)*

## Jacob's history

- Jacob sent to Laban's house — *Genesis 28:1–5*
- Dream at Bethel — *Genesis 28:10–22*
- Arrives in Haran — *Genesis 29:1–14*
- Works seven years for Rachel — *Genesis 29:15–20*
- Marriage to Leah then to Rachel — *Genesis 29:21–31*
- Twelve children born while working for Rachel — *Genesis 29:32–34, 30:1–6, 29:35, 30:9, 7–8, 10–11, 14–18, 12–13, 19–20, 22–24 & 21*
- Jacob's closing days with Laban — *Genesis 30:25–43, 31:1–16*

**FOR THOUGHT AND CONTEMPLATION**

Have your heard of the 'Laban Principle'? It says that those who scheme to have their own way, as opposed to God's way, often have a head-on collision with someone who is their equal as a schemer.

"The heart is deceitful above all things and beyond cure. Who can understand it?" (Jer. 17:9, NIV)

---

## Esau's history

- Esau marries Mahalath — *Genesis 28:6–9*
- Esau's marriages and descendants — *Genesis 36:1–30, 1 Chronicles 1:35–42*
- Kings of Edom: Bela, first king — *Genesis 36:31–33, 1 Chronicles 1:43–44*
- Other kings — *Genesis 36:34–39, 1 Chronicles 1:45–50*
- Dukes of Edom — *Genesis 36:40–43, 1 Chronicles 1:51–54*
- Departure from Laban — *Genesis 31:17–32*

**FOR THOUGHT AND CONTEMPLATION**

God often accomplishes His purposes with us despite our waywardness and stubbornness. But how much grief we would spare ourselves if we would learn to wait on God, and follow His bidding to the letter.

"The Lord delights in the way of the man whose steps he has made firm" (Psa. 37:23, NIV)

---

## Jacob changes name

- Departure from Laban continued — *Genesis 31:33–55*
- Jacob's apprehension before his reunion with Esau — *Genesis 32:1–23*
- Jacob wrestles with angel — *Genesis 32:24–32*
- Jacob's name changed — *Genesis 35:10*
- Jacob meets Esau — *Genesis 33:1–16*
- Jacob's return to Shechem — *Genesis 33:17–20*
- Dinah's defilement — *Genesis 34:1–12*

**FOR THOUGHT AND CONTEMPLATION**

Have you ever stopped everything and said this one thing to God—your name? What is your name? Ego? Fear? Resentment? Self-pity? A new name doesn't come until we say the old one. In other words, confession is catharsis.

"… I will also write on him my new name." (Rev. 3:12, NIV). "… rejoice that your names are written in heaven." (Lk. 10:20, NIV)

## SATURDAY Week 3 — The selling of Joseph

- Jacob's sons take revenge — *Genesis 34:13–31*
- Jacob's return to Bethel — *Genesis 35:1–9, 11–15*
- Death of Rachel at Benjamin's birth — *Genesis 35:16–19, 48:7, 35:20–22*
- Jacob's return to Hebron — *Genesis 35:27, 37:1*
- Joseph's early days and dreams — *Genesis 37:2–11*
- His brother's conspiracy — *Genesis 37:12–35*
- Sold into Egypt — *Genesis 37:36, 39:1*
- Judah's three sons — *Genesis 38:1–5, 1 Chronicles 2:3*

**FOR THOUGHT AND CONTEMPLATION**

Some use unpleasant situations and difficulties as an excuse for becoming bitter and hostile. But God intends that life's trials should make us better — not bitter. How are you reacting to what is happening in your life at the moment — with despair or delight?

"… If God is for us, who can be against us?" (Rom. 8:31, NIV)

## SUNDAY Week 4 — The ascent of Joseph

- Joseph's early days in Egypt — *Genesis 39:2–6*
- Joseph flees from committing adultery — *Genesis 39:7–19*
- Joseph put in jail — *Genesis 39:20–23*
- Sons of Levi — *Exodus 6:16, Numbers 3:17, 1 Chronicles 6:1 & 16*
- Joseph interprets dreams — *Genesis 40:1–23*
- Death of Isaac — *Genesis 35:28–29*
- Joseph interprets Pharaoh's dream — *Genesis 41:1–37*
- Joseph made governor of Egypt — *Genesis 41:38–44*

**FOR THOUGHT AND CONTEMPLATION**

God has a marvellous and brilliant way of camouflaging opportunities to look like difficulties. Hundreds of Bible characters, including Joseph, discovered this. Have you?

"But God chose the foolish things of the world to shame the wise; God chose the weak things of the world to shame the strong." (1 Cor. 1:27, NIV)

## MONDAY Week 4 — God reunites a family

- Joseph marries Asenath — *Genesis 41:45*
- The seven years of plenty — *Genesis 41:46–49*
- Joseph's sons born — *Genesis 41:50–52*
- Seven years of plenty ended — *Genesis 41:53*
- Judah and Tamar — *Genesis 38:6–26*
- The seven years of famine — *Genesis 41:54–57*
- Birth of Pharez and Zarah — *Genesis 38:27–30, 1 Chronicles 2:4*
- Joseph reunited with his brothers — *Genesis Ch. 42, 43:1–14*

**FOR THOUGHT AND CONTEMPLATION**

We must be careful not to interpret the days of obscurity and isolation as meaningless and unimportant. It is there that God prepares His servants for the spiritual challenges that lie ahead.

"… being confident of this, that he who began a good work in you will carry it on to completion until the day of Christ Jesus." (Phil. 1:6, NIV)

# Provision instead of famine

☑ Joseph reunited with his brothers — *Genesis 43:15–34, & Ch. 44*

☑ Joseph reveals himself to his brothers — *Genesis 45:1–15*

☑ Jacob hears news — *Genesis 45:16–28*

☑ Jacob goes to Egypt — *Genesis 46:1–7 & 28*

☑ Summary of those who went to Egypt — *Genesis 46:8–27, Exodus 1:1–5*

☑ Joseph's family settle in Egypt — *Genesis 46:29–34, 47:1–12*

☑ His wise leadership continues — *Genesis 47:13–26*

☑ Jacob's last days — *Genesis 47:28–31*

☑ Jacob's blessing — *Genesis 48:1–6, 8–22*

FOR THOUGHT AND CONTEMPLATION

Few people can be rejected, insulted, slandered and vilified without carrying a grudge and harbouring hatred in their hearts — but it's possible. Joseph did it. Jesus did it. And, in God's strength, so can you.

---

"For if you forgive men when they sin against you, your heavenly Father will also forgive you." (Matt. 6:14, NIV)

---

# A faithful Patriarch

☑ Jacob speaks to his twelve sons — *Genesis 49:1–32*

☑ Death of Jacob — *Genesis 49:33*

☑ Burial of Jacob — *Genesis 50:1–14*

☑ Joseph reassures his brothers — *Genesis 50:15–21*

☑ Birth of Hezron — *Ruth 4:18, 1 Chronicles 2:5*

☑ Zerah's descendants — *1 Chronicles 2:6–8*

☑ Joseph's latter days — *Genesis 50:22–23*

☑ Joseph's last words — *Genesis 50:24–25*

☑ Death of Joseph and his brothers — *Genesis 50:26, Exodus 1:6*

FOR THOUGHT AND CONTEMPLATION

God does not promise us a life free from difficulties or dangers. He does, however, promise us that, in all situations and problems, His wisdom will be at work to turn the dross into purest gold.

---

"These have come so that your faith — of greater worth than gold, which perishes even though refined by fire — may be proved genuine and may result in praise, glory and honour when Jesus Christ is revealed." (1 Pet. 1:7, NIV)

---

## A BIRD'S EYE VIEW OF EXODUS

**Place in the Bible:**
Second Old Testament book; second book of the Law:

**Main character:**
Moses.

**Special features:**
The account of the deliverance from Egypt, the Plagues, the Passover, the Exodus, and the giving of the Law.

**Jesus and the book of Exodus:**
The New Testament draws out the many ways in which people as well as events in Exodus teach us about Christ: for example, Aaron the High Priest (Jesus Christ is "our great high priest", Heb. 4:14); the Passover (Jesus Christ is the killed passover lamb, 1 Cor. 5:7).

**Teaching:**
Exodus teaches that God is the God who in His love delivers His people from oppression. The day of the Exodus is the symbol and illustration of this truth.

**A verse to remember:**
"Now if you obey me fully and keep my covenant, then out of all nations you will be my treasured possession" (Exod. 19:5).

**The birth and commission of Moses**

- [ ] Population of Israel grows — *Genesis 47:27, Exodus 1:7*
- [x] Egypt's bondage and oppression — *Exodus 1:8–14*
- [x] Moses' early days — *Numbers 26:59, Exodus 6:20*
- [x] Death of Israel's baby boys decreed — *Exodus 1:15–22*
- [x] Birth of Aaron — *1 Chronicles 23:13*
- [x] Birth of Moses — *Exodus 2:1–9*
- [x] Moses' childhood — *Exodus 2:10*
- [x] Aaron's family — *Exodus 6:23, Numbers 26:60, 1 Chronicles 6:49*
- [x] Moses slays Egyptian — *Exodus 2:11–15*
- [x] God hears Israel's groanings — *Exodus 2:23–25*
- [x] Moses flees to Midian — *Exodus 2:16–20*
- [ ] Moses marries Zipporah — *Exodus 2:21–22*
- [x] Moses' sons — *1 Chronicles 23:14–15*
- [x] Birth of Phinehas — *Exodus 6:25*
- [x] Moses receives his commission — *Exodus Ch. 3*
- [x] Moses' objections — *Exodus 4:1–13*
- [ ] Moses complies — *Exodus 4:14–18*

FOR THOUGHT AND CONTEMPLATION

No one can do God's work effectively in this world until they have graduated from His 'School of Patience'. And patience, according to one definition, is 'the ability to count down before blasting off'.

"Therefore, since we are surrounded by such a great cloud of witnesses, let us throw off everything that hinders and the sin that so easily entangles, and let us run with perseverance the race marked out for us. Let us fix our eyes on Jesus, the author and perfecter of our faith ..." (Heb. 12:1–2, NIV)

---

FRIDAY Week 4  **Moses becomes leader**

- [x] Moses, the deliverer — *Exodus 4:19–29*
- [x] Moses reports to the people — *Exodus 4:30–31*
- [x] Moses contends with Pharaoh — *Exodus 5:1–3*
- [x] Pharaoh increases burdens — *Exodus 5:4–23*
- [x] Final instructions to Moses — *Exodus 6:1–13, 26–30, 7:1–6*
- [x] First meeting with Pharaoh — *Exodus 7:7*
- [x] Rods turn to serpents — *Exodus 7:8–14*

  The ten plagues
- [x] 1. Rivers turned to blood — *Exodus 7:15–25*
- [x] 2. Frogs — *Exodus 8:1–15*

FOR THOUGHT AND CONTEMPLATION

If we are to be successful in this life, then we must regard this as a central truth: there are no detours around God's will, and anything short of total obedience to God is disobedience.

"For he chose us in him before the creation of the world to be holy and blameless in his sight." (Eph. 1:4, NIV)

## THE BOOKS OF THE LAW

The first five books of the Old Testament, Genesis, Exodus, Leviticus, Numbers, Deuteronomy, are known as the Pentateuch (literally: the five-volumed book).

In the Old Testament the Pentateuch is referred to as:
— the Law (Ezra 10:3)
— the book of the Law of Moses (Neh. 8:1)
— the Book of Moses (Neh. 13:1)
— the Law of the Lord (1 Chron. 16:40)
— the Law of God (Neh. 10:28)
— the Book of the Law of God (Neh. 8:18)
— the Book of the Law of the Lord (Neh. 9:3)
— the Law of Moses (Dan. 9:11)

In the New Testament the Pentateuch is referred to as:
— the Book of the Law (Gal. 3:10)
— the Book of Moses (Mark 12:26)
— the Law of the Lord (Luke 2:23–24)

The first five books of the Bible set down God's laws for mankind.

**God continues the Plagues**

- ☑ 3. Lice — *Exodus 8:16–19*
- ☑ 4. Flies — *Exodus 8:20–32*
- ☑ 5. Death of livestock — *Exodus 9:1–7*
- ☑ 6. Boils — *Exodus 9:8–12*
- ☑ 7. Hail — *Exodus 9:13–35*
- ☑ 8. Locusts — *Exodus 10:1–13, 12:1–2, 10:14–20*
- ☑ 9. Darkness — *Exodus 10.21–27*

FOR THOUGHT AND CONTEMPLATION

The more we resist God's Word and the more we refuse to do the divine bidding, the harder and more stubborn our hearts become. The tragedy is that, when we insist on having our own way, God may let us have it.

"It is a dreadful thing to fall into the hands of the living God." (Heb. 10:31, NIV)

---

**The Passover**

- ☑ 10. Killing of firstborn: warning — *Exodus 11:1–8*
- ☑ Pharaoh cancels negotiations — *Exodus 10:28–29*
- ☑ Pharaoh's heart hardened — *Exodus 11:9–10*
- ☑ Passover instructions — *Exodus 12:3–12*
- ☑ Importance of the blood — *Exodus 12:13–27*
- ☑ Israel's obedience — *Exodus 12:28*
- ☑ Firstborn of Egypt killed — *Exodus 12:29*
- ☑ Egyptians demand immediate departure — *Exodus 12:30–36*
- ☑ Deliverance begins — *Exodus 12:40–42, Numbers 33:1–4*

  The Exodus approx. 1462 BC
- ☑ From Rameses to Succoth — *Exodus 12:37, Numbers 33:5*

- ☑ At Succoth — *Exodus 12:38–39, 43–51*

FOR THOUGHT AND CONTEMPLATION

The greatest celebration in the life of Israel is Passover. They rejoice with great gladness as they remember their deliverance from Egypt. You have experienced a greater deliverance. Does it cause your heart to rejoice?

"… For Christ, our passover lamb, has been sacrificed." (1 Cor. 5:7, NIV)

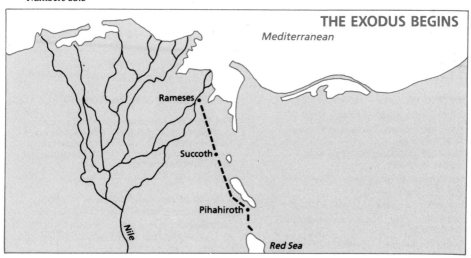

**THE EXODUS BEGINS**

*Mediterranean*

Rameses

Succoth

Pihahiroth

*Nile*

**Red Sea**

29

## MONDAY Week 5 — Crossing the Red Sea

- ☑ Passover instructions — *Exodus 13:1–19*
- ☑ From Succoth to Etham — *Exodus 13:20, Numbers 33:6*
- ☑ Pillar of fire and cloud — *Exodus 13:21–22, 14:1–2*
- ☑ From Etham to Pihahiroth — *Numbers 33:7*
- ☑ Pursuit of Pharaoh — *Exodus 14:3–20*
- ☑ Crossing the Red Sea — *Exodus 14:21–31*
- ☑ Song of victory — *Exodus 15:1–21*

FOR THOUGHT AND CONTEMPLATION

Has God placed you in a wilderness at this particular time? If so, then He has done it in order to teach you the important lesson of dependency. God will have you dependent on no one but Himself.

"He has delivered us from such a deadly peril, and he will deliver us. On him we have set our hope that he will continue to deliver us." (2 Cor. 1:10, NIV)

## TUESDAY Week 5 — Into the wilderness

- ☑ To the wilderness of Shur — *Exodus 15:22*
- ☑ From Shur to Marah — *Numbers 33:8, Exodus 15:23–26*
- ☑ From Marah to Elim — *Exodus 15:27, Numbers 33:9*
- ☑ From Elim to wilderness of Sin — *Exodus 16:1, Numbers 33:10–11*
- ☑ Murmuring about lack of food — *Exodus 16:2–3*
- ☑ Manna promised — *Exodus 16:4–13*
- ☑ Manna provided — *Exodus 16:14–22, 31–36*
- ☑ Law of the Sabbath — *Exodus 16:23–30*
- ☑ From wilderness of Sin to Rephidim — *Exodus 17:1, Numbers 33:12–14*
- ☑ Murmuring about the lack of water — *Exodus 17:2–4*
- ☑ Water from rock on Mount Horeb — *Exodus 17:5–7*

- ☑ Conflict with Amalek — *Exodus 17:8–16*
- **Sinai approx 1461 BC**
- ☑ From Rephidim to Sinai — *Exodus 19:1–2, Numbers 33:15*
- ☑ Giving of the Law: Covenant reviewed and preliminary instructions — *Exodus 19:3–8*

FOR THOUGHT AND CONTEMPLATION

Have you ever considered why it is that God allows us to go through bad days as well as good ones? Because we can learn things through adversity that we would never learn through prosperity.

"These things happened to them as examples and were written down as warnings for us ..." (1 Cor, 10:11, NIV)

## WEDNESDAY Week 5 — The Ten Commandments

- ☑ Relatives visit Moses — *Exodus 18:1–12*
- ☑ Jethro's wise counsel — *Exodus 18:13–27*
- ☑ Moses prepares Israel to meet with God — *Exodus 19:9–15*
- ☑ Moses holds Israel back from the mount — *Exodus 19:16–25*
- ☑ Ten Commandments given — *Exodus 20:1–10, 12–20*
- ☑ Instructions for altar — *Exodus 20:21–26*
- ☑ Various laws given: Masters and servants — *Exodus 21:1–11*
- ☑ Injuries to persons — *Exodus 21:12–36*

FOR THOUGHT AND CONTEMPLATION

The Ten Commandments are God's moral guidelines for all people in all generations. If God wanted us to live in moral uncertainty, He would have given us Ten Suggestions, not Ten Commandments!

"This is the covenant I will make with them after that time, says the Lord. I will put my laws in their hearts, and I will write them on their minds." (Heb. 10:16, NIV)

## THURSDAY Week 5 — God's covenant with Israel

- Rights of property — *Exodus 22:1–15*
- Crimes against humanity — *Exodus 22:16–31, 23:1–9*
- Land and the Sabbath — *Exodus 23:10–13*
- Three national feasts — *Exodus 23:14–19*
- God's covenant with Israel: future conquest — *Exodus 23:20–33*
- Altar built — *Exodus 24:3–8*
- Moses goes up Mount Sinai — *Exodus 24:1–2, 9–15*
- Forty days of instruction begin — *Exodus Exodus 24:16–18*

Tabernacle items
- Materials — *Exodus 25:1–9*

FOR THOUGHT AND CONTEMPLATION

Confucius said, "The faintest ink is better than the strongest memory." How easy it would be to forget God's principles if they were not written down. Aren't you thankful for the Bible?

"'But the word of the Lord stands for ever'. And this is the word that was preached to you." (1 Pet. 1:25, NIV)

## FRIDAY Week 5 — The Tabernacle

- Ark — *Exodus 25:10–22*
- Table of shewbread — *Exodus 25:23–30, Leviticus 24:5–9*
- Golden candlestick — *Exodus 25:31–40*
- Curtains of linen — *Exodus 26:1–6*
- Curtains of goats' hair — *Exodus 26:7–13*
- Covering of rams' skins — *Exodus 26:14*
- Boards and sockets — *Exodus 26:15–25*
- Outside bars — *Exodus 26:26–27*
- Middle bar — *Exodus 26:28*
- Overlay of gold — *Exodus 26:29–30*
- Inner veil — *Exodus 26:31–35*
- Outer veil — *Exodus 26:36–37*
- Brazen altar — *Exodus 27:1–8*

- Court — *Exodus 27:9–15*

FOR THOUGHT AND CONTEMPLATION

God's greatest longing is not simply to visit His people, but to live with them. Divine visitation is wonderful, but how much more glorious is divine habitation. Blessed *Immanuel*.

"When Christ came as high priest of the good things that are already here, he went through the greater and more perfect tabernacle that is not man-made, that is to say, not a part of this creation." (Heb. 9:11, NIV)

## SATURDAY Week 5 — Tabernacle items

- Hangings for gate of court — *Exodus 27:16–19*
- Oil for the light — *Exodus 27:20–21, Leviticus 24:1–4*
- Altar of incense — *Exodus 30:1–16*
- Laver of brass — *Exodus 30:17–21*
- Incense and spices — *Exodus 30:22–38*
- Workmen — *Exodus 31:1–11*
- Priesthood items — *Exodus 28:1*
- Garments of the priests — *Exodus 28:2–30*

FOR THOUGHT AND CONTEMPLATION

If you are a believer, you are also a priest. You can come into God's presence and *linger* there — without dread or fear. What an exciting ministry! Are you using it?

"Now we know that if the earthly tent we live in is destroyed, we have a building from God, an eternal house in heaven, not built by human hands." (2 Cor. 5:1, NIV)

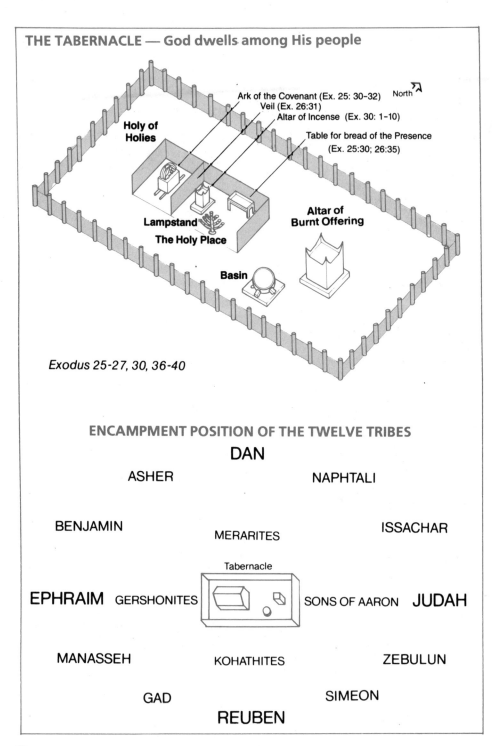

# THE TABERNACLE — God dwells among His people

Ark of the Covenant (Ex. 25: 30–32)
Veil (Ex. 26:31)
Altar of Incense (Ex. 30: 1–10)
North

**Holy of Holies**

Table for bread of the Presence (Ex. 25:30; 26:35)

**Lampstand**

**The Holy Place**

**Altar of Burnt Offering**

**Basin**

*Exodus 25-27, 30, 36-40*

## ENCAMPMENT POSITION OF THE TWELVE TRIBES

### DAN

ASHER                    NAPHTALI

BENJAMIN                                              ISSACHAR

MERARITES

Tabernacle

**EPHRAIM**  GERSHONITES          SONS OF AARON  **JUDAH**

MANASSEH          KOHATHITES          ZEBULUN

GAD                    SIMEON

### REUBEN

**The Priesthood**

- ☑ Garments of the priests continued — *Exodus 28:31–43*
- ☐ Consecration of the priests — *Exodus 29:1–25*
- ☑ Food for the priests — *Exodus 29:26–37*
- ☑ Continual burnt offering — *Exodus 29:38–46*
- ☐ Sabbath rest — *Exodus 31:12–18*

**FOR THOUGHT AND CONTEMPLATION**

If you were asked to write down the thought on which your mind most often focuses, what would it be? Money? Fame? Pleasure? Or God? If God doesn't have the central place in our thoughts, then whatever takes His place is an idol.

"For Christ did not enter a man-made sanctuary that was only a copy of the true one; he entered heaven itself, now to appear for us in God's presence." (Heb. 9:24, NIV)

**Moses' anger and tablets broken**

- ☑ The golden calf — *Exodus 32:1–6*
- ☑ Moses' anger — *Exodus 32:7–29*
- ☑ Moses' plea and God's answer — *Exodus 32:30–35*
- ☑ Temporary tabernacle erected — *Exodus 33:7–11*
- ☑ Moses communes with God — *Exodus 33:12–23*
- ☑ Instructions to hew stone — *Exodus 34:1–3*
- ☑ Forty more days on mount: Tablets remade — *Exodus 34:4*
- ☑ Directions renewed — *Exodus 34:5–28*
- ☑ Law of the land given: Sabbatic year — *Leviticus 25:1–7*
- ☑ Years of Jubilee — *Leviticus 25:8–24*

**FOR THOUGHT AND CONTEMPLATION**

Whenever we fall into sin, the way out is not by indulging in excuses, but by an act of genuine repentance. When man covers his sin, he adds to it, but when God covers sin, He absolves it — eternally.

"If we confess our sins, he is faithful and just and will forgive us our sins and purify us from all unrighteousness." (1 Jn. 1:9, NIV)

**Further laws**

- ☐ Redemption of inheritance — *Leviticus 25:25–34*
- ☑ Care of the poor — *Leviticus 25:35–46*
- ☑ Redemption of poor — *Leviticus 25:47–55*
- ☑ Other laws given: conditions for blessing — *Leviticus 26:1–13*
- ☑ Warnings of chastisement — *Leviticus 26:14–31*
- ☑ Dispersion predicted — *Leviticus 26:32–39*
- ☑ Covenant remains (conditional) — *Leviticus 26:40–46*
- ☐ Dedicated persons and things (tax) — *Leviticus 27:1–13*

**FOR THOUGHT AND CONTEMPLATION**

God's warnings are clearly signposted everywhere in life — for those who have eyes to see. And no one can accuse God of enforcing any law that He has not clearly 'posted'.

"It is because of him that you are in Christ Jesus, who has become for us wisdom from God — that is, our righteousness, holiness and redemption." (1 Cor. 1:30, NIV)

**Tabernacle contents**

- ☑ Dedicated persons and things (tax) continued — *Leviticus 27:14–25*
- ☑ Three items that are the Lord's — *Leviticus 27:26–34*

- ☑ Moses' face shines with God's glory — *Exodus 34:29–35*
- ☑ Tabernacle built: materials given by people — *Exodus 35:4–29, 36:1–7*
- ☑ Ark — *Exodus 37:1–9*
- ☑ Table of shewbread — *Exodus 37:10–16*
- ☑ Golden candlestick — *Exodus 37:17–24*
- ☑ Curtains of linen — *Exodus 36:8–13*

**FOR THOUGHT AND CONTEMPLATION**

It is a Scriptural principle to give according to one's income. Those whose giving is not according to their income, may find that God adjusts their income according to their giving.

"Give, and it will be given to you. A good measure, pressed down, shaken together and running over, will be poured into your lap. For with the measure you use, it will be measured to you." (Lk. 6:38, NIV)

## THE HIGH PRIEST AND HIS GARMENTS

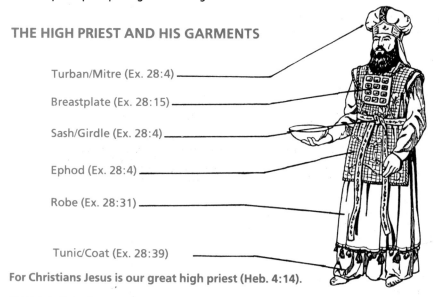

Turban/Mitre (Ex. 28:4) ————

Breastplate (Ex. 28:15) ————

Sash/Girdle (Ex. 28:4) ————

Ephod (Ex. 28:4) ————

Robe (Ex. 28:31) ————

Tunic/Coat (Ex. 28:39) ————

**For Christians Jesus is our great high priest (Heb. 4:14).**

---

**THURSDAY Week 6** ## Tabernacle built

- ☑ Tabernacle items continued: curtains of goats' hair — *Exodus 36:14–18*
- ☑ Covering of rams' skins — *Exodus 36:19*
- ☑ Boards and sockets — *Exodus 36:20–30*
- ☑ Outside bars — *Exodus 36:31–32*
- ☑ Middle bar — *Exodus 36:33*
- ☑ Overlay of gold — *Exodus 36:34*
- ☑ Inner veil — *Exodus 36:35–36*
- ☑ Outer veil — *Exodus 36:37–38*
- ☑ Brazen altar — *Exodus 38:1–7*
- ☑ Court — *Exodus 38:9–17*
- ☑ Hangings for gate of court — *Exodus 38:18–20*
- ☑ Altar of incense made — *Exodus 37:25–28*
- ☑ Laver of brass — *Exodus 38:8*
- ☑ Incense and spices — *Exodus 37:29*

- ☑ Workmen — *Exodus 35:30–35*
- ☑ Priesthood items: garments of the priests — *Exodus 39:1–31*

**FOR THOUGHT AND CONTEMPLATION**

Christ, our Great High Priest, when undertaking the work of our redemption, put on the garments of humility, girded Himself with resolution, took charge of God's spiritual Israel — the Church — and one day will present us perfect to the Father.

"Therefore, since we have a great high priest who has gone through the heavens, Jesus the Son of God, let us hold firmly to the faith we profess." (Heb. 4:14, NIV)

# Levitical duties

- ☑ Sabbath rest — *Exodus 35:1–3*
- ☑ Summary of the building of tabernacle — *Exodus 38:21–31, 39:32–43*
- ☑ Trumpets used to alert congregation — *Numbers 10:1–10*
- ☑ Tabernacle made ready for service — *Exodus 40:1–15*
- ☑ Instructions and duties prior to leaving wilderness of Sinai: to tribe of Levi — *Numbers 3:5–13*
- ☑ To families of Levi — *Numbers 3:14–16, 21–24*
- ☑ Responsibilities of Levi's sons — *Numbers 3:25–39*

FOR THOUGHT AND CONTEMPLATION

It took Israel a whole year before they learned the lessons of Sinai and were ready to move forward. How long does God have to keep us encamped at one spot because of our unco-operative and unsubmissive spirit?

"... to obey is better than sacrifice ..." (1 Sam. 15:22, NIV)

# Duties apportioned

- ☑ Firstborn redeemed — *Numbers 3:40–51*
- ☑ Cleansing of the Levites — *Numbers 8:5–26*
- ☑ Office of Eleazar — *Numbers 4:16–20*
- ☑ Service of the Kohathites — *Numbers 4:1–15*
- ☑ Service of the Gershonites — *Numbers 4:21–28*
- ☑ Service of the Merarites — *Numbers 4:29–49*

FOR THOUGHT AND CONTEMPLATION

An old cliche in Christian circles runs like this: We are saved to serve. It's true. And joy comes in exercising the gifts God has given us. An unhappy Christian is usually an indolent Christian.

"Therefore, I urge you, brothers, in view of God's mercy, to offer your bodies as living sacrifices, holy and pleasing to God — which is your spiritual worship." (Romans 12:1, NIV)

# Tabernacle completed

- ☑ Moses performs all as directed — *Exodus 40:16–33*
- ☑ Aaron lights the lamps — *Numbers 8:1–4*
- ☑ Cloud covers tabernacle — *Exodus 40:34–35*
- ☐ Gifts and offerings brought at the dedication of the tabernacle and the altar — *Numbers 7:1–77*

FOR THOUGHT AND CONTEMPLATION

No matter how efficiently or effectively the hands of men contribute to God's work, the one thing that gives it meaning and purpose is the glory of God resting upon it. Without Him, the best we can produce is — nothing.

"The Word became flesh and lived for a while among us. We have seen his glory, the glory of the one and only Son, who came from the Father, full of grace and truth." (Jn. 1:14, NIV)

# Priestly ministry

- ☑ Gifts and offerings brought — *Numbers 7:78–88*
- ☑ Moses hears God's voice — *Numbers 7:89*
- ☑ Aaron's sons' ministry described — *Numbers 3:1–3, Leviticus 7:35–36*
- ☑ Consecration of Aaron — *Leviticus 8:1–36*

☑ Ministry of priests begins — *Leviticus 9:1–24*

☑ Unauthorised ("Strange"—AV) fire of Nadab and Abihu — *Leviticus 10:1–7, Numbers 3:4*

**FOR THOUGHT AND CONTEMPLATION**

Is the fire that burns on the altar of your heart strange fire or spiritual fire? *Strange* fire is fire that has its origin on earth. *Spiritual* fire is fire that comes down from heaven.

"... To him who loves us and has freed us from our sins by his blood, and has made us to be a kingdom and priests to serve his God and Father — to him be glory and power for ever and ever! ..." (Rev. 1:5–6, NIV)

---

**TUESDAY Week 7** ## Laws about sacrifice

☑ Day of Atonement — *Leviticus 16:1–34*

☑ Necessity of blood sacrifice — *Leviticus 17:1–16*

☑ Offerings described: sacrifice system and priest's duties — *Leviticus 7:37–38*

☑ The burnt offering from the herds — *Leviticus 1:1–9*

☑ The burnt offering from the flocks, and from the fowls — *Leviticus 1:10–17*

☑ Concerning the burnt offering — *Leviticus 6:8–13*

**FOR THOUGHT AND CONTEMPLATION**

How would you go about the task of atoning for your own sin? Would you offer the deeds of your home, your bank account, or some other material asset? Such things would be totally inadequate. God has paid your debt freely and fully in His Son. Think about it — and be glad!

"Not only is this so, but we also rejoice in God through our Lord Jesus Christ, through whom we have now received reconciliation." (Rom. 5:11, NIV)

**A BIRD'S EYE VIEW OF LEVITICUS**

**Place in the Bible:**
Third Old Testament book; third book of the Law:

**Special features:**
Sacrifices, the day of atonement, detailed laws covering the whole of life.

**Jesus and the book of Leviticus:**
The details about sacrifices in Leviticus teach us about God's holiness and help us to understand Jesus' sacrifice. One way to appreciate this is to read the book of Hebrews as a commentary on the book of Leviticus.

**Teaching:**
God's people are told how they can have access to God and how they are to live their lives in obedience to God: they are to be holy.

**A verse to remember:**
"I am the Lord your God; consecrate yourselves and be holy, because I am holy" (Lev. 11:44).

---

**WEDNESDAY Week 7** ## The offerings

☑ The meal offering of flour — *Leviticus 2:1–11*

☑ The offering of first fruits — *Leviticus 2:12–16*

☑ Concerning the meal offering — *Leviticus 6:14–23*

☑ The peace offering of the herd — *Leviticus 3:1–5*

☑ The peace offering of the flock — *Leviticus 3:6–17*

☑ Concerning the fellowship and wave offerings, and food prohibitions — *Leviticus 7:11–36*

☑ The sin offering of ignorance for the priest — *Leviticus 4:1–12*

**FOR THOUGHT AND CONTEMPLATION**
Israel were commanded to present many sacrifices, but the only sacrifice God asks of His Church is a "sacrifice of praise" (Heb. 13:15). And it is a sacrifice He requires continually. How consistently does this flame burn on the altar of your heart?

"... so Christ was sacrificed once to take away the sins of many people; and he will appear a second time, not to bear sin, but to bring salvation to those who are waiting for him." (Heb. 9:28, NIV)

## Atonement for sin

- ☑ The sin offering for the whole congregation — *Leviticus 4:13–21*
- ☑ The sin offering for a ruler and for any of the people — *Leviticus 4:22–35*
- ☑ Concerning the sin offering — *Leviticus 6:24–30*
- ☑ Concerning various sins — *Leviticus 5:1–13*
- ☑ Concerning sins against the Lord — *Leviticus 5:14–19*
- ☑ Concerning sins against our neighbour — *Leviticus 6:1–7*
- ☑ Concerning the guilt offering — *Leviticus 7:1–10*
- ☑ Instructions about offerings — *Leviticus 10:8–20*

FOR THOUGHT AND CONTEMPLATION

Someone has said that the first step towards thanking is thinking. Think, therefore, of how marvellously God has dealt with your sin in Christ, and let your thinking turn into thanking.

---

"For Christ died for sins once for all, the righteous for the unrighteous, to bring you to God. He was put to death in the body but made alive by the Spirit." (1 Pet. 3:18, NIV)

---

## Laws for the people

- ☑ Food: clean and unclean animals — *Leviticus 11:1–47*
- ☑ Ceremonial purification: cleansing after childbirth — *Leviticus 12:1–8*
- ☑ Directions to the priest to judge concerning leprosy — *Leviticus 13:1–17*
- ☑ Further directions — *Leviticus 13:18–44*

FOR THOUGHT AND CONTEMPLATION

God has a personal concern for the holiness and well-being of His people. And why? Because the holier we are, the more clearly others see Him in us. How clearly do others see God in you?

---

"… through Christ Jesus the law of the Spirit of life set me free from the law of sin and death." (Rom. 8:2, NIV)

---

## The problem of leprosy

- ☑ The treatment of lepers — *Leviticus 13:45–46*
- ☑ Concerning the leprosy in garments — *Leviticus 13:47–59*
- ☑ Rules to be observed after cleansing of leprosy: declaring the leper to be clean — *Leviticus 14:1–9*
- ☑ The sacrifices to be offered by him — *Leviticus 14:10–32*
- ☑ Leprosy in a house — *Leviticus 14:33–53*
- ☑ Summary of the law concerning leprosy — *Leviticus 14:54–57*
- ☑ Laws concerning ceremonial uncleanness — *Leviticus 15:1–33*

FOR THOUGHT AND CONTEMPLATION

No wonder preachers refer to leprosy as an illustration of sin, for it is one of the most disfiguring and debilitating of all diseases. How wonderful a leper must have felt when healed. How much more wonderful to be cleansed from sin!

---

"Jesus reached out his hand and touched the man … Immediately he was cured of his leprosy." (Matt. 8:3, NIV)

---

## The Feasts of Israel

- ☑ Regulations concerning marriage — *Leviticus 18:1–30*
- ☑ Idolatry forbidden — *Leviticus 20:1–6 & 27*

# FELLOWSHIP WITH GOD: THE FIVE MAIN LEVITICAL OFFERINGS

| Offering | Reference | Purpose |
|---|---|---|
| **Burnt offering** | **Lev. 1** | **Dedication** |

Bullocks, lambs, goats, doves, pigeons — were wholly consumed on the altar. It was offered every day, each morning and night.

| | | |
|---|---|---|
| **Cereal offering** | **Lev. 2** | **Thanksgiving** |

Fine flour, unleavened bread, cakes, wafers, grain — always with salt. A handful was burned on the altar; the rest was for the priests, who ate it in a holy place — always followed the morning and evening burnt offerings.

| | | |
|---|---|---|
| **Peace offering** | **Lev. 3** | **Fellowship** |

Oxen, sheep, goats. This was a shared sacrifice. The fat was burned: the rest was eaten by priests, and by the sacrificer and his friends. A meal and drink offering always accompanied this sacrifice.

| | | |
|---|---|---|
| **Sin offering** | **Lev. 4** | **Cleansing** |

Bullocks, goats, lambs. The whole animal was burned outside the camp. A sin offering was made for the whole congregation on all the feast days, especially on the Day of Atonement.

| | | |
|---|---|---|
| **Trespass offering** | **Lev. 5** | **Reconciliation** |

Always a lamb, with one exception (Lev. 14:12). The ritual was the same as in the sin offering except that the blood was poured and not sprinkled over the surface of the altar. Where wrong had been done to another, restitution was made, including an additional 20% of its value.

- ☑ The feasts of the Lord: the Sabbath — *Leviticus 23:1–3*
- ☑ The Passover; the feast of unleavened bread; the offering of first fruits — *Leviticus 23:4–14*
- ☑ The Feast of Weeks/Pentecost — *Leviticus 23:15–22*
- ☑ The Feast of Trumpets — *Leviticus 23:23–25*
- ☑ The Day of Atonement — *Leviticus 23:26–32*
- ☑ The Feast of Tabernacles — *Leviticus 23:33–44*

FOR THOUGHT AND CONTEMPLATION

The Christian life is characterised by both fasting and feasting, by curtailment and celebration. Those who do not take this into account have a very lopsided Christian experience.

"I know what it is to be in need, and I know what it is to have plenty. I have learned the secret of being content in any and every situation, whether well fed or hungry, whether living in plenty or in want." (Phil. 4:12, NIV)

---

## MONDAY Week 8    A time of sanctification

- ☑ Conduct of God's people — *Leviticus 19:1–8*
- ☑ Laws concerning neighbours, the land, and foreigners — *Leviticus 19:9–37*
- ☑ Punishments for disobedience — *Leviticus 20:7–26*
- ☑ Instructions for priests — *Leviticus 21:1–9*
- ☑ Concerning the High Priest — *Leviticus 21:10–15*
- ☑ Physical requirements for priests — *Leviticus 21:16–24*
- ☑ Priests and the holy things — *Leviticus 22:1–16*

FOR THOUGHT AND CONTEMPLATION

Before God's people can take possession of God's fulness (Canaan), there must, of necessity, be a time of preparation, training and testing. God always prepares His children before He entrusts them with greater possessions and responsibility.

"... But you were washed, you were sanctified, you were justified in the name of the Lord Jesus Christ and by the Spirit of our God." (1 Cor. 6:11, NIV)

---

## A BIRD'S EYE VIEW OF NUMBERS

**Place in the Bible:**
Fourth Old Testament book; fourth book of the Law:

**Main characters:**
Moses, the Levites, Miriam, Aaron, Caleb, Balaam.

**Special features:**
Two censuses, the spies in the promised land, wandering in the wilderness, Balaam's talking donkey.

**Jesus and the book of Numbers:**
In chapter 3 of John's Gospel Jesus speaks of Moses' raising of the bronze snake (Num. 21:4–9) as a picture of His own lifting up "that all who believe in Him may receive eternal life".

**Teaching:**
God's people spend forty long years wandering around in the wilderness and learn that they can only make progress as they trust and obey God. In chapter 14 they rebel against God and so the Lord tells them "For forty years — one year for each of the forty days you explored the land — you will suffer for your sins and know what it is like to have me against you (v.34)."

**A verse to remember:**
"... my servant Caleb has a different spirit and follows me wholeheartedly ..." (Num. 14:24).

# FEASTS OF THE LORD

**Passover**                    Lev. 23 vv. 5–8
*Purpose*

Beginning of the religious year, commemorating the Exodus and the establishment of Israel as a nation by God's redeeming power.

*NT Spiritual significance*

Calvary and Christ's death

**Pentecost**                    vv. 15–22
*Purpose*

Commemorating the firstfruits of harvest and later the giving of the Law. Observed 50 days after the Passover (also see Ex. 23:16; 34:22; Num. 28:26; Deut. 16:9–10).

*NT Spiritual significance*

The coming of the Holy Spirit

**Trumpets**                    vv. 23–25
*Purpose*

Beginning of the civil year, corresponding to our New Year's Day.

*NT Spiritual significance*

The coming again of the Lord Jesus

**Atonement**                    vv. 26–32
*Purpose*

A day of remembrance when the High Priest made confession of all the sins of the past year and made atonement in the Most Holy Place.

*NT Spiritual significance*

Redemption and righteousness in Christ

**Tabernacles**                    vv. 33–43
*Purpose*

Commemorating life in the wilderness; thanksgiving for harvest; the last feast of the religious year.

*NT Spiritual significance*

The rule and reign of Christ

The purpose of these feasts was a spiritual one — for God to meet with His people.

## TUESDAY Week 8 — The second Passover

- ☑ Requirements for animals to be sacrificed — *Leviticus 22:17–33*
- ☑ Death penalties: blasphemy — *Leviticus 24:10–16 & 23*
- ☑ Murder — *Leviticus 24:17–22*
- ☑ Camp laws explained — *Numbers 5:1–10*
- ☑ Law of jealous husband — *Numbers 5:11–31*
- ☑ Vow of Nazarites — *Numbers 6:1–27*
- ☐ God reminds Israel to keep Passover — *Numbers 9:1–4*
- ☐ Passover held in Sinai — *Numbers 9:5–14*

FOR THOUGHT AND CONTEMPLATION

How grateful we ought to be that, in Jesus Christ, God has provided a lamb—not merely for the sins of an individual, not merely for the sins of a family, not even for the sins of a nation. Jesus Christ is the Lamb of God who takes away the sins of the *world*.

"… 'This is my body, which is for you; do this in remembrance of me.' In the same way, after supper he took the cup, saying, 'This cup is the new covenant in my blood; do this, whenever you drink it, in remembrance of me.'" (1 Cor. 11:24–25, NIV)

## WEDNESDAY Week 8 — Getting ready to move

- ☑ Preparations for leaving Sinai: numbering of the people — *Numbers 1:1–54*
- ☑ General arrangement of the camp — *Numbers 2:1–2, 17, 32–34*
- ☑ Eastern division — *Numbers 2:3–9*
- ☑ Southern division — *Numbers 2:10–16*
- ☑ Western division — *Numbers 2:18–24*
- ☑ Northern division — *Numbers 2:25–31*
- ☑ Journey to resume — *Numbers 33:1–6*
- ☑ Moses recommissioned — *Deuteronomy 1:6–18*
- ☑ From Sinai to Kadesh-Barnea: journey starts — *Numbers 10:11 & 13*

FOR THOUGHT AND CONTEMPLATION

A relationship with God always begins with the knowledge of the law and humiliation for sin. After that comes the long march toward Canaan and all the fulness of His blessings.

"The wind blows wherever it pleases. You hear its sound, but you cannot tell where it comes from or where it is going. So it is with everyone born of the Spirit." (Jn. 3:8, NIV)

## THURSDAY Week 8 — Journeyings continue

- ☑ Order of the divisions — *Numbers 10:14–28*
- ☑ Cloud leads them — *Exodus 40:36–38, Numbers 9:15–23*
- ☑ In Paran wilderness — *Numbers 10:12, 29–32*
- ☑ Fire at Taberah — *Numbers 10:33–36, 11:1–3*
- ☑ Arrival at Kibroth — *Numbers 33:16*
- ☑ Murmuring about manna — *Numbers 11:4–9*
- ☑ Moses complains — *Numbers 11:10–15*
- ☑ Seventy elders chosen — *Numbers 11:16–25*
- ☑ Prophecy in the camp — *Numbers 11:26–30*
- ☑ Plague of quails — *Numbers 11:31–34*
- ☑ From Kibroth to Hazeroth — *Numbers 11:35, 33:17*
- ☑ Miriam's leprosy — *Numbers 12:1–15*

FOR THOUGHT AND CONTEMPLATION

Today's pressing problems sometimes create within us a hankering for times past—'the good old days'. If we forget God's promise of *future* blessing, we will suffer from a lack of perspective.

"… But one thing I do: Forgetting what is behind and straining towards what is ahead, I press on towards the goal to win the prize for which God has called me heavenwards in Christ Jesus." (Phil. 3:13–14, NIV)

## A BIRD'S EYE VIEW OF DEUTERONOMY

**Place in the Bible:**
Fifth Old Testament book; fifth book of the Law:

**Main characters:**
Moses, Joshua.

**Special features:**
The title of the book of Deuteronomy comes from the Greek, meaning "Second Law", since it expands on the laws God had already given at Sinai. Deuteronomy gives God's laws for His people as they prepare to live in Canaan.

**Jesus and the book of Deuteronomy:**
The writer to the Hebrews picks up the covenant theme and states that, "... Jesus is the mediator of a new covenant" (Heb. 12:24).

**Teaching:**
Most of Deuteronomy consists of three long speeches made by Moses to the Israelites in which he emphasises how God has saved the people He loves. As they get ready to move into the Promised Land Moses calls the Israelites to keep God's great power and faithfulness in mind. Blessing or disaster will depend on their response.

**A verse to remember:**
"Love the Lord your God with all your heart and with all your soul and with all your strength" (Deut. 6:5).

---

**FRIDAY Week 8**

# Turning back from Canaan

- From Hazeroth to Kadesh-Barnea — *Numbers 33:18–36, 12:16, Deuteronomy 1:19–20*
- From Kadesh-Barnea to Jordan crossing: spies sent out to Canaan — *Numbers 13:1–24, Deuteronomy 1:21–24*
- Spies return — *Numbers 13:25–33, Deuteronomy 1:25–33*
- Unbelief of Israel — *Numbers 14:1–24*
- Generation cursed to die in wilderness — *Numbers 14:25–30*

FOR THOUGHT AND CONTEMPLATION

How often have we stepped right up to the edge of God's fulness, only to draw back because of unbelief? Are you there right now? Press on, despite the giants. God will give you all the ground you place your feet upon.

"So we see that they were not able to enter, because of their unbelief. Therefore, since the promise of entering his rest still stands, let us be careful that none of you be found to have fallen short if it." (Heb. 3:19—4:1, NIV)

---

**SATURDAY Week 8**

# Wilderness wanderings

- Generation cursed continued — *Numbers 14:31–38, Deuteronomy 1:34–40*
- Defeat at Hormah — *Numbers 14:39–45, Deuteronomy 1:41–44*
- Repentance too late — *Deuteronomy 1:45–46*
- Earliest Psalm — *Psalm 90:1, 3–17*
- Instructions: offerings — *Numbers 15:1–31*
- Separation — *Numbers 15:37–41*
- Man stoned for working on Sabbath — *Numbers 15:32–36*
- The rebellion of Korah, Dathan and Abiram — *Numbers 16:1–2*

FOR THOUGHT AND CONTEMPLATION

God often allows His people a second chance when they fail to enter into a blessing, but only after they have undergone some painful discipline. Make up your mind to say 'Yes' to God, no matter what fears arise within you.

"So, as the Holy Spirit says: 'Today, if you hear his voice, do not harden your hearts as you did in the rebellion, during the time of testing in the desert...'" (Heb. 3:7–8, NIV)

# The people murmur

- ☑ The rebellion of Korah, Dathan and Abiram continued: Korah contends for the priesthood — *Numbers 16:3–11*
- ☑ The disobedience of Dathan and Abiram — *Numbers 16:12–15*
- ☑ The glory of the Lord appears and the intercession of Moses and Aaron — *Numbers 16:16–22*
- ☑ The ground swallows up Dathan and Abiram — *Numbers 16:23–34*
- ☑ The company of Korah consumed — *Numbers 16:35–40*
- ☑ The people murmur and a plague is sent — *Numbers 16:41–50*
- ☑ The budding of Aaron's rod — *Numbers 17:1–13*

- ☑ Levite responsibilities — *Numbers 18:1–24*

FOR THOUGHT AND CONTEMPLATION

How easy it is when things go wrong in our lives to lash out at others and say, "It's all your fault." This is the oldest defence in history. Adam and Eve used it in the Garden of Eden. Is it also a favourite defence of yours?

---

"With the tongue we praise our Lord and Father, and with it we curse men, who have been made in God's likeness. Out of the same mouth come praise and cursing. My brothers, this should not be." (Jas. 3:9–10, NIV)

---

# Water from the Rock

- ☑ Levite responsibilities — *Numbers 18:25–32*
- ☑ Red heifer ordinance: instructions about dead — *Numbers 19:1–22*
- ☑ Death of Miriam — *Numbers 20:1*
- ☑ Water from Meribah — *Numbers 20:2–13*
- ☑ Birth of Moses' grandchildren — *1 Chronicles 23:16–17*
- ☑ Permission to pass through Edom denied — *Numbers 20:14–21*
- ☑ To Mount Hor — *Numbers 20:22, 33:37*
- ☑ Death of Aaron — *Numbers 20:23–28, 33:38–39, Deuteronomy 10:6–7*
- ☑ Mourning for Aaron — *Numbers 20:29*

- ☑ Victory at Hormah — *Numbers 33:40, 21:1–3*

FOR THOUGHT AND CONTEMPLATION

Our vulnerability does not always lie in our weaknesses: it can also lie in our strengths. Moses, the meekest man on the face of the earth, sinned through losing his temper. We are strong only in Christ.

---

"In your anger do not sin. Do not let the sun go down while you are still angry, and do not give the devil a foothold." (Eph. 4:26–27, NIV)

---

# Healing for sickness

- ☑ From Mount Hor around Edom — *Deuteronomy 2:1–12, Numbers 21:4, 33:41–42*
- ☑ The brass serpent — *Numbers 21:5–9*
- ☑ To Oboth and Ije-Abarim — *Numbers 21:10–11, 33:43–44*
- ☑ Northward through Moab — *Numbers 21:12–15, Deuteronomy 2:13–18, Numbers 33:45*
- ☑ Victory over Amorites: in Gilead (over Sihon) — *Numbers 21:16, 33:46–47, 21:17–32, Deuteronomy 2:19–37*
- ☐ In Bashan (over Og) — *Deuteronomy 3:1–11, Numbers 21:33–35*

FOR THOUGHT AND CONTEMPLATION

A history of failure does not mean that victory is not possible. When we align ourselves with God, no matter the defeats of the past, victory is not only possible, but assured.

---

"Just as Moses lifted up the snake in the desert, so the Son of Man must be lifted up, that everyone who believes in him may have eternal life." (Jn. 3:14–15, NIV)

---

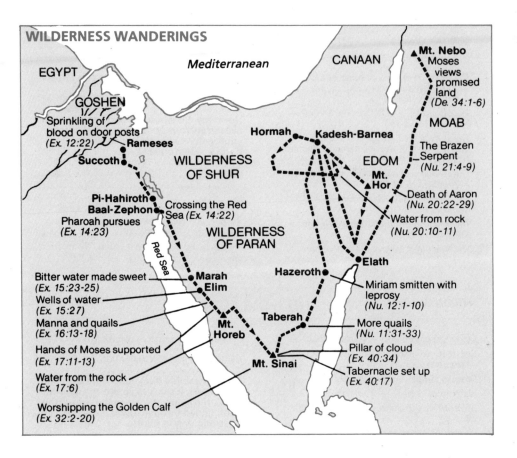

## WILDERNESS WANDERINGS

EGYPT

GOSHEN
Sprinkling of
blood on door posts
(Ex. 12:22)
Rameses

Succoth

Mediterranean

CANAAN

Mt. Nebo
Moses
views
promised
land
(De. 34:1-6)

MOAB

Hormah
Kadesh-Barnea

WILDERNESS
OF SHUR

EDOM

The Brazen
Serpent
(Nu. 21:4-9)

Mt.
Hor

Pi-Hahiroth
Baal-Zephon
Pharoah pursues
(Ex. 14:23)

Crossing the Red
Sea (Ex. 14:22)

Death of Aaron
(Nu. 20:22-29)

WILDERNESS
OF PARAN

Water from rock
(Nu. 20:10-11)

Red Sea

Bitter water made sweet
(Ex. 15:23-25)
Wells of water
(Ex. 15:27)
Manna and quails
(Ex. 16:13-18)
Hands of Moses supported
(Ex. 17:11-13)
Water from the rock
(Ex. 17:6)
Worshipping the Golden Calf
(Ex. 32:2-20)

Marah
Elim

Hazeroth

Elath

Miriam smitten with
leprosy
(Nu. 12:1-10)

Mt.
Horeb

Taberah

More quails
(Nu. 11:31-33)

Mt. Sinai

Pillar of cloud
(Ex. 40:34)
Tabernacle set up
(Ex. 40:17)

---

## WEDNESDAY Week 9   Balak meets Balaam

☑ The Israelites settle in Moab — *Numbers 22:1, 33:48–49*

☑ Balak sends for Balaam — *Numbers 22:2–14*

☑ Balaam goes to Balak — *Numbers 22:15–21*

☑ Balaam's ass talks — *Numbers 22:22–35*

☑ Balaam and Balak meet — *Numbers 22:36–41*

☑ Balak's sacrifice and Balaam's blessing — *Numbers 23:1–10*

☑ Balak's disappointment — *Numbers 23:11–15*

☑ Balaam again blesses Israel — *Numbers 23:16–24*

☑ Balak's third sacrifice — *Numbers 23:25–30*

☑ Balaam predicts Israel's happiness — *Numbers 24:1–9*

☑ Balak dismisses Balaam — *Numbers 24:10–14*

FOR THOUGHT AND CONTEMPLATION

Failure to obey God's commands leads inevitably to spiritual insensitivity. This is illustrated by Balaam's inability to see the angel barring his way. Even the ass seemed to have more spiritual sensitivity than Balaam!

---

"Trust in the Lord with all your heart and lean not on your own understanding; in all your ways acknowledge him, and he will make your paths straight." (Prov. 3:5–6, NIV)

---

## Second numbering of Israel

☑ Balaam's prophecies — *Numbers 24:15–25*
☑ The Israelites enticed — *Numbers 25:1–5*
☑ Phinehas puts Zimri and Cozbi to death — *Numbers 25:6–15*
☑ The Midianites to be punished — *Numbers 25:16–18*
☑ Second numbering of Israel — *Numbers 26:1–51*
☑ Division of the land — *Numbers 26:52–56*
☑ Number of Levites — *Numbers 26:57–58, 61–62*
☑ None remaining of first numbering — *Numbers 26:63–65*
☑ The inheritance law — *Numbers 27:1–11*

FOR THOUGHT AND CONTEMPLATION

How sad that between the first census and this second census a whole generation— with the exceptions of Caleb and Joshua— had died in the wilderness. Disobedience makes havoc of God's purposes.

"…you will cross the Jordan here to go in and take possession of the land the Lord your God is giving you for your own." (Josh. 1:11, NIV)
"Not one of you will enter the land I swore with uplifted hand to make your home, except Caleb son of Jephunneh and Joshua son of Nun." (Num. 14:30, NIV)

---

## Sacrifices and offerings

☑ The daily sacrifice — *Numbers 28:1–8*
☑ Sabbath and new moon offerings — *Numbers 28:9–15*
☑ Passover and Firstfruits offerings — *Numbers 28:16–31*
☑ Feast of Trumpets and Day of Atonement offering — *Numbers 29:1–11*
☑ Offerings at the Feast of Tabernacles — *Numbers 29:12–40*
☑ Laws about vows — *Numbers 30:1–2*
☑ When vows might be released — *Numbers 30:3–16*

FOR THOUGHT AND CONTEMPLATION

Of the many varied sacrifices and offerings in ancient Israel, one offering was a daily occurence — *the sin offering*. How beautifully this illustrates the fact that our 'burnt offerings' are of no interest to God until we have first showed an interest in the great Sin-offering which He Himself made for us on Calvary.

"For Christ died for sins once for all, the righteous for the unrighteous, to bring you to God. He was put to death in the body but made alive by the Spirit." (1 Pet. 3:18 NIV)

---

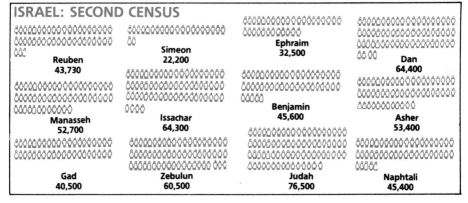

ISRAEL: SECOND CENSUS

Reuben 43,730

Simeon 22,200

Ephraim 32,500

Dan 64,400

Manasseh 52,700

Issachar 64,300

Benjamin 45,600

Asher 53,400

Gad 40,500

Zebulun 60,500

Judah 76,500

Naphtali 45,400

45

# WILDERNESS WANDERINGS

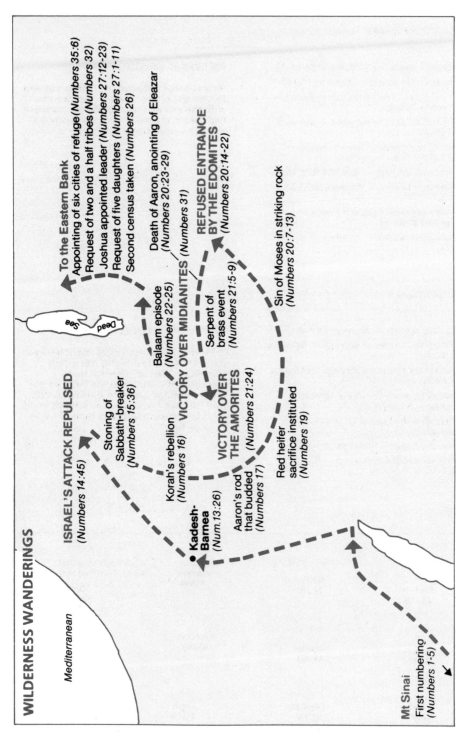

Mediterranean

**ISRAEL'S ATTACK REPULSED**
*(Numbers 14:45)*

Stoning of Sabbath-breaker *(Numbers 15:36)*

Korah's rebellion *(Numbers 16)*  **VICTORY OVER MIDIANITES** *(Numbers 31)*

Aaron's rod that budded *(Numbers 17)*

**VICTORY OVER THE AMORITES** *(Numbers 21:24)*

Red heifer sacrifice instituted *(Numbers 19)*

● **Kadesh-Barnea** *(Num.13:26)*

Balaam episode *(Numbers 22-25)*

Serpent of brass event *(Numbers 21:5-9)*

Sin of Moses in striking rock *(Numbers 20:7-13)*

**REFUSED ENTRANCE BY THE EDOMITES** *(Numbers 20:14-22)*

Death of Aaron, anointing of Eleazar *(Numbers 20:23-29)*

Dead Sea

**To the Eastern Bank**
Appointing of six cities of refuge *(Numbers 35:6)*
Request of two and a half tribes *(Numbers 32)*
Joshua appointed leader *(Numbers 27:12-23)*
Request of five daughters *(Numbers 27:1-11)*
Second census taken *(Numbers 26)*

Mt Sinai
First numbering *(Numbers 1-5)*

## The Reubenites and Gadites

☑ War with Midian — *Numbers 31:1–7*

☑ Balaam and kings of Midian slain — *Numbers 31:8–12*

☑ Those slain who caused sin — *Numbers 31:13–18*

☑ Purification of Israelites — *Numbers 31:19–24*

☑ Division of the spoil — *Numbers 31:25–47*

☑ Offerings to the Lord — *Numbers 31:48–54*

☑ Tribes of Reuben and Gad request an inheritance — *Numbers 32:1–5*

☑ Moses reproves Reubenites and Gadites — *Numbers 32:6–15*

☑ Their views explained — *Numbers 32:16–27*

☑ They settle to the east of the Jordan — *Numbers 32:28–42*

FOR THOUGHT AND CONTEMPLATION

What a tragedy that some of God's people, within sight of the *Land of Promise*, should prefer to settle for something less than God's best. How is it with you? Are you content to remain this side of Jordan? Are you settling for less than God's best?

---

"Therefore, I urge you, brothers, in view of God's mercy, to offer your bodies as living sacrifices, holy and pleasing to God — which is your spiritual worship." (Rom. 12:1, NIV)

---

## Preparing to enter Canaan

☑ Inheritance of the tribes — *Deuteronomy 3:12–17, Joshua 13:8–13, 15–32*

☑ Recap of victories — *Joshua 12:1–6*

☑ Command for conquest — *Numbers 33:50–56, Deuteronomy 3:18–29*

☑ Boundaries given — *Numbers 34:1–15*

☑ Men chosen to divide the land — *Numbers 34:16–29*

☑ Cities promised to Levites — *Numbers 35:1–8*

FOR THOUGHT AND CONTEMPLATION

In dividing the land *before* they entered it, the Israelites demonstrated their faith in God's great promise. Has God made you a personal promise? Then remember that faith is acting as if you are already in possession of it.

---

"For no matter how many promises God has made, they are 'Yes' in Christ. And so through him the 'Amen' is spoken by us to the glory of God." (2 Cor. 1:20, NIV)

---

## Review of Jewish law and history

☑ The laws about murder — *Numbers 35:9–34*

☑ Cities of refuge appointed — *Deuteronomy 4:41–49*

☑ Law settled regarding murder — *Deuteronomy 19:1–13*

☑ Inheritance law reviewed — *Numbers 36:1–12*

☑ Review of Jewish law and history: Moses' words to Israel — *Deuteronomy 1:1–5*

☑ Moses' exhortation to obedience — *Deuteronomy 4:1–24*

FOR THOUGHT AND CONTEMPLATION

Have you ever wondered why some enjoy the blessing of God more than others? One great key is *obedience*. That key opened up the whole of Canaan to the Israelites. It will open up your own personal 'Canaan' too — but only as you use it.

---

"Don't you know that when you offer yourselves to someone to obey him as slaves, you are slaves to the one whom you obey — whether you are slaves to sin, which leads to death, or to obedience, which leads to righteousness?" (Rom. 6:16, NIV)

---

# Restating of the Ten Commandments

☑ God's warning and promise of mercy — *Deuteronomy 4:25–40*

☑ The covenant in Horeb — *Deuteronomy 5:1–5*

☑ The ten commandments repeated — *Deuteronomy 5:6–22*

☑ The people's request — *Deuteronomy 5:23–33*

☑ An incentive to obedience — *Deuteronomy 6:1–3*

☑ An exhortation to obedience — *Deuteronomy 6:4–5*

☑ Obedience taught — *Deuteronomy 6:6–16*

☑ Instruction of children — *Deuteronomy 6:17–25*

☑ Caution against association with idolaters — *Deuteronomy 7:1–11*

FOR THOUGHT AND CONTEMPLATION

In restating the Ten Commandments, Moses underlined the command: "Thou shalt have no other gods before me." Why this emphasis? Moses knew the ever-present danger of substituting *something* for the all-important *Someone*.

---

"For although they knew God, they neither glorified him as God nor gave thanks to him, but their thinking became futile and their foolish hearts were darkened. They exchanged the truth of God for a lie, and worshipped and served created things rather than the Creator …" (Rom. 1:21, 25, NIV)

---

# Exhortations and cautions

☑ Rewards for obedience — *Deuteronomy 7:12–26*

☑ Exhortations and cautions — *Deuteronomy 8:1–9*

☑ Exhortations and cautions further enforced — *Deuteronomy 8:10–20*

☑ Success not due to worthiness — *Deuteronomy 9:1–6*

☑ Moses reminds the Israelites of God's mercies — *Deuteronomy 9:7–29*

☑ Moses makes new stone tablets — *Deuteronomy 10:1–5*

☑ Moses' exhortation to obedience — *Deuteronomy 10:8–22*

FOR THOUGHT AND CONTEMPLATION

Moses' reminder that success is due, not to human worthiness, but Divine mercy, is something that relates equally to His Church of today. Hold it as an axiom and repeat it as often as you can: *I am what I am because He is what He is!*

---

"I know what it is to be in need, and I know what it is to have plenty. I have learned the secret of being content in any and every situation, whether well fed or hungry, whether living in plenty or in want. I can do everything through him who gives me strength." (Phil. 4:12–13, NIV)

---

## HISTORICAL BOOKS

After the first five books of the Bible come a collection of books which are often known as the historical books of the Old Testament (Joshua, Judges, Ruth, 1 and 2 Samuel, 1 and 2 Kings, 1 and 2 Chronicles, Ezra, Nehemiah and Esther). These twelve books trace the history of God's people from their entry into the Promised Land under Joshua's leadership, their settling there with their rulers (judges and then kings), the division of the kingdom, their capture, deportation and return to Jerusalem.

## THURSDAY, Week 10 — Further exhortations and instructions

- ☑ Results of obedience and disobedience — *Deuteronomy 11:1–7*
- ☑ Promises and warnings — *Deuteronomy 11:8–17*
- ☑ Study of God's Word imperative — *Deuteronomy 11:18–25*
- ☑ Choice between blessing or curse — *Deuteronomy 11:26–32*
- ☑ Monuments of idolatry to be destroyed — *Deuteronomy 12:1–4*
- ☑ The place of God's service — *Deuteronomy 12:5–32*
- ☑ Punishment of the wicked — *Deuteronomy 13:1–11*
- ☑ Idolatrous cities to be destroyed — *Deuteronomy 13:12–18*

FOR THOUGHT AND CONTEMPLATION

In all our duties as Christians the reading and study of God's Word is one of the highest priorities, for the more we love God, the more we will love the Bible, and the more we love the Bible, the more we will love God. Don't give up. The benefits of reading through the Bible and meditation are worth more than the cost in the time and effort involved.

"Do your best to present yourself to God as one approved, a workman who does not need to be ashamed and who correctly handles the word of truth." (2 Tim. 2:15, NIV)

## FRIDAY Week 10 — Laws and directives

- ☑ Israelites to be a distinguished people — *Deuteronomy 14:1–21*
- ☑ Regarding tithes — *Deuteronomy 14:22–29*
- ☑ The seventh year of release — *Deuteronomy 15:1–11*
- ☑ The release of servants — *Deuteronomy 15:12–18*
- ☑ Regarding the firstlings of cattle — *Deuteronomy 15:19–23*
- ☑ The yearly feasts — *Deuteronomy 16:1–17*
- ☑ Appointment of judges, and other directives — *Deuteronomy 16:18–22*
- ☑ Sacrifices to be perfect — *Deuteronomy 17:1*
- ☑ Penalty for idolatry — *Deuteronomy 17:2–7*

FOR THOUGHT AND CONTEMPLATION

God's purpose for Israel was that they might be His *distinguished* people — a nation *in* the world, yet *different* from it. This is equally His purpose for you and me — today. But how sad that our similarities to the world are sometimes more clearly seen than our differences.

"But you are a chosen people, a royal priesthood, a holy nation, a people belonging to God, that you may declare the praises of him who called you out of darkness into his wonderful light." (1 Pet. 2:9, NIV)

## SATURDAY Week 10 — National laws

- ☑ Settling of controversies — *Deuteronomy 17:8–13*
- ☑ The choice of a king — *Deuteronomy 17:14–20*
- ☑ Provision for the Levites — *Deuteronomy 18:1–8*
- ☑ Abominations to be avoided — *Deuteronomy 18:9–14*
- ☑ Christ the great Prophet — *Deuteronomy 18:15–22*
- ☑ Landmarks not to be removed — *Deuteronomy 19:14*
- ☑ The punishment of false witnesses — *Deuteronomy 19:15–21*
- ☑ Proclamation regarding war — *Deuteronomy 20:1–9*

- ☑ Instructions about captured cities — *Deuteronomy 20:10–20*
- ☑ Various instructions — *Deuteronomy 21:1–14*

FOR THOUGHT AND CONTEMPLATION

The rules and regulations of God may seem at times to be onerous and unnecessary. But God's laws are designed to help us — not hurt us. It is better to build a fence at the top of a cliff than a hospital at the bottom.

"For in my inner being I delight in God's law." (Rom. 7:22, NIV)

# Further regulations for Israel

✓ The firstborn — *Deuteronomy 21:15–17*
✓ A stubborn son — *Deuteronomy 21:18–21*
✓ Rule about hanging — *Deuteronomy 21:22–23*
✓ Extent of punishment — *Deuteronomy 25:1–3*
✓ Regarding the ox — *Deuteronomy 25:4*
✓ Marriage of a brother's wife — *Deuteronomy 25:5–12*
✓ Regarding unjust weights — *Deuteronomy 25:13–16*
✓ War against Amalek — *Deuteronomy 25:17–19*
✓ Second table of laws — *Deuteronomy 22:1–30*
✓ Regulations of the congregation — *Deuteronomy 23:1–25*

FOR THOUGHT AND CONTEMPLATION

The wisdom which Moses shows by anticipating problems that might arise in Canaan, and then giving clear answers for them, is the kind of wisdom that is characteristic of a true leader. Has God given you a leadership role in your home, the church or the community? Then pray for wisdom. Remember — it's yours for the asking.

---

"If any of you lacks wisdom, he should ask God, who gives genersously to all without finding fault, and it will be given to him." (Jas. 1:5, NIV)

---

# Personal laws

✓ Divorce and other laws — *Deuteronomy 24:1–22*
✓ Firstfruits offering — *Deuteronomy 26:1–11*
✓ Obedience and prayer — *Deuteronomy 26:12–19*
✓ Law to be written on stones — *Deuteronomy 27:1–10*
✓ The curses to be pronounced — *Deuteronomy 27:11–26*
✓ Prophecy concerning Israel's future — *Deuteronomy 28:1–14*

FOR THOUGHT AND CONTEMPLATION

As free agents, we may choose for ourselves which path to take, but in the divine scheme of things it always works out like this: obedience brings results; disobedience brings consequences. We are free to choose, but we are not free to choose the consequences of our choosing. Today, therefore — choose life!

---

"No man will be able to stand against you. The Lord your God . . . will put the terror and fear of you on the whole land . . . See, I am setting before you today a blessing and a curse — the blessing if you obey the commands of the Lord your God . . ." (Deut. 11:25–27, NIV)

---

# Prophecy concerning Israel's future

✓ Cures for disobedience — *Deuteronomy 28:15–44*
✓ Result of disobedience — *Deuteronomy 28:45–68*
✓ Moses calls God's mercies to remembrance — *Deuteronomy 29:1–9*
✓ Divine wrath — *Deuteronomy 29:10–21*
✓ The result of idolatry — *Deuteronomy 29:22–28*
✓ Secret things belong to God — *Deuteronomy 29:29*

FOR THOUGHT AND CONTEMPLATION

Never be afraid of the Almighty's chastisement. God's disciplines are designed not to demean and deter, but develop us. Parents who are afraid to put their foot down usually have children who step on their toes!

---

"'. . . the Lord disciplines those he loves, and he punishes everyone he accepts as a son.' Endure hardship as discipline; God is treating you as sons. For what son is not disciplined by his father?" (Heb. 12:6–7, NIV)

- Mercies promised to repentant — *Deuteronomy 30:1–10*
- Life and death set before them — *Deuteronomy 30:11–20, Numbers 36:13*
- Joshua replaces Moses — *Numbers 27:15–23*
- Final words of Moses to people — *Deuteronomy 31:1–6*
- Final words of Moses to Joshua — *Deuteronomy 31:7–8, 23*
- Final words of Moses to priests — *Deuteronomy 31:9–13*
- Final words of Moses to Levites — *Deuteronomy 31:24–29*
- Israelites' apostasy foretold — *Deuteronomy 31:14–22, 30, 32:1–18*

FOR THOUGHT AND CONTEMPLATION

The last words of any great man are usually of great importance and have special significance. It was so with Moses, and it was so with Jesus. Remember the last words of Jesus? They have cosmic significance! "Go into all the world and preach the good news to all creation" (Mark 16:15, NIV).

---

"… 'Write on a scroll what you see and send it to the seven churches … I am the Living One; I was dead, and behold I am alive for ever and ever! And I hold the keys of death and Hades.'" (Rev. 1:11, 18, NIV)

## MOSES — GOD'S MESSENGER

**God's Faithfulness** Deuteronomy 2:7; 4:33–38; 7:6–8; 8:3, 4; 9:4–6; 29:5, 6; 32:9–14

**God's Character** 6:4, 5; 7:9; 32:39

**God's Love** 7:13

**God's Glory** 4:39; 10:17, 18

**God's Grace** 7:6–9; 9:4–6

**God's Will** 10:12–16

**God's Coming Messiah** 18:15–19

**God's Word** 4:1, 2, 7, 9; 11:18–21; 30:11–14

"The Lord would speak to Moses face to face, as a man speaks with his friend." (Ex. 33:11)

---

- Judgments for sins — *Deuteronomy 32:19–25*
- God's deliverance — *Deuteronomy 32:26–43*
- Moses' exhortation — *Deuteronomy 32:44–47*
- Moses goes to Mount Nebo — *Numbers 27:12–14, Deuteronomy 32:48–52*
- Final words to the tribes — *Deuteronomy 33:1, 6–25, 2–5, 26–29, Psalm 91:1–16*
- Death of Moses — *Deuteronomy 34:1–7*

FOR THOUGHT AND CONTEMPLATION

It is always a sad moment when a great leader, particularly a spiritual leder, goes to his reward in heaven. But we must never fail to hold fast to the truth that though God may bury His workman, He carried on His work.

---

"… the time has come for my departure. I have fought the good fight, I have finished the race, I have kept the faith. Now there is in store for me the crown of righteousness, which the Lord … will award to me … and not only to me, but also to all who have longed for his appearing." (2 Tim. 4:6–8, NIV)

# A summary of Israel's history

- ☑ Thirty days of mourning for Moses — *Deuteronomy 34:8, 10–12*
- ☑ Joshua, the new leader — *Deuteronomy 34:9*
- ☑ Psalms summing up previous history of Israel — *Psalm 78:12–66, 105:16–45, 106:1–33, 135:1–20*

FOR THOUGHT AND CONTEMPLATION

When God called Joshua to lead the nation, He did not ask him to be another Moses. Leading Israel *out* was a task for a Moses, leading Israel *in* was a task for a Joshua. Joshua could not be Moses, nor Moses Joshua. You, too, have a place in God's eternal scheme of things, but you can only fit into it as you are yourself.

"Just as each of us has one body with many members, and these members do not all have the same function, so in Christ we who are many form one body, and each member belongs to all the others. We have different gifts, according to the grace given us ..." (Rom. 12:4–6, NIV)

---

# The crossing into Canaan

- ☑ God appoints Joshua — *Joshua 1:1–4*
- ☑ God promises His assistance — *Joshua 1:5–9*
- ☑ Joshua and the Israelites go to Jordan — *Joshua 3:1*
- ☑ Rahab protects the spies — *Joshua 2:1–21*
- ☑ The return of the spies — *Joshua 2:22–24*
- ☑ Joshua instructs the people — *Joshua 1:10–18*
- ☑ The ark's importance — *Joshua 3:2–13*
- ☑ Crossing the Jordan — *Joshua 3:14–17*
- ☑ The memorial stones — *Joshua 4:1–18*

FOR THOUGHT AND CONTEMPLATION

When our focus is on what God has for us in the future, it is so easy to forget the past. But reminding ourselves of God's past victories buttresses our faith in His continuing goodness in the future. What 'memorial stones' can you raise in your mind today?

"... I have written ... to stimulate you to wholesome thinking — I want you to recall the words spoken in the past by the holy prophets and the command given by our Lord and Saviour through your apostles." (2 Pet. 3:1–2, NIV)

---

## A BIRD'S EYE VIEW OF JOSHUA

**Place in the Bible:**
Sixth Old Testament book; first book of history.

**Main character:**
Joshua.

**Special features:**
The Promised Land is the dominating theme of this book. Much of the book reads like an exciting epic with spies being sent on ahead into the Promised Land, Canaan, the Israelites crossing the Jordan and then the conquest and settlement of the Promised Land under Joshua's leadership.

**Jesus and the book of Joshua:**
Many examples of salvation are given in this book. Joshua, who leads the Israelites to take possession of Canaan, is a 'type' of Jesus Christ who is "bringing many sons to glory!'" (Heb. 2:10).

**Teaching:**
The main message of this book is that God always keeps His promises. The land that He had promised to Moses is now possessed by the Israelites. In this God's will, His goodness and His great power are all demonstrated.

**A verse to remember:**
"Not one of all the Lord's good promises to the house of Israel failed; every one was fulfilled" (Josh. 21:45).

# The battle of Jericho

- ☑ An exhortation to fear God — *Psalm 114:1–8*
- ☑ Camp at Gilgal — *Joshua 4:19–24, 5:1*
- ☑ Circumcision renewed — *Joshua 5:2–9*
- ☑ Change of food — *Joshua 5:10–12*
- ☑ Jericho shut up — *Joshua 6:1*
- ☑ The Captain of the Lord's host — *Joshua 5:13–15*
- ☑ The siege of Jericho — *Joshua 6:2–5*
- ☑ The city is compassed — *Joshua 6:6–16*
- ☑ Jericho is taken — *Joshua 6:17–20*
- ☑ Rahab and her family are saved — *Joshua 6:21–27*
- ☑ Defeat at Ai — *Joshua 7:1–5*
- ☑ Joshua's humiliation and prayer — *Joshua 7:6–9*
- ☑ God instructs Joshua — *Joshua 7:10–15*

FOR THOUGHT AND CONTEMPLATION

Victory at Jericho — but defeat at Ai. Why? A simple reason — *sinful disobedience*. When the sin is purged, then victory is given. Is there something in your heart that is holding up the victories you ought to be experiencing? Then root it out — today.

"'A little yeast works through the whole batch of dough.'" (Gal. 5:9, NIV) "Catch for us the foxes, the little foxes that ruin the vineyards ..." (Song of Sol. 2:15, NIV)

# The victory at Ai

- ☑ Achan is detected and destroyed — *Joshua 7:16–26*
- ☑ God encourages Joshua — *Joshua 8:1–2*
- ☑ The capture of Ai — *Joshua 8:3–22*
- ☑ The destruction of Ai — *Joshua 8:23–29*
- ☑ Altar built at Mount Ebal — *Joshua 8:30–35*
- ☑ The kings against Israel — *Joshua 9:1–2*
- ☑ The Gibeonites apply for peace — *Joshua 9:3–13*
- ☑ They are soon detected — *Joshua 9:14–21*
- ☑ They are to be bondmen — *Joshua 9:22–27*

FOR THOUGHT AND CONTEMPLATION

What a perilous path we walk when we rely upon our own wisdom and neglect to include God in our decisions (Josh. 9:14–15). Are you facing a major decision today? Then don't make a move until you have prayed and invited God's involvement in your decision-making.

"Guide me in your truth and teach me, for you are God my Saviour, and my hope is in you all day long." (Psa. 25:5, NIV)

# Continued victory in Canaan

- ☑ The angel of the Lord rebukes the people — *Judges 2:1–5*
- ☑ Five kings attack Gibeon — *Joshua 10:1–6*
- ☑ Joshua aids Gibeon — *Joshua 10:7–14*
- ☑ The kings' armies are defeated — *Joshua 10:15–27*
- ☑ Other victories — *Joshua 10:28–43*
- ☑ The kings at Merom — *Joshua 11:1–9*
- ☑ Hazor is burned — *Joshua 11:10–14*
- ☑ The country is subdued — *Joshua 11:15–23*

FOR THOUGHT AND CONTEMPLATION

Need a miracle in your life today? Then ponder again the story of the sun and moon standing still. This miracle of 'daylight saving time' has stretched the credulity of millions. But is anything too hard for the Lord? Well — is there anything?

"'Ah, Sovereign Lord, you have made the heavens and the earth by your great power and outstretched arm. Nothing is too hard for you.'" (Jer. 32:17, NIV)

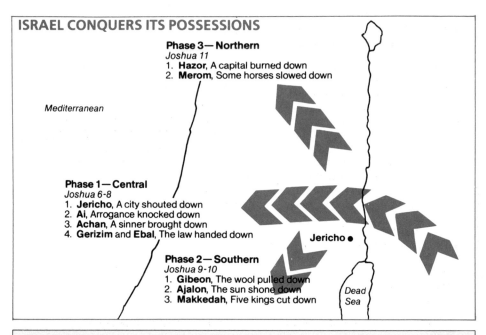

## ISRAEL CONQUERS ITS POSSESSIONS

**Phase 3— Northern**
*Joshua 11*
1. **Hazor**, A capital burned down
2. **Merom**, Some horses slowed down

*Mediterranean*

**Phase 1— Central**
*Joshua 6-8*
1. **Jericho**, A city shouted down
2. **Ai**, Arrogance knocked down
3. **Achan**, A sinner brought down
4. **Gerizim** and **Ebal**, The law handed down

Jericho ●

**Phase 2— Southern**
*Joshua 9-10*
1. **Gibeon**, The wool pulled down
2. **Ajalon**, The sun shone down
3. **Makkedah**, Five kings cut down

Dead
Sea

---

## WEDNESDAY Week 12 Caleb and Joshua

☑ Kings defeated by Joshua — *Joshua 12:7–24*
☑ The land not yet conquered — *Joshua 13:1–6*
☑ The division of Canaan — *Joshua 13:7, 14:1–5*
☑ Caleb obtains Hebron and his daughter receives a blessing — *Joshua 14:6–15, 15:13–19, Judges 1:20, 10–16, 1 Chronicles 6:56*
☑ Judah's portion — *Joshua 15:1–12*
   Israel's first sabbatical year 1415 BC
☑ The cities of Judah — *Joshua 15:20–47*

FOR THOUGHT AND CONTEMPLATION

After 400 years of waiting in Egypt, 40 years of strife in the wilderness and months of bitter warfare, the Israelites finally occupy the whole of Canaan. And guess what? It could all have been accomplished in far less time had they been obedient. Got the point?

"'Do not let this Book of the Law depart from your mouth; meditate on it day and night, so that you may be careful to do everything written in it. Then you will be prosperous and successful.'" (Josh. 1:8, NIV)

---

## THURSDAY Week 12 Division of the land

☑ The cities of Judah — *Joshua 15:48–63, Judges 1:21*
☑ The portion of Joseph's sons — *Joshua 16:1–10*
☑ Manasseh's portion — *Joshua 17:1–6*
☑ The boundaries of Manasseh — *Joshua 17:7–13*
☑ Joseph desires a larger portion — *Joshua 17:14–18*

☑ The tabernacle set up — *Joshua 18:1*
☑ The remainder of the land divided — *Joshua 18:2–10*
☑ The lot of Benjamin — *Joshua 18:11–28*
☑ The lot of Simeon — *Joshua 19:1–9, 1 Chronicles 4:28–33*

Many people 'yawn' their way through this part of the Bible. But as "all Scripture is profitable" (2 Tim. 3:16), there are nuggets of gold in every page. Here's one — the word 'inheritance'. It occurs many times. You, too, have an inheritance in God. Do you know what it is? Have you entered into it?

"I pray also that the eyes of your heart may be enlightened in order that you may know the hope to which he has called you, the riches of his glorious inheritance in the saints." (Eph. 1:18, NIV)

## FRIDAY Week 12    The cities of refuge

### CITIES OF REFUGE

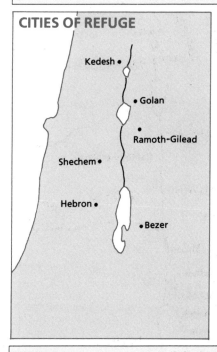

Kedesh •

• Golan

•
Ramoth-Gilead

Shechem •

Hebron •

• Bezer

☑ The lot of Zebulun — *Joshua 19:10–16*
☑ The lot of Issachar — *Joshua 19:17–23*
☑ The lot of Asher — *Joshua 19:24–31*
☑ The lot of Naphtali — *Joshua 19:32–39*
☑ The lot of Dan — *Joshua 19:40–48*
☑ Joshua's portion — *Joshua 19:49–51*
☑ The cities of refuge — *Joshua 20:1–9*
☑ No inheritance for the Levites — *Joshua 13:14, 33*
☑ Cities allotted to the Levites out of the other Israelites' inheritance — *Joshua 21:1–42*

FOR THOUGHT AND CONTEMPLATION

The cities of refuge were so appointed that a person who had committed unintentional murder could reach them within a day. They were easily accessible, well signposted, and their gates were open day and night. How beautifully illustrative of our Lord Jesus Christ — our eternal City of Refuge — to whom we run, when in trouble, and find perfect peace and rest. Hallelujah!

"God is our refuge and strength, an ever present help in trouble." (Psa. 46:1, NIV)

## SATURDAY Week 12    Establishment of the Judges

☑ Cities of the Levites — *1 Chronicles 6:54–55, 57–81*
☑ The Lord's promise fulfilled — *Joshua 21:43–45*
☑ Reuben and Gad sent to their homes — *Joshua 22:1–9*
☑ Altar of testimony built which offends the Israelites — *Joshua 22:10–20*
☑ The Reubenites' answer — *Joshua 22:21–29*
☑ The Israelites are satisfied — *Joshua 22:30–34*
☑ Establishment of the Judges — *Judges 2:16–19*
☑ First apostasy and servitude (Mesopotamia) — *Judges 3:5–8*

FOR THOUGHT AND CONTEMPLATION

Misunderstandings and disagreements between God's people over spiritual matters are often the most difficult to resolve. This is why we must heed the Scripture's advice, and *endeavour* (strive earnestly) to maintain "the unity of the Spirit in the bond of peace" (Eph. 4:3).

"Then Peter came to Jesus and asked, 'Lord, how many times shall I forgive my brother when he sins against me? Up to seven times?' Jesus answered, 'I tell you, not seven times, but seventy times seven.'" (Matt. 18:21–22, NIV)

THE TWELVE TRIBES

Mediterranean

Sidon

Damascus

Tyre

ASHER

NAPHTALI

DAN (North)

Kedesh

BASHAN

Hazor

MANASSEH (East)

Accho

ZEBULUN
ISSACHAR

Dor

Mt. Tabor

Megiddo

Ramoth-gilead

MANASSEH (West)

Jordan River

GAD

GILEAD

AMMON

Shechem

Joppa

DAN (South)

EPHRAIM

Shiloh

Bethel

Jericho

BENJAMIN

Ashdod

PHILISTINES

Jerusalem

Ashkelon

JUDAH

Bethlehem

REUBEN

Gaza

Lachish

Hebron

Dead
Sea

Beer-sheba

MOAB

SIMEON

EDOM

# The death of Joshua

☑ Othniel, the first Judge, delivers Israel — *Judges 3:9–10*

☑ Joshua's final exhortation — *Joshua 23:1–10*

☑ Joshua warns the people — *Joshua 23:11–16*

☑ God's benefits to their fathers — *Joshua 24:1–14*

☑ Joshua renews the covenant — *Joshua 24:15–28, Judges 2:6–7*

☑ Death of Joshua — *Joshua 24:29–31, Judges 2:8–9*

☑ Joseph's bones buried — *Joshua 24:32*

☑ Battles of the tribes of Judah and Simeon — *Judges 1:1–9, 17–19*

☑ Tribe of Joseph attacks Bethel — *Judges 1:22–26*

**FOR THOUGHT AND CONTEMPLATION**

Israel had lost Moses, and now they lose Joshua. But the nation continued to serve the Lord because of the spiritual impact of its elders. Spiritual leadership begets spiritual leadership.

---

"'Be strong and courageous, because you will lead these people to inherit the land I swore to their forefathers to give them.'" (Josh. 1:6, NIV) "Israel served the Lord throughout the lifetime of Joshua and of the elders who outlived him and who had experienced everything the Lord had done for Israel." (Josh. 24:31, NIV)

---

## A BIRD'S EYE VIEW OF JUDGES

**Place in the Bible:**
Seventh Old Testament book; second book of history.

**Main characters:**
Gideon, Samson.

**Special features:**
The special feature of this book is what has become known as the 'sin-cycle'. Six times the prospering Israelites forget God, are oppressed, then repent and are delivered by Him before they neglect Him and start the cycle all over again!

**Jesus and the book of Judges:**

Jesus came as a despised carpenter from Nazareth to save the humble, the weak and oppressed, and often in Judges it is the lowly and insignificant man, or tribe, whom God uses. Gideon asked: "How can I save Israel? My clan is the weakest in Manasseh ..." (6:15).

**Teaching:**
Judges is a sobering illustration of what disastrous consequences occur when God is rejected by a nation.

**A verse to remember:**
"But when they cried out to the Lord, he raised up for them a deliverer ..." (Judg. 3:9).

---

# Micah's idolatry

☑ Some Canaanites remain — *Judges 1:27–36*

☑ Israel's backsliding — *Judges 2:10–15, 20*

☑ Some nations left — *Judges 2:21–23, 3:1–4, 11*

☑ Second apostasy and servitude (Moab) — *Judges 3:12–14*

☑ Death of Eleazar — *Joshua 24:33*

☑ Second Judge, Ehud, delivers Israel — *Judges 3:15–30*

☑ Micah and his mother — *Judges 17:1–6*

☑ Micah hires a Levite to be his priest — *Judges 17:7–13*

☑ The Danites seek to enlarge their inheritance — *Judges 18:1–15*

**FOR THOUGHT AND CONTEMPLATION**

Micah thought it a sign of God's favour to him and his images that a Levite should knock on his door. His mistake was that he interpreted Scripture in the light of circumstances rather than circumstances in the light of Scripture.

---

"But when he, the Spirit of truth, comes, he will guide you into all truth. He will not speak on his own; he will speak only what he hears, and he will tell you what is yet to come." (Jn. 16:13, NIV)

**Civil war in Israel**

- ☑ The Danites rob Micah and invade Laish — *Judges 18:16–31*
- ☑ A Levite and his concubine — *Judges 19:1–13*
- ☑ The wickedness of the men of Gibeah — *Judges 19:14–30*
- ☑ Israel prepares for civil war — *Judges 20:1–17*
- ☑ War against the Benjamites and their defeat — *Judges 20:18–36a*

FOR THOUGHT AND CONTEMPLATION

Why do God's people one moment climb to great heights of spiritual attainment, then the next descend into the depths of degradation and despair? There is only one answer — the waywardness of the human heart. keep that in mind when next you stand on a peak of spiritual attainment.

"The heart is deceitful above all things and beyond cure. Who can understand it?" (Jer. 17:9, NIV)

## A BIRD'S EYE VIEW OF RUTH

**Place in the Bible:**
Eighth Old Testament book; third book of history.
**Main characters:**
Naomi, Ruth, Boaz.
**Special features:**
The book shows how a Gentile, Ruth, becomes an ancestor of Jesus Christ (she was King David's great-grandmother).

**Jesus and the book of Ruth:**
The book of Ruth mentions the word 'kinsman-redeemer' (see 3:9) thirteen times. Boaz, Ruth's 'kinsman-redeemer' prefigures our Redeemer, Jesus.
**Teaching:**
The book is a wonderful portrayal of God's care for an insignificant widow.
**A verse to remember:**
"'Your people will be my people and your God my God.'" (Ruth 1:16).

---

WEDNESDAY Week 13 **Ruth and Naomi**

- ☑ How the Israelites won — *Judges 20:36b–48*
- ☑ Mourning for the tribe of Benjamin — *Judges 21:1–25*
- ☑ Third judge, Shamgar — *Judges 3:31*
- ☑ Third apostasy and servitude (Canaan) — *Judges 4:1–3*
- ☑ The death of Elimelech and his sons — *Ruth 1:1–5*
- ☑ Naomi returns home — *Ruth 1:6–13*
- ☑ Ruth goes with Naomi — *Ruth 1:14–18*
- ☑ Ruth and Naomi arrive at Bethlehem — *Ruth 1:19–22*

FOR THOUGHT AND CONTEMPLATION

The decisions of Ruth and Orpah present a picture of what is involved in true conversion. Orpah draws back to end her days in heathen idolatry. Ruth moves on to have her name inscribed in the divine record. How sad that some can travel with God's people, yet fail to make that 'leap of faith' and entrust all to the Saviour.

" ...Agrippa said to Paul, 'Do you think that in such a short time you can persuade me to be a Christian?' Paul replied, 'Short time or long — I pray God that not only you but all who are listening to me today may become what I am...'" (Acts 26:28–29, NIV)

---

THURSDAY Week 13 **Ruth and Boaz**

- ☑ Ruth gleans in Boaz' fields — *Ruth 2:1–3*
- ☑ Boaz' kindness to Ruth — *Ruth 2:4–16*
- ☑ Ruth returns to Naomi — *Ruth 2:17–23*
- ☑ Naomi's instructions — *Ruth 3:1–5*
- ☑ Boaz acknowledges the duty of a kinsman — *Ruth 3:6–13*
- ☑ Ruth's return to Naomi — *Ruth 3:14–18*
- ☑ The kinsman refuses to redeem Ruth's inheritance — *Ruth 4:1–8*

- ☑ Boaz marries Ruth — *Ruth 4:9–12*
- ☑ Birth of Obed — *Ruth 4:13–17*
- ☑ Deborah and Barak, the fourth and fifth Judges — *Judges 4:4–9*
- ☑ Sisera defeated — *Judges 4:10–16*

FOR THOUGHT AND CONTEMPLATION

In the controlled life nothing happens by chance. Ruth's meeting with Boaz was not an accident, it was providentially arranged. Aren't you glad that your life is guided, not by luck, but by the *Lord* — not by the stars, but by the *Saviour*?

"The Lord delights in the way of the man whose steps he has made firm." (Psa. 37:23, NIV)

---

## FRIDAY Week 13  Israel — a world power

- ☑ Sisera put to death — *Judges 4:17–24*
- ☑ Praise and glory ascribed to God — *Judges 5:1–5*
- ☐ The deliverance of Israel — *Judges 5:6–11* **Israel is the world power (1200–750 BC)**
- ☑ Some commended, others censured — *Judges 5:12–23*
- ☑ Sisera's mother disappointed — *Judges 5:24–31*
- ☑ Fourth apostasy and servitude (Midian) — *Judges 6:1–6*
- ☑ Israel rebuked — *Judges 6:7–10*
- ☑ Sixth Judge, Gideon, set to deliver Israel — *Judges 6:11–24*
- ☑ Gideon destroys Baal's altar — *Judges 6:25–35*

- ☑ Gideon's fleece — *Judges 6:36–40*

FOR THOUGHT AND CONTEMPLATION

Israel's rise as a world power came about only through *God's* blessing and the people's obedience. As long as they remained faithful, their power was certain. When they became disobedient, their power diminished. This is not only the story of nations, it is the story of individuals too.

"My eyes will be on the faithful in the land, that they may dwell with me; he whose walk is blameless will minister to me." (Psa. 101:6, NIV)

---

## THE JUDGES OF ISRAEL

| OTHNIEL | *v. Nomads* | Judges 3:5–11 |
|---|---|---|
| EHUD | *v. Moabites* | Judges 3:12–30 |
| SHAMGAR | *v. Philistines* | Judges 3:31 |
| DEBORAH | *v. Canaanites* | Judges 4—5 |
| GIDEON | *v. Midianites* | Judges 6:11—8:33 |
| TOLA | *of Issachar* | Judges 10:1–2 |
| JAIR | *of Gilead* | Judges 10:3–5 |
| JEPHTHAH | *v. Ammonites* | Judges 10:6 to 12:7 |
| IBZAN | *of Bethlehem* | Judges 12:8–10 |
| ELON | *of Zebulun* | Judges 12:11–12 |
| ABDON | *of Ephraim* | Judges 12:13–15 |
| SAMSON | *v. Philistines* | Judges 13—16 |

## SATURDAY Week 13 — The story of Gideon

- ☑ Gideon's army reduced — *Judges 7:1–8*
- ☑ Gideon encouraged — *Judges 7:9–15*
- ☑ The defeat of the Midianites — *Judges 7:16–22*
- ☑ The Ephraimites take Oreb and Zeeb — *Judges 7:23–25*
- ☑ Gideon pacifies the Ephraimites — *Judges 8:1–3*
- ☑ Succoth and Penuel are punished — *Judges 8:4–17*
- ☑ Gideon avenges his brethren — *Judges 8:18–21*
- ☑ Gideon gives occasion for idolatry — *Judges 8:22–30*
- ☑ Birth of Abimelech — *Judges 8:31*
- ☑ Gideon's death — *Judges 8:32–35*

- ☑ Abimelech made king — *Judges 9:1–6*

FOR THOUGHT AND CONTEMPLATION

Just as God gave Gideon a strategy to overcome the Midianites, so He is able to provide you with a divine plan to resolve your most pressing problems. Who and what are the 'Midianites' in your life? Pinpoint a problem right now, and ask God to give you His strategy for dealing with it.

"What, then, shall we say in response to this? If God is for us, who can be against us?" (Rom. 8:31, NIV)

## SUNDAY Week 14 — The story of Abimelech

- ☑ Jotham rebukes the Shechemites — *Judges 9:7–21*
- ☑ The Shechemites' conspiracy — *Judges 9:22–29*
- ☑ Abimelech destroys Shechem — *Judges 9:30–49*
- ☑ Abimelech slain — *Judges 9:50–57*
- ☑ Seventh Judge, Tola, defends Israel — *Judges 10:1–2*
- ☑ Eighth Judge, Jair — *Judges 10:3–5 (Ninth Judge, Eli)*
- ☑ Samson's conception — *Judges 13:2–7*
- ☑ The angel appears to Manoah — *Judges 13:8–14*

- ☑ Manoah's sacrifice — *Judges 13:15–23*

FOR THOUGHT AND CONTEMPLATION

"The measure of a man," said a great philosopher, "is what he does with power." Gideon's son, Abimelech, misused it, and ended his life in failure and defeat. How do you use the power God has given you? Carefully — or carelessly?

"For God did not give us a spirit of timidity, but a spirit of power, of love and of self-discipline." (2 Tim. 1:7, NIV)

## MONDAY Week 14 — The story of Samson

- ☑ Samson's birth — *Judges 13:24–25*
- ☑ Jephthah's youth — *Judges 11:1–3*
- ☑ Elkanah and his family — *1 Samuel 1:1–8*
- ☑ Hannah's prayer — *1 Samuel 1:9–18*
- ☑ Samuel's birth — *1 Samuel 1:19–23*
- ☑ Samuel's dedication — *1 Samuel 1:24–28*
- ☑ Hannah's song — *1 Samuel 2:1–10*
- ☑ The oppression of Israel — *Judges 10:6–9*
- ☑ Israel's repentance — *Judges 10:10–18*
- ☑ The Philistines in the west — *Judges 13:1, Psalm 106:34–46*
- ☑ Samson desires a Philistine wife — *Judges 14:1–4*
- ☑ Samson kills a lion — *Judges 14:5–9*

- ☑ Samson's riddle — *Judges 14:10–14*

FOR THOUGHT AND CONTEMPLATION

One important fact spells out Samson's downfall — he was careless in the day of his power. Those who are careless about their God-given duties and responsibilities end up like Samson — disappointed, disillusioned and powerless.

"Now it is required that those who have been given a trust must prove faithful." (1 Cor. 4:2, NIV)

## TUESDAY Week 14 God calls Samuel

- Samson's riddle continued — *Judges 14:15–20*
- Samson denied his wife — *Judges 15:1–2*
- Eli's wicked sons — *1 Samuel 2:12–17*
- Samuel's childhood — *1 Samuel 2:11, 18–21, 26*
- Warning to Eli — *1 Samuel 2:22–25, 27–36*
- Birth of Saul — *1 Samuel 9:1, 14:51*
- God calls Samuel — *1 Samuel 3:1–10*
- God tells Samuel of the destruction of Eli's house — *1 Samuel 3:11–18*
- Samuel established as a prophet — *1 Samuel 3:19–21*
- Jephthah and the Gileadites — *Judges 11:4–11*
- He attempts to make peace — *Judges 11:12–28*

FOR THOUGHT AND CONTEMPLATION

Who can tell the far-reaching effects of prayer? Hannah prayed, and from her prayer came Samuel, the first great prophet and the last Judge in Israel. Pray on — your *persistent* praying can produce results you never dreamed possible.

---

"This is the assurance we have in approaching God: that if we ask anything according to his will, he hears us. And if we know that he hears us — whatever we ask — we know that we have what we asked of him." (1 Jn. 5:14–15, NIV)

---

## WEDNESDAY Week 14 The Ark taken

- Jephthah's vow — *Judges 11:29–40*
- The Ephraimites quarrel with Jephthah — *Judges 12:1–6*
- Tenth Judge, Jephthah, dies — *Judges 12:7*
- Eleventh Judge, Samson — *Judges 15:20*
- The ark is taken — *1 Samuel 4:1–11*
- Eli's death and Ichabod's birth — *1 Samuel 4:12–22*
- Dagon is broken — *1 Samuel 5:1–5*
- The Philistines afflicted — *1 Samuel 5:6–12, 6:1*
- Ark restored — *1 Samuel 6:2–12*

FOR THOUGHT AND CONTEMPLATION

Why did Israel lose the battle even though the ark was with them? Perhaps they came to rely more on the ark than on God. When faith in God wavers, faith in inanimate objects increased. And when that happens, victory is no longer assured.

---

"By faith we understand that the universe was formed at God's command, so that what is seen was not made out of what was visible." (Heb. 11:3, NIV)

---

## THURSDAY Week 14   Samson and Delilah

- Ark at Bethshemesh — *1 Samuel 6:13–18*
- The people destroyed — *1 Samuel 6:19–21*
- The ark taken to Kirjath-jearim — *1 Samuel 7:1–2*
- Twelfth Judge, Ibzan — *Judges 12:8–10*
- Samson and the Philistines — *Judges 15:3–19*
- Samson's escape — *Judges 16:1–3*
- Saul's marriage and family — *1 Samuel 14:49, 50*
- Thirteenth Judge, Elon — *Judges 12:11–12*
- Samson and Delilah — *Judges 16:4–22*
- Samson's death — *Judges 16:23–31*
- Revival at Mizpeh — *1 Samuel 7:3–8*

### FOR THOUGHT AND CONTEMPLATION

How reassuring is the truth that God is the God of the 'second chance' — Samson's hair began to grow again! Have you failed in something God gave you to do? Then be encouraged — tell Him you are sorry, ask His forgiveness, and He will give you another chance.

"I will repay you for the years the locusts have eaten — the great locust and the young locust … my great army that I sent among you. You will have plenty to eat, until you are full, and you will praise the name of the Lord your God, who has worked wonders for you; never again will my people be shamed." (Joel 2:25–26, NIV)

## FRIDAY Week 14   The Story of Saul

- The Philistines defeated — *1 Samuel 7:9–14*
- Samuel's leadership — *1 Samuel 7:15–17*
- Fourteenth Judge, Abdon — *Judges 12:13–15*
- The evil government — *1 Samuel 8:1–3*
- Israel desires a king — *1 Samuel 8:4–9*
- The manner of a king — *1 Samuel 8:10–22*
- Saul brought to Samuel — *1 Samuel 9:2–10*
- Samuel told about Saul — *1 Samuel 9:11–17*
- Samuel's treatment of Saul — *1 Samuel 9:18–27*
- **Reign of Saul 1065–1025 BC**
- Samuel anoints Saul — *1 Samuel 10:1–16*
- Saul chosen to be king — *1 Samuel 10:17–27*

### FOR THOUGHT AND CONTEMPLATION

Israel's desire for a king was really a cover-up. Deep down inside, they resented the rule of God over them. They were like the boy who said, "My father told me to sit down, but I was still standing up on the inside." Remind you of anyone?

"If you love me, you will obey what I command." (Jn. 14:15, NIV)

## SATURDAY Week 14   War with the Philistines

- Jabesh-gilead delivered — *1 Samuel 11:1–11*
- Saul confirmed as king — *1 Samuel 11:12–15*
- Saul defeats Hagarites — *1 Chronicles 5:10, 18–22*
- Samuel declares his integrity — *1 Samuel 12:1–5*
- Samuel reproves the people — *1 Samuel 12:6–15*
- Thunder sent in harvest time — *1 Samuel 12:16–25*
- The Philistines' invasion — *1 Samuel 13:1–7, 19–23*
- Saul sacrifices and is reproved — *1 Samuel 13:8–18*

### FOR THOUGHT AND CONTEMPLATION

God never acts out of character. Despite the rebellion of His people, He promises not to forsake them "for the sake of his great name" (1 Sam. 12:22). And for that same reason, God will not forsake you. Remember that the next time you feel discouraged.

" …because God has said, 'Never will I leave you; never will I forsake you.'" (Heb. 13:5, NIV)

# The decline of Saul

☑ Jonathan's victory — *1 Samuel 14:1–23*

☑ The people forbidden to eat — *1 Samuel 14:24–35*

☑ Jonathan — the offender — *1 Samuel 14:36–46*

☑ Continual war with the Philistines — *1 Samuel 14:47–48, 52*

☑ Saul sent to destroy Amalek — *1 Samuel 15:1–9*

☑ Saul commends himself — *1 Samuel 15:10–23*

☑ Saul's imperfect humiliation — *1 Samuel 15:24–31*

☑ Agag put to death, Samuel and Saul part — *1 Samuel 15:32–35*

FOR THOUGHT AND CONTEMPLATION

Failure to carry out God's instructions, however contradictory to reason they may appear to be, always results in great spiritual loss. Make it a life principle to do whatever God asks, even though you may not feel like it. God says, "To obey is better than sacrifice." It is.

"'For my thoughts are not your thoughts, neither are your ways my ways,' declares the Lord. 'As the heavens are higher than the earth, so are my ways higher than your ways and my thoughts than your thoughts.'" (Isa. 55:8–9, NIV)

# The rise of David

☑ Samuel sent to Bethlehem — *1 Samuel 16:1–11*

☑ Samuel anoints David — *1 Samuel 16:12–13*

☑ The glory of God's creation — *Psalm 19:1–14, 8:1–9*

☑ David calms Saul — *1 Samuel 16:14–23*

☑ Goliath's challenge — *1 Samuel 17:1–11*

☑ David comes to the camp — *1 Samuel 17:12–30*

FOR THOUGHT AND CONTEMPLATION

Anger can be righteous as well as unrighteous. David's anger at Goliath's taunting of the Israelites was righteous because it arose from grief at what was happening to others, not from a grudge because of what was happening to him. Discerning the difference is vital.

"'In your anger do not sin': Do not let the sun go down while you are still angry." (Eph. 4:26, NIV)

# David's popularity increases

☑ David and Goliath — *1 Samuel 17:31–41, 55–56, 42–51, 57–58, 52–54*

☑ Jonathan's friendship — *1 Samuel 18:2, 1, 3–4*

☑ David's confidence in God's grace and care — *Psalm 23:1–6*

☑ David is praised — *1 Samuel 18:5–9*

☑ Saul tries to kill David — *1 Samuel 18:10–13*

☑ David prays for protection — *Psalm 5:1–12*

☑ David's wisdom — *1 Samuel 18:14–19*

☑ David marries Michal — *1 Samuel 18:20–30*

☑ David's prayer for help — *Psalm 12:1–8*

FOR THOUGHT AND CONTEMPLATION

David dressing up in Saul's armour was not the way to victory over Goliath. His defeat required special insight and sanctified cunning. When facing your 'Goliath' today, keep in mind that it is "Not by might nor by power, but by my Spirit," says the Lord Almighty" (Zech. 4:6, NIV).

"If any of you lacks wisdom, he should ask God, who gives generously to all without finding fault, and it will be given to him." (Jas. 1:5, NIV)

# KING SAUL — HIS RISE AND FALL

## The Rise of Saul

1. Israel demands a king. (1 Sam. 8)
Israel wanted to be like other nations.

2. Saul is chosen. (1 Sam. 9)
God instructs Samuel to look Saul out.

3. Samuel anoints him. (1 Sam. 10)
God's Spirit comes on him and he prophesies.

4. His leadership is confirmed.
(1 Sam. 11)
Saul raises an army and delivers the city.

## The Fall of Saul

1. He desecrates the priesthood.
(1 Sam. 13)
He offers a burned offering. Samuel reproves him.

2. He spares Amalek.
God had commanded them to be destroyed. Samuel reproves him.

3. He is possessed by an evil spirit.
(1 Sam. 16)
He attempts to kill and destroy David. David escapes, then confronts him.

4. He commands the killing of the priests of God. (1 Sam. 22)
He was jealous of David and thought they were his supporters.

5. He visits the witch of Endor.
(1 Sam. 28)
Saul is full of fear and commits suicide with his armour bearer. (1 Sam. 31)

"Now the Spirit of the Lord had departed from Saul..." (1 Sam. 16:14)

---

## WEDNESDAY Week 15 David turns to his God

- ☑ Jonathan warns David — *1 Samuel 19:1–3*
- ☑ David's confidence in the Lord — *Psalm 11:1–7*
- ☑ Saul's behaviour towards David — *1 Samuel 19:4–11*
- ☑ Michal helps David — *1 Samuel 19:12–17*
- ☑ David's prayer for safety — *Psalm 59:1–17*
- ☑ David flees to Samuel — *1 Samuel 19:18–24*
- ☑ David's prayer for justice — *Psalm 7:1–17*
- ☑ David's prayer for guidance and protection — *Psalm 25:1–22*
- ☑ David consults Jonathan — *1 Samuel 20:1–11*

FOR THOUGHT AND CONTEMPLATION

Where do you turn for confidence when you are up against the wall? To art? To literature? To music? To alcohol? David turned to the Lord, and reminded himself that God was on the throne (Psa. 11:4). In the midst of life's insecurities, He is the greatest security.

"God is our refuge and strength, an ever present help in trouble." (Psa. 46:1, NIV)

**David in difficulties**

- [x] Jonathan's covenant with David — *1 Samuel 20:12–23*
- [ ] Saul seeks to kill Jonathan — *1 Samuel 20:24–34*
- [ ] Jonathan and David part — *1 Samuel 20:35–42*
- [ ] David's prayer — *Psalm 26:1–12*
- [ ] David flees to Ahimelech — *1 Samuel 21:1–9*
- [ ] David's praise of God's goodness — *Psalm 34:1–22*
- [ ] David's prayer of trust in God — *Psalm 56:1–13*

FOR THOUGHT AND CONTEMPLATION

While fleeing from Saul, David finds time to compose two magnificent psalms. This is what is meant by turning a setback into a springboard. Can you turn life's trials and setbacks into a song? Try it today.

"I am not saying this because I am in need, for I have learned to be content whatever the circumstances." (Phil. 4:11, NIV)

---

**David's victory**

- [ ] David at cave of Adullam — *1 Samuel 22:1, 1 Chronicles 12:16*
- [ ] David's prayer for help — *Psalm 142:1–7*
- [ ] Many come to David — *1 Samuel 22:2, 1 Chronicles 12:17–18*
- [ ] David's evening prayer — *Psalm 141:1–10*
- [ ] David flees to Moab — *1 Samuel 22:3–5*
- [ ] David's prayer for protection — *Psalm 64:1–10*
- [ ] Doeg slays the priests — *1 Samuel 22:6–20*
- [ ] David's prayer for help — *Psalm 35:1–28*
- [ ] David saves the people of Keilah — *1 Samuel 23:1–5*
- [ ] David offers Abiathar protection — *1 Samuel 22:21–23*

FOR THOUGHT AND CONTEMPLATION

Imagine taking a band of men who were "in distress or in debt or discontented" and turning them into a formidable army! What a picture it presents of One greater than David — Jesus — who takes utterly unworthy men and women and turns them into a might army — the Church of the Living God!

"These ... follow the Lamb wherever he goes. They were purchased from among men and offered as firstfruits to God and the Lamb." (Rev. 14:4, NIV)

---

**Saul in pursuit of David**

- [ ] David speaks of God's judgment and grace — *Psalm 52:1–9*
- [ ] David's complaint — *Psalm 109:1–31*
- [ ] David's prayer for protection — *Psalm 140:1–13*
- [ ] God warns David — *1 Samuel 23:6–13*
- [ ] David's prayer of trust in God — *Psalm 31:1–24*
- [ ] David still sought by Saul — *1 Samuel 23:14–15*
- [ ] David's prayer for help — *Psalm 13:1–6*
- [ ] Jonathan comforts David — *1 Samuel 23:16–18*
- [ ] David betrayed by the Ziphites — *1 Samuel 23:19–23*
- [ ] David escapes — *1 Samuel 23:24–28*

- [ ] David's prayer for protection — *Psalm 54:1–7*

FOR THOUGHT AND CONTEMPLATION

Do you feel at this moment that Satan seems to be pursuing you to an unusual degree? Then do as David did, and focus your thoughts upon God. This is why God recorded David's words in His book, the Bible. He wants you to focus your thoughts on Him. And when you do, you will find the same comfort that David did.

" ...when the enemy comes in like a flood, the Spirit of the Lord will put him to flight" (Isa. 59:19, NIV)

## David spares Saul's life

- ☑ David goes to Engedi — *1 Samuel 23:29*
- ☑ David's prayer — *Psalm 17:1–15*
- ☑ David spares Saul's life — *1 Samuel 24:1–7*
- ☑ David shows his innocence — *1 Samuel 24:8–15*
- ☑ Saul acknowledges his fault — *1 Samuel 24:16–22*
- ☑ David's confidence in God — *Psalm 57:1–11, 108:1–5*
- ☑ Death of Samuel — *1 Samuel 25:1*
- ☑ David's request — *1 Samuel 25:2–11*
- ☑ David's intention to destroy Nabal — *1 Samuel 25:12–17*
- ☑ Abigail pacifies David and Nabal dies — *1 Samuel 25:18–38*

FOR THOUGHT AND CONTEMPLATION

One of the great principles of spiritual success is to honour leadership, even when that leadership seems to be working against you or shows signs of failure. David knew that Saul's authority was given him by God. He respected that — and moved on to success.

"Obey your leaders and submit to their authority. They keep watch over you as men who must give an account. Obey them so that their work will be a joy, not a burden, for that would be of no advantage to you." (Heb. 13:17, NIV)

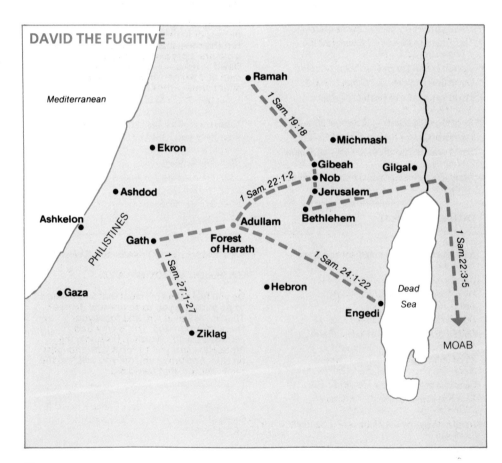

DAVID THE FUGITIVE

# David builds a great army

- David marries Abigail — *1 Samuel 25:39–44*
- David again spares Saul's life — *1 Samuel 26:1–12*
- David confronts Saul — *1 Samuel 26:13–25*
- David retires to Gath — *1 Samuel 27:1–7*
- David deceives Achish — *1 Samuel 27:8–12*
- David's friends — *1 Chronicles 12:1–7*
- The Philistines gather for battle: Achish's confidence in David — *1 Samuel 28:1–2*
- David prevented from fighting — *1 Samuel 29:1–11*
- Men who joined David — *1 Chronicles 12:19–22*

FOR THOUGHT AND CONTEMPLATION

Building anything for God requires dedication, determination and persistence. There are sure to be times of doubt and difficulty. David had his time of doubt, but he acknowledged it, resisted it, and moved ahead in the direction God told him to go. And so must you.

"We are hard pressed on every side, but not crushed; perplexed, but not in despair; persecuted, but not abandoned; struck down, but not destroyed." (2 Cor. 4:8–9, NIV)

## A BIRD'S EYE VIEW OF 1 CHRONICLES

**Place in the Bible:**
Thirteenth Old Testament book; eighth book of history.

**Main character:**
David.

**Special feature:**
Family histories (genealogies).

**Jesus and the book of 1 Chronicles:**
This book teaches how the relationship of the people of Israel to the Lord God should include worship and obedience. Jesus said that "God is spirit, and his worshippers must worship in spirit and in truth" (Jn. 4:24), and, "if anyone loves me, he will obey my teaching" (Jn. 14:23).

**Teaching:**
The story of Israel up to the end of David's reign is now retold from the point of view of a priest. The aim is to give the reader spiritual insight into these historical events. The events are the same as those covered in 2 Samuel and Kings. But Chronicles was originally intended for those returning from exile in Babylon to Jerusalem. Consequently, its spotlight falls almost entirely on the kings and kingdom of Judah.

**A verse to remember:**
"'Be strong and courageous, and do the work. Do not be afraid or discouraged, for the Lord God, my God, is with you'" (1 Chron. 28:20).

# The deaths of Saul and Jonathan

- Ziklag spoiled — *1 Samuel 30:1–6*
- David pursues the Amalekites — *1 Samuel 30:7–15*
- He recovers everything — *1 Samuel 30:16–20*
- David's distribution of the spoil — *1 Samuel 30:21–31*
- Battle positions — *1 Samuel 28:4*
- Saul consults the witch of Endor — *1 Samuel 28:3, 5–19*
- Saul's terror — *1 Samuel 28:20–25*
- Saul's defeat and death — *1 Samuel 31:1–13, 1 Chronicles 10:1–14*

FOR THOUGHT AND CONTEMPLATION

In God's sovereignty the destruction of David's home — which outwardly seemed a calamity — was but the preparation for his next phase of service — kingship. The words 'calamity' and 'sovereignty' are incompatible.

"And we know that in all things God works for the good of those who love him who have been called according to his purpose." (Rom. 8:28, NIV)

## A BIRD'S EYE VIEW OF 2 SAMUEL

**Place in the Bible:**
Tenth Old Testament book; fifth book of history.

**Main characters:**
Saul, David, Bathsheba, Nathan, Absalom.

**Special features:**
The establishment of Jerusalem and the reign of David, Israel's greatest king.

**Jesus and the book of 2 Samuel:**
2 Samuel 7:16, referring to David, records, "Your house and your kingdom shall endure for ever before me; your throne shall be established for ever." This promise was fulfilled in Jesus Christ, who is called the "Son of David" (Matt. 21:9), and who will be given "the throne of his father David" (Luke 1:32).

**Teaching:**
For all his conspicuous faults and sins, notably adultery and murder, King David stands out as a man who loved God. In public he showed his joy in God openly. In private he prayed frequently and confessed that God's grace accounted for all that he was. "The Lord is my rock, my fortress and my deliverer" (2 Sam. 22:1).

**A verse to remember:**
"... I will raise up your offspring to succeed you ... and I will establish his kingdom. He is the one who will build a house for my Name, and I will establish the throne of his kingdom for ever" (2 Samuel 7:12–13).

---

**WEDNESDAY Week 16  David becomes King**

- Mephibosheth's lameness — *2 Samuel 4:4*
- David hears of Saul's death — *2 Samuel 1:1–16*
- David's lamentation — *2 Samuel 1:17–27*
- Saul's descendants — *1 Chronicles 8:29–40, 9:35–44*
- David becomes king — *2 Samuel 5:4, 1 Kings 2:11, 1 Chronicles 29:27*
  Reign of David 1025–985 BC
- David anointed King of Judah — *2 Samuel 2:1–7*
- Ish-bosheth made King of Israel — *2 Samuel 2:8–11*
- Civil war in Israel — *2 Samuel 2:12–32, 2 Samuel 3:1*
- Children born in Hebron — *2 Samuel 3:2–5, 1 Chronicles 3:1–4*

FOR THOUGHT AND CONTEMPLATION

David's lament over Jonathan's death — "Your love for me was wonderful" — is one of the most beautiful passages in the Bible. When you consider the death of Christ, and what it meant for you, do not those selfsame words describe your feelings also?

"This is love: not that we loved God, but that he loved us and sent his Son as an atoning sacrifice for our sins." (1 Jn. 4:10, NIV)

---

**THURSDAY Week 16  Israel united**

- Michal and Abner return to David — *2 Samuel 3:6–21*
- Joab murders Abner — *2 Samuel 3:22–29*
- Murder of Ish-bosheth — *2 Samuel 4:1–3, 5–12*
- David made king over Israel — *2 Samuel 5:1–3, 1 Chronicles 11:1–3*
- List of David's warriors — *1 Chronicles 12:23–40*
- Israel united under David — *1 Chronicles 29:26*

FOR THOUGHT AND CONTEMPLATION

What explains David's great success? One thing above all else — early in his life he made a commitment to the God of the covenant. And the God of the covenant made a commitment to him. Without this understanding, no life can be secure.

"This is my blood of the new covenant, which is poured out for many for the forgiveness of sins." (Matt. 26:28, NIV)

# David: King of Israel and Judah

Length of David's reign — *2 Samuel 5:5*

Punishment of the wicked — *Psalm 58:1–11*

God the great King — *Psalm 93:1–5*

A song of praise — *Psalm 95:1–11*

Jerusalem becomes the capital city —
*2 Samuel 5:6–10, 1 Chronicles 11:4–9*

A prayer of thanksgiving — *Psalm 118:5–28*

House built for David — *2 Samuel 5:11–12,
1 Chronicles 14:1–2*

David's promise — *Psalm 101:1–8*

Children born in Jerusalem — *2 Samuel
5:13–16, 1 Chronicles 3:5–9, 14:3–7*

Wars against the Philistines — *2 Samuel 5:17,
1 Chronicles 14:8*

The Gadites join David — *1 Chronicles
12:8–15*

The Philistines gather — *2 Samuel 5:18,
1 Chronicles 14:9*

David brought water from Bethlehem —
*2 Samuel 23:13–17, 1 Chronicles 11:15–19*

FOR THOUGHT AND CONTEMPLATION

David's act of sacrifice in pouring out the
water that came from the well of Bethlehem
shows the depth of his sincerity and
dedication. How does his action compare
with your own willingness for self-sacrifice?
Moderately? Closely? Or remotely?

---

"Therefore, I urge you, brothers, in view of
God's mercy, to offer your bodies as living
sacrifices, holy and pleasing to God — which is
your spiritual worship." (Rom. 12:1, NIV)

---

# Israel's victory

Victory at Baal-perazim — *2 Samuel 5:19–21,
1 Chronicles 14:10–12*

The second conflict — *2 Samuel 5:22–25,
1 Chronicles 14:13–17*

Decision to bring ark back — *1 Chronicles
13:1–4*

God's complete knowledge and care — *Psalm
139:1–24*

Journey of ark from Kirjath-jearim —
*2 Samuel 6:1–2, 1 Chronicles 13:5–6,
2 Samuel 6:3–5, 1 Chronicles 13:7–8*

God and His people — *Psalm 78:1–11, 67–72*

Ark brought to Obed-edom — *2 Samuel
6:6–11, 1 Chronicles 13:9–14*

David's song of triumph — *Psalm 68:1–18*

FOR THOUGHT AND CONTEMPLATION

For God's blessing to flow, He must have the
central place. The ark, which was the symbol
of God's presence, had to be brought to
Jerusalem — the city of God. Where does
God dwell in your life? Is He marginal? Or
central?

---

"Being confident of this, that he who began a
good work in you will carry it on to completion
until the day of Christ Jesus." (Phil. 1:6, NIV)

---

## FROM SHEPHERD TO KING

David, the shepherd and son of a
Bethlehem farmer, was a man of many
parts and endowed with outstanding
abilities. He was an accomplished
musician, the poet who gave us so many
of the Psalms, a shrewd statesman and a
fearless general. He was responsible for
uniting the divided tribes of Israel and is
remembered as Israel's greatest king. 1
Samuel 13:14 reveals the key to David's
passionate devotion to his Lord. David,
it says, was a man "after God's own
heart".

**The ark restored**

David's song of triumph — *Psalm 68:19–35*

Preparation for the ark — *1 Chronicles 15:1–14*

The temple praised — *Psalm 132:1–18*

Musicians chosen — *1 Chronicles 15:15–24*

Ark brought to Jerusalem — *2 Samuel 6:12–15, 1 Chronicles 15:25–28*

God the supreme Ruler — *Psalm 97:1–12*

Ark set in its place — *2 Samuel 6:16, 17, 1 Chronicles 15:29, 16:1, 2 Chronicles 1:4*

What God requires — *Psalm 15:1–5*

The great King — *Psalm 24:1–10*

David blesses the people — *2 Samuel 6:18–19, 1 Chronicles 16:2–3*

FOR THOUGHT AND CONTEMPLATION

When the ark of God's presence is given its rightful place, the inevitable result is jubilation and rejoicing. If your heart is not singing today, perhaps this is the reason — God does not have His rightful place in your life.

"Let them give thanks to the Lord for his unfailing love and his wonderful deeds for men. Let them sacrifice thank-offerings and tell of his works with songs of joy." (Psa. 107:21–22, NIV)

*1 may 2016*

**Psalms of praise**

Hymn of praise prepared — *1 Chronicles 16:4–7*

Hymn of praise sung — *1 Chronicles 16:8–22*

God and His people — *Psalm 105:1–15, 1 Chronicles 16:23, Psalm 96:1–2, 1 Chronicles 16:24–33, Psalm 96:3–13, 98:1–9, 1 Chronicles 16:34–36, Psalm 106:47–48*

Daily sacrifices instituted — *1 Chronicles 16:37–43*

Michal despises David — *2 Samuel 6:20–23*

David's care for the ark — *2 Samuel 7:1–3, 1 Chronicles 17:1–2*

God's covenant with David — *2 Samuel 7:4–17*

FOR THOUGHT AND CONTEMPLATION

When God has His rightful place in the hearts of not just some, but all of His people, then the Church becomes like the temple in David's day — a habitation of continuous delight and endless praise. Why is it not so?

"The Lord is my strength and my song; he has become my salvation. Shouts of joy and victory resound in the tents of the righteous: 'The Lord's right hand has done mighty things!'" (Psa. 118:14–15, NIV)

**Israel increases her territory**

God's covenant with David — *1 Chronicles 17:3–15*

David's prayer and thanksgiving — *2 Samuel 7:18–29, 1 Chronicles 17:16–27*

God's chosen King — *Psalm 2:1–12, 110:1–7*

David's prayer of confidence — *Psalm 16:1–11*

Territorial gains: Philistine — *2 Samuel 8:1, 1 Chronicles 18:1*

Moab — *2 Samuel 8:2, 1 Chronicles 18:2*

Zobah — *2 Samuel 8:3–4, 7–8, 1 Chronicles 18:3–4, 7–8*

Syria — *2 Samuel 8:5–6, 1 Chronicles 18:5–6*

David's thanksgiving — *Psalm 9:1–20*

FOR THOUGHT AND CONTEMPLATION

Despite all that Israel had gained, God led them to embark upon gaining even more territory. How is it with you in your Christian life? Is God leading you on to even greater gains? Then don't hold back. S-t-r-e-t-c-h yourself. God is with you.

"Enlarge the place of your tent, stretch your tent curtain wide, do not hold back; lengthen your cords, strengthen your stakes." (Isa. 54:2, NIV)

**David's military victories**

- ☑ Territories gained: Hamath — *2 Samuel 8:9–11, 1 Chronicles 18:9–10*
- ☑ David's prayer for deliverance — *Psalm 60:1–12, 108:6–13*
- ☑ Edom subdued — *2 Samuel 8:13–14, 1 Chronicles 18:12–13*
- ☑ Hadad flees to Egypt — *1 Kings 11:15–20*
- ☑ Spoils dedicated — *2 Samuel 8:12, 1 Chronicles 18:11*
- ☑ David's mighty men — *2 Samuel 23:8–12, 18–39, 1 Chronicles 11:10–14, 20–47*
- ☑ David's government and officers — *2 Samuel 8:15–18, 1 Chronicles 18:14–17*

FOR THOUGHT AND CONTEMPLATION

The list of David's victories is staggering. But had he gone to battle without God, it would not be his victories we would be reading about, but his defeats. When God sends, He fends — wards off all fatal harm on the way.

"But thanks be to God! He gives us the victory through our Lord Jesus Christ." (1 Cor. 15:57, NIV)

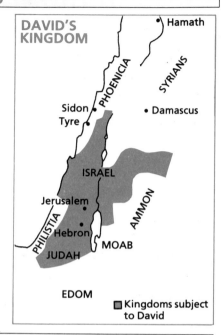

DAVID'S KINGDOM

Hamath

PHOENICIA

SYRIANS

Sidon
Tyre

• Damascus

ISRAEL

Jerusalem

AMMON

Hebron

MOAB

PHILISTIA

JUDAH

EDOM

■ Kingdoms subject to David

---

**David's songs of thanksgiving**

- ☑ David's psalm of thanksgiving — *2 Samuel 22:1–51*
- ☑ David's song of victory — *Psalm 18:1–50*
- ☑ He thanks God for victory — *Psalm 144:1–15*

FOR THOUGHT AND CONTEMPLATION

One of the things God delights in is His people's praise. Has God given you a victory in the last few days or weeks? Then do as David did, and compose your own psalm of praise. You'll be surprised at the result.

"I will extol the Lord at all times; his praise will always be on my lips." (Psa. 34:1, NIV)

---

**David and Bathsheba**

- ☑ David and Mephibosheth — *2 Samuel 9:1–13*
- ☑ Decisive victories over Ammonite-Syrian forces — *2 Samuel 10:1–14, 1 Chronicles 19:1–15*
- ☑ David defeats Syrian forces — *2 Samuel 10:15–19, 1 Chronicles 19:16–19*
- ☑ David's prayer for victory — *Psalm 20:1–9*
- ☑ David's sin — *1 Kings 15:5*
- ☑ David's adultery — *2 Samuel 11:1–5*
- ☑ His attempt at concealment — *2 Samuel 11:6–13*
- ☑ Uriah murdered — *2 Samuel 11:14–27*

FOR THOUGHT AND CONTEMPLATION

How sad that David — "the man after God's own heart" — could fall into the sins of adultery and murder. Somewhere inside David's heart, spiritual erosion had set in. Is there any spiritual erosion taking place in your life? Check now — before it is too late!

"If we confess our sins, he is faithful and just and will forgive us our sins and purify us from all unrighteousness." (1 Jn. 1:9, NIV)

# The birth of Solomon

☑ Nathan's parable and David's confession — *2 Samuel 12:1–15*

☑ His prayer for forgiveness — *Psalm 51:1–19, 32:1–11, 38:1–22*

☑ God's love and mercy — *Psalm 103:1–22*

☐ David's intercession — *2 Samuel 12:16*

☐ His prayer for help — *Psalm 6:1–10*

☑ David's child dies — *2 Samuel 12:17–23*

☑ Solomon's birth — *2 Samuel 12:24–25*

**FOR THOUGHT AND CONTEMPLATION**

The greatest deception in life is self-deception. David had deceived himself to such an extent that it took Nathan's barbed parable to bring him out into the open. "To thine own self be true, then it follows as the night the day — thou canst not then be false to any man."

---

"Surely you desire truth in the inner parts; you teach me wisdom in the inmost place." (Psa. 51:6, NIV)

---

# David's family troubles

☑ David and Joab capture Rabbah — *2 Samuel 12:26–31, 1 Chronicles 20:1–3*

☑ Praise for victory — *Psalm 21:1–13*

☑ Amnon rapes his sister Tamar — *2 Samuel 13:1–20*

☑ Absalom murders Amnon — *2 Samuel 13:21–29*

☑ Absalom flees to Geshur — *2 Samuel 13:30–39*

☑ Absalom persuaded to return — *2 Samuel 14:1–7, 15–17, 8–14, 18–33*

**FOR THOUGHT AND CONTEMPLATION**

"Most problems in children," said one famous family counsellor, "are the reflecton of what lies in the hearts of the parents." Did David's weaknesses work themselves out in his own offspring? We can only speculate — but it's a thought worth pondering.

---

"Train a child in the way he should go, and when he is old he will not turn from it." (Prov. 22:6, NIV)

---

## NAMES OF GOD

**ELOHIM** — used 2,570 times, refers to God's power and might (Gen. 1:1; Psa. 19:1).

**EL** — *four compounds of this name* —
**ELYON**, the strongest strong One (Gen. 14:17–20; Isa. 14:13, 14)
**ROI**, the strong One who sees (Gen. 16:13)
**SHADDAI**, the breasted One (used 48 times in Old Testament; see Gen. 17:1; Psa. 91:1)
**OLAM**, the everlasting God (Isa. 40:28)

**ADONAI** — Master, Lord. God owns all His creation (Mal. 1:6).

**JEHOVAH** — the most common name. Occurs 6,823 times. The Self-existent One, the God of the covenant (Gen. 2:4). *There are nine compound names of this name:*
**JIREH** — the Lord will provide (Gen. 22:13, 14)
**NISSI** — the Lord, my banner (Ex. 17:15)
**SHALOM** — the Lord is Peace (Judg. 6:24)
**SABBAOTH** — the Lord of Hosts (1 Sam. 1:3; Isa. 6:1–3)
**MACCADDESHOEM** — the Lord thy Sanctifier (Ex. 31:13)
**ROHI** (Raah) — the Lord my Shepherd (Psa. 23:1)
**TSIDKENU** — the Lord our Righteousness (Jer. 23:6)
**SHAMMAH** — the Lord who is present (Ezek. 48:35)
**RAPHA** — the Lord our Healer (Ex. 15:26)

*Begin - 9-05-16* ✓

**Absalom's rebellion**

- Absalom's ambition — *2 Samuel 15:1–6*
- David's trust in God — *Psalm 62:1–12*
- Absalom's conspiracy — *2 Samuel 15:7–12*
- David's prayer — *Psalm 41:1–13*
- David leaves Jerusalem — *2 Samuel 15:13–16*
- His confidence in God's protection — *Psalm 63:1–11*
- Ittai's loyalty — *2 Samuel 15:17–23*
- David sends ark back — *2 Samuel 15:24–28*
- His prayer for protection — *Psalm 61:1–8*
- David on Mount Olivet — *2 Samuel 15:29–30*
- David's prayer for help — *Psalm 3:1–8*
- His cry of anguish — *Psalm 22:1–18*

FOR THOUGHT AND CONTEMPLATION

David's response to the conspiracy against him was not to wallow in self-pity, but to draw from it the lessons that would make him a better servant of the Lord. When we see God's hand in all events, then we shall see all events in God's hand.

---

"This is what the Lord says — your Redeemer, the Holy One of Israel: 'I am the Lord your God, who teaches you what is best for you, who directs you in the way you should go.'" (Isa. 48:17, NIV)

---

**Absalom's advisors** ✓

- David's prayer and praise — *Psalm 22:19–31*
- Man's wickedness — *Psalm 14:1–7, 53:1–6*
- David and Hushai — *2 Samuel 15:31–37*
- David and Ziba — *2 Samuel 16:1–4*
- Shimei curses David — *2 Samuel 16:5–14*
- David cries to God — *Psalm 39:1–13*
- Absalom enters Jerusalem — *2 Samuel 16:15–23*
- Ahithophel and Hushai advise Absalom — *2 Samuel 17:1–14*
- David escapes — *2 Samuel 17:15–24*

FOR THOUGHT AND CONTEMPLATION

How do you feel when you are ridiculed or abused? David did not allow Shimei's cursing to provoke him to anger, but viewed it as a 'divine reproof'. How much easier it is to stand up to life when we can make all things serve.

---

"'Blessed are you when people insult you, persecute you and falsely say all kinds of evil against you because of me. Rejoice and be glad, because great is your reward in heaven ...'" (Matt. 5:11–12, NIV)

---

**Absalom pursues David**

- David's prayer for help — *Psalm 4:1–8*
- Absalom pursues David — *2 Samuel 17:25–26*
- David is provided for — *2 Samuel 17:27–29*
- The prayer of an exiled man — *Psalm 42:1–11, 43:1–5*
- David's prayer after his betrayal — *Psalm 55:1–23*
- An old man's prayer — *Psalm 71:1–24*
- David' prayer for help — *Psalm 28:1–9, 143:1–12*
- His praises to God — *Psalm 40:1–12*

FOR THOUGHT AND CONTEMPLATION

Someone has said that there are two ways of handling life's problems: we can either let them drive us to despair — or drive us to prayer. David learned how to turn his irritations into intercessions. Have you?

---

" ...I have learned to be content whatever the circumstances." (Phil. 4:11, NIV)

---

## The Battle of Mount Ephraim

*14 . 05 . 16*

- ☑ David's prayer for help — *Psalm 40:13–17.* ✓ *70:1–5*
- ☑ His prayer of praise — *Psalm 27:1–14* ✓
- ☑ His cry for help — *Psalm 69:1–36* ✓
- ☑ A prayer for help — *Psalm 120:1–7* ✓
- ☑ The Lord our protector — *Psalm 121:1–8* ✓
- ☑ Absalom is slain — *2 Samuel 18:9–18* ✓

FOR THOUGHT AND CONTEMPLATION

How ironic that Absalom's glory — a head of hair, from which seven pounds in weight was trimmed annually — proved to be the cause of his death. Be careful about your *strengths* — they may turn out to be your greatest weaknesses.

---

"That is why, for Christ's sake, I delight in weaknesses, in insults, in hardships, in persecutions, in difficulties. For when I am weak, then I am strong." (2 Cor. 12:10, NIV)

---

## David restored to the throne

*15 . 05 . 16*

- ☑ David learns of Absalom's death — *2 Samuel 18:19–33*
- ☑ Prayer for justice — *Psalm 10:1–18*
- ☑ Joab reproaches David — *2 Samuel 19:1–10*
- ☑ David's praise of Jerusalem — *Psalm 122:1–9*
- ☑ David returns to Jerusalem — *2 Samuel 19:11–15*
- ☑ He pardons Shimei — *2 Samuel 19:16–23*
- ☑ A song of praise — *Psalm 92:1–15*
- ☑ David and Mephibosheth — *2 Samuel 19:24–30*

FOR THOUGHT AND CONTEMPLATION

"The true measure of a person," said someone, "is seen not only in their readiness to ask forgiveness of those against whom they have sinned, but in their willingness to forgive those who have sinned against them." By that standard, David was great. How about you?

---

"'And when you stand praying, if you hold anything against anyone, forgive him, so that your Father in heaven may forgive you your sins.'" (Mk. 11:25, NIV)

---

## SAMUEL — THE CIRCUIT-RIDING PREACHER

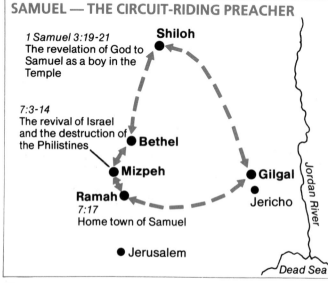

1 Samuel 3:19-21
The revelation of God to Samuel as a boy in the Temple

7:3-14
The revival of Israel and the destruction of the Philistines

Shiloh
Bethel
Mizpeh
Ramah
7:17
Home town of Samuel
Gilgal
Jericho
Jordan River
Jerusalem
Dead Sea

"And Samuel judged Israel all the days of his life. And he went from year to year in circuit to Bethel, and Gilgal, and Mizpeh, and judged Israel in all those places. And his return was to Ramah; for there was his house, and there he judged Israel, and there he built an altar unto the Lord"
1 Samuel 7:15-17

*16. 05. 16.*

## SATURDAY Week 18 — Israel and Judah quarrel

- David and Barzillai — *2 Samuel 19:31–40*
- Israel quarrels with Judah — *2 Samuel 19:41–43*
- Sheba's rebellion — *2 Samuel 20:1–3*
- Joab kills Amasa — *2 Samuel 20:4–12*
- Sheba seeks refuge but is killed — *2 Samuel 20:13–22*
- David's officers — *2 Samuel 20:23–26*
- The Gibeonites avenged — *2 Samuel 21:1–9*
- Rizpah's care — *2 Samuel 21:10–14*
- David honours God's majesty — *Psalm 29:1–11*
- His thanksgiving — *Psalm 65:1–13*

FOR THOUGHT AND CONTEMPLATION

The quarrel between the men of Israel and the men of Judah (whose words were "fiercer than the words of the men of Israel") might have been avoided if they had acted according to the key truth below. Try it the next time you find yourself on the verge of a quarrel.

"A gentle answer turns away wrath, but a harsh word stirs up anger." (Prov. 15:1, NIV)

## SUNDAY Week 19 — David numbers the people

- Battles with the Philistines — *2 Samuel 21:15–22, 1 Chronicles 20:4–8*
- David speaks of man's wickedness and God's goodness — *Psalm 36:1–12*
- David numbers the people — *2 Samuel 24:1–9, 1 Chronicles 21:1–6*
- Numbering hindered — *1 Chronicles 27:23–24*
- David's choice — *2 Samuel 24:10–14, 1 Chronicles 21:7–13*
- The pestilence — *2 Samuel 24:15–17, 1 Chronicles 21:14–17*
- David's sacrifice — *2 Samuel 24:18–25, 1 Chronicles 21:18–30*

FOR THOUGHT AND CONTEMPLATION

In the light of David's sacrificial giving, examine your own attitude to this important matter. Some give like a sponge — only when they are squeezed. Others give like Moses' rock — only when they are hit. But others give like a flower opening up to the sun — they *delight* to give. The latter was David's method. What's yours?

"Each man should give what he has decided in his heart to give, not reluctantly or under compulsion, for God loves a cheerful giver." (2 Cor. 9:7, NIV)

## A BIRD'S EYE VIEW OF 1 KINGS

**Place in the Bible:**
Eleventh Old Testament book; sixth book of history.

**Main characters:**
David, Solomon, Elijah, Ahab.

**Special features:**
1 Kings is the story of two nations: Judah and Israel. The building of Solomon's temple is followed by the division of David's kingdom into two. Elijah dramatically confronts the prophets of Baal who play a major role in the country's spiritual life.

**Jesus and the book of 1 Kings:**
The Queen of Sheba mentions Solomon's wisdom (1 Kings 10:8). Solomon is taken to be a "type" of Christ who "has become for us wisdom from God" (1 Cor. 1:30).

**Teaching:**
Chapters 12—14 record the division of the united kingdom of the original twelve tribes of Israel. As the book traces the histories of the kings of the southern kingdom of Judah (based in Jerusalem), and the northern kingdom of Israel (based in Samaria), we see the destruction caused by failure to obey God.

**A verse to remember:**
"God gave Solomon wisdom and very great insight, and a breadth of understanding as measureless as the sand of the seashore" (1 Kings 4:29).

# Solomon is made king

- ☑ David's thanksgiving — *Psalm 30:1–12*
- ☑ A song of praise — *Psalm 33:1–22*
- ☑ David's humble trust — *Psalm 131:1–3*
- ☑ David's old age — *1 Kings 1:1–4*
- ☑ Adonijah's plot — *1 Kings 1:5–9*
- ☑ David makes Solomon king — *1 Kings 1:10–37*
- ☑ Solomon is anointed — *1 Kings 1:38–40*
- ☑ The supreme ruler — *Psalm 47:1–9*
- ☑ Adonijah's submission — *1 Kings 1:41–53*

FOR THOUGHT AND CONTEMPLATION

The knowledge that David's son, Solomon, had come to the throne of Israel caused the heart of every true Israelite to rejoice. But here is a reason for greater joy: Jesus — "the son of David" — has ascended a throne from which He will never be deposed. Hallelujah! Our God reigns!

" …the appearing of our Lord Jesus Christ, which God will bring about in his own time — God, the blessed and only Ruler, the King of kings and Lord of lords." (1 Tim. 6:14–15, NIV)

---

# David's preparations for the Temple

- ☑ David's preparations — *1 Chronicles 22:1–5*
- ☑ His instructions to Solomon — *1 Chronicles 22:6–16*
- ☑ His commands to the princes — *1 Chronicles 22:17–19*
- ☑ The Levites and their duties — *1 Chronicles 23:2–6, 24–32, 24:20–31*
- ☑ Divisions of priests — *1 Chronicles 24:1–19*
- ☑ Singers and musicians — *1 Chronicles 25:1–31*

FOR THOUGHT AND CONTEMPLATION

In Christ's Church, as in Solomon's Temple, everyone has a place and a purpose. Have you discovered your place in the Body of Christ?* If not, you may end up trying to do someone else's job instead of your own. And that's frustrating!

" …in Christ we who are many form one body, and each member belongs to all the others. We have different gifts, according to the grace given us …" (Rom. 12:5–6, NIV)

*For more guidance on this subject, see the chart 'Discovering Your Basic Gift', available from CWR, or Selwyn Hughes' book 'Discovering Your Place in the Body of Christ' (Marshalls; available from CWR).

---

# Temple duties

- ☑ The temple guards — *1 Chronicles 26:1–19*
- ☑ The temple treasurers — *1 Chronicles 26:20–28*
- ☑ Administrative duties — *1 Chronicles 26:29–32*
- ☑ David's military force — *1 Chronicles 27:1–15*
- ☑ Chiefs of the 12 tribes — *1 Chronicles 27:16–22*
- ☑ David's overseers and officers — *1 Chronicles 27:25–34*
- ☑ David assembles the people — *1 Chronicles 28:1*
- ☑ Solomon is made king — *1 Chronicles 23:1*
- ☑ David's address — *1 Chronicles 28:2–10*

☑ David's hymn of praise — *Psalm 145:1–8*

FOR THOUGHT AND CONTEMPLATION

David wisely provided not only for worship, but also for war. The spiritual life involves not only benedictions, but battles. Alert Christians learn to worship with their armour on!

"Finally, be strong in the Lord and in his mighty power. Put on the full armour of God so that you can take your stand against the devil's schemes.' (Eph. 6:10–11, NIV)

**David's instructions**

☑ David's hymn of praise — *Psalm 145:9–21*
☑ David's directions concerning the temple — *1 Chronicles 28:11–21*
☑ In praise of the Creator — *Psalm 104:1–35*
☑ David speaks of God's protection — *Psalm 124:1–8*
☑ He praises brotherly love — *Psalm 133:1–3*
☐ His prayer for help — *Psalm 86:1–17*
☑ His instructions regarding giving — *1 Chronicles 29:1–9*
☐ His thanksgiving — *1 Chronicles 29:10–13*

FOR THOUGHT AND CONTEMPLATION

David had only to contemplate the glories of creation and his heart would swell in endless praise. Ever tried to compose a psalm? Try it today. Meditate on God's love and goodness as it relates to your life, and then compose your own personal paean of praise.

"Speak to one another with psalms, hymns and spiritual songs. Sing and make music in your heart to the Lord, always giving thanks to God the Father for everything, in the name of our Lord Jesus Christ." (Eph. 5:19–20, NIV)

---

**David's final words**

☑ David's prayer — *1 Chronicles 29:14–19*
☑ His prayer for the king — *Psalm 72:1–20*
☑ Solomon enthroned — *1 Chronicles 29:20–22*
☑ David's last words — *2 Samuel 23:1–7, 1 Kings 2:1–9*
☑ His death — *1 Kings 2:10, 1 Chronicles 29:28–30*
☑ Unclassified psalms of David — *Psalm 37:1–40, 138:1–8*

FOR THOUGHT AND CONTEMPLATION

A great man's final words are usually carefully noted and recorded for posterity. This is how it was with Moses, David, Elijah — and with many others. You have read David's last words — now read the last words of Jesus. Are they saying something to you — today?

"' ...you will receive power when the Holy Spirit comes on you; and you will be my witnesses in Jerusalem, and in all Judea and Samaria, and to the ends of the earth.'" (Acts 1:8, NIV)

---

## A BIRD'S EYE VIEW OF 2 CHRONICLES

**Place in the Bible:**
Fourteenth Old Testament book; ninth book of history.

**Main characters:**
Solomon, Queen of Sheba.

**Special features:**
The reigns of twenty-one kings and one queen are recounted. 2 Chronicles starts with Solomon — especially emphasising the building and finishing of the temple, and ends with Cyrus' decree permitting the exiled Jews of Babylon to return home.

**Jesus and the book of 2 Chronicles:**
In chapter 9 the Queen of Sheba visited Solomon and was overwhelmed by his wisdom and wealth. In Matthew 12:42, speaking of Himself, Jesus says, "... now one greater than Solomon is here."

**Teaching:**
The theme of this book is the consequences which stem from the keeping or the breaking of God's covenant. God will reward those who faithfully keep His laws. The book also outlines numerous characteristics of the Lord of the covenant: He is great (2:6), good (5:13), just (12:6), and patient (21:7).

**A verse to remember:**
"' ... if my people, who are called by my name, will humble themselves and pray and seek my face and turn from their wicked ways, then will I hear from heaven and will forgive their sin and will heal their land.'" (2 Chron. 7:14)

# King Solomon

☑ Solomon's reign begins — *1 Kings 2:12, 1 Chronicles 29:23–25, 2 Chronicles 1:1*

☑ Adonijah put to death — *1 Kings 2:13–25*

☑ Abiathar banished — *1 Kings 2:26–27*

**Reign of Solomon 985–945 BC**

☑ Joab put to death — *1 Kings 2:28–34*

☑ Solomon's instructions to Shimei — *1 Kings 2:35–38*

☑ Solomon and Pharaoh's daughter — *1 Kings 3:1*

☑ A royal wedding song — *Psalm 45:1–17*

☑ Solomon's love of God — *1 Kings 3:2–3*

☑ His sacrifice — *1 Kings 3:4, 2 Chronicles 1:2–3, 5–6*

☑ His prayer for wisdom — *1 Kings 3:5–15, 2 Chronicles 1:7–12*

☐ His return to Jerusalem — *2 Chronicles 1:13*

**FOR THOUGHT AND CONTEMPLATION**

Great though Solomon became in wisdom, riches and honour, the most significant thing that was ever said about him was that "he loved the Lord" (1 Kings 3:3). Would those words be true of you if they were written on your epitaph?

---

"Keep yourselves in God's love as you wait for the mercy of our Lord Jesus Christ to bring you to eternal life." (Jude 21, NIV)

---

## SOLOMON

Solomon's prayer for wisdom assured his place in Israel's history, for God generously answered that request. Wisdom in the Old Testament has a very practical emphasis — the skilful application of knowledge to daily life. The ancient Near East in Solomon's day, and before, was full of wise men and seekers of wisdom. Egyptian and Mesopotamian sages have left us their writings, but Solomon surpassed them all. One is always amazed how Solomon the wise man, the Temple builder, the king of God's choosing, could also become Solomon the despot and apostate. Wisdom, wealth, and wives were a potent combination that Solomon could not handle.

Solomon's reign has sometimes been called the Augustan age of the Jewish nation. But Solomon was not only its Augustus — he was also, according to tradition, its Aristotle. With the accession of Solomon, a new world of thought was opened to the Israelites. We find the first beginnings of that wider view which ended, at last, in the development of Judaism into Christianity.

---

# Preparations for building the Temple

☑ Solomon's judgment — *1 Kings 3:16–28*

☑ Reaction to David's death — *1 Kings 11:21–22*

☑ Solomon's court — *1 Kings 4:1–19*

☑ His daily provision — *1 Kings 4:22–23, 27–28*

☑ His agreement with Hiram — *1 Kings 5:1–12, 7:13–14*

☑ His treaty with Hiram — *2 Chronicles 2:1, 3–16*

☑ His workmen — *1 Kings 5:13–18, 2 Chronicles 2:2, 17–18*

**FOR THOUGHT AND CONTEMPLATION**

Building a temple for the worship of God was a colossal task. It involved careful planning, skilful negotiaton and great faith. But Solomon discovered, as will you, that God's work done in God's way will receive God's support.

---

"May the God of peace ... equip you with everything good for doing his will, and may he work in us what is pleasing to him, through Jesus Christ, to whom be glory for ever and ever ..." (Heb. 13:20–21, NIV)

---

# The Temple is built

- [x] Shimei's execution — *1 Kings 2:39–46*
- [x] A mother's advice — *Proverbs 31:1–9*
- [x] God's ideal woman — *Proverbs 31:10–31*
- [x] Solomon begins to build — *1 Kings 6:1, 37, 2 Chronicles 3:1–2*
- [x] God's promise — *1 Kings 6:11–13*
- [x] The dimensions — *1 Kings 6:2, 2 Chronicles 3:3*
- [x] The materials — *1 Kings 6:7 & 9, 2 Chronicles 3:5–7*
- [x] The porch — *1 Kings 6:3, 2 Chronicles 3:4*
- [x] The windows — *1 Kings 6:4*
- [x] The stories — *1 Kings 6:5–6, 8 & 10*
- [x] Most holy place — *1 Kings 6:16–22, 2 Chronicles 3:8–9*
- [x] The cherubim — *1 Kings 6:23–28, 2 Chronicles 3:10–13*
- [x] The veil — *2 Chronicles 3:14*

*28. 5. 13.*

- [x] The walls, floor and doors — *1 Kings 6:15, 29–35*
- [x] The completion — *1 Kings 6:14, Psalm 127:1–5*

FOR THOUGHT AND CONTEMPLATION

Solomon's temple was constructed not only with infinite care, but with the minimum of noise: "no hammer, chisel or any other iron tool was heard" (1 Kings 6:7). Clamour and frenzy hinder rather than foster spiritual growth. God's kingdom develops, not with great noise and the fanfare of trumpets, but quietly, effortlessly and silently.

" ...'In repentance and rest is your salvation, in quietness and trust is your strength...'"
(Isa. 30:15, NIV)

---

# The Temple furnishings

- [x] The reward of obedience — *Psalm 128:1–6, 1 Kings 6:38*
- [x] Solomon's buildings — *1 Kings 7:1–12*
- [x] Temple furnishings — *1 Kings 7:15–22, 2 Chronicles 3:15–17*
- [x] Altar of brass — *2 Chronicles 4:1*
- [x] Molten sea — *1 Kings 7:23–26, 2 Chronicles 4:2–5, 10*
- [x] Ten bases — *1 Kings 7:27–37*
- [x] Ten basins — *1 Kings 7:38–39, 2 Chronicles 4:6*
- [x] The courts — *1 Kings 6:36, 2 Chronicles 4:9*
- [x] Hiram's brass work — *1 Kings 7:40–47, 2 Chronicles 4:11–18*
- [x] Golden vessels — *1 Kings 7:48–50, 2 Chronicles 4:7–8, 19–22*

*28. 5. 13.*

FOR THOUGHT AND CONTEMPLATION

The priests who ministered in Solomon's temple were required to cleanse themselves frequently as they ministered before the Lord. As God's 'royal priesthood', we, too, must take advantage of the full means provided for our cleansing, the blood of Christ and the water of the Word.

" ...Christ loved the church and gave himself up for her to make her holy, cleansing her by the washing with water through the word."
(Eph. 5:25–26, NIV)

---

# The dedication of the Temple

- [ ] Final completion — *1 Kings 7:51, 2 Chronicles 5:1*
- [ ] The dedication of the temple — *1 Kings 8:1–11, 2 Chronicles 5:2–14*
  Dedication of Temple 972 BC
- [x] A prayer of thanks — *Psalm 118:1–4, 29*
- [x] The one true God — *Psalm 115:1–18*

- [x] A call to praise God — *Psalm 134:1–3, 135:21*
- [x] A hymn of thanksgiving — *Psalm 136:1–26*
- [ ] Solomon's address — *1 Kings 8:12–16, 2 Chronicles 6:1–6, 1 Kings 8:17–20, 2 Chronicles 6:7–10, 1 Kings 8:21, 2 Chronicles 6:11*

God required not only that the temple be built for Him but also *dedicated* to Him. Dedication goes further than hoping God will accept what we offer — it gathers up those hopes in a distinct and definite commitment. Don't just hope God will use you — dedicate your talents to Him — now.

" ...I urge you, brothers, in view of God's mercy, to offer your bodies as living sacrifices, holy and pleasing to God — which is your spiritual worship." (Rom. 12:1, NIV)

## THURSDAY Week 20   Solomon's prayer

☑ Solomon reminds God of His promises — *1 Kings 8:22–26, 2 Chronicles 6:12–17*

☑ He pleads for forgiveness — *1 Kings 8:27–30, 2 Chronicles 6:18–21*

☑ He prays for God's justice — *1 Kings 8:31–32, 2 Chronicles 6:22–23*

☑ He prays for mercy — *1 Kings 8:33–40, 2 Chronicles 6:24–31*

☑ He asks God to answer the foreigner's prayer — *1 Kings 8:41–43, 2 Chronicles 6:32–33*

☑ Prayer for victory — *1 Kings 8:44–45, 2 Chronicles 6:34–35*

☑ Prayer for Israelites — *1 Kings 8:46–53, 2 Chronicles 6:36–39*

☑ His final petitions — *2 Chronicles 6:40–42*

☑ Solomon's blessing and exhortation — *1 Kings 8:54–61*

FOR THOUGHT AND CONTEMPLATION

The prayers of God's servants in the Old Testament, Solomon's included, contain a common characteristic — spiritual boldness. This boldness stemmed from their knowledge that God was under an obligation to fulfil his promises (see 1 Kings 8:25). Follow this principle, and it could add a whole new dimension to your prayer life.

"Let us then approach the throne of grace with confidence, so that we may receive mercy and find grace to help us in our time of need." (Heb. 4:16, NIV)

## FRIDAY Week 20   Building programme completed

☑ God's blessing — *2 Chronicles 7:1–3*

☑ Solomon's peace-offerings — *1 Kings 8:62–66, 2 Chronicles 7:4–10*

☑ God, the supreme King — *Psalm 99:1–9*

☑ A hymn of praise — *Psalm 100:1–5*

☑ Building programme finished — *1 Kings 9:1, 2 Chronicles 7:11*

☑ God warns Solomon — *1 Kings 9:2–9, 2 Chronicles 7:12–22*

☑ Solomon and Hiram — *1 Kings 9:10–14, 2 Chronicles 8:1–2*

☑ Hamath conquered — *2 Chronicles 8:3*

☑ Solomon's wife's house — *1 Kings 9:24, 2 Chronicles 8:11*

☑ Love's beginning — *Song of Solomon 1:1–17*

FOR THOUGHT AND CONTEMPLATION

Another evidence of Solomon's wisdom was the fact that he had his priorities in the right order — he built a house for God before he built one for himself. When we put God *first*, then prosperity and blessing follow. Whose interests come first in your life? Yours — or God's?

"' ...seek first his kingdom and his righteousness, and all these things will be given to you as well.'" (Matt. 6:33, NIV)

# SOLOMON'S TEMPLE

A permanent resting place for the Ark of the Covenant. Similar to the tabernacle, but the Holy Place and the Holy of Holies were doubled in size. Known in the ancient world for its breathtaking beauty and craftsmanship. It stood for four hundred years until destroyed by the Babylonians.

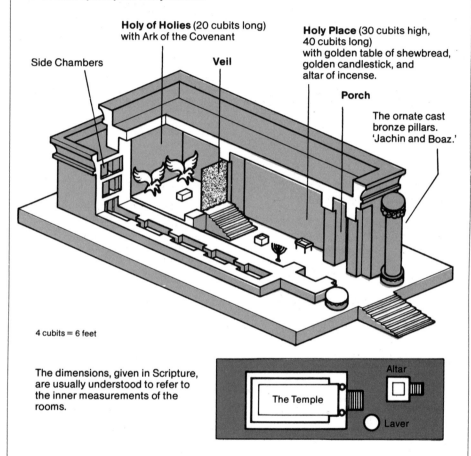

**Holy of Holies** (20 cubits long) with Ark of the Covenant

Side Chambers

**Veil**

**Holy Place** (30 cubits high, 40 cubits long) with golden table of shewbread, golden candlestick, and altar of incense.

**Porch**

The ornate cast bronze pillars. 'Jachin and Boaz.'

4 cubits = 6 feet

The dimensions, given in Scripture, are usually understood to refer to the inner measurements of the rooms.

The Temple

Altar

Laver

"And the house which King Solomon built for the Lord, the length thereof was threescore cubits, and the breadth thereof twenty cubits, and the height thereof thirty cubits. . ."

*1 Kings 6:2*

David wanted to build a permanent house where the people could worship God. He made very full plans for the building of a Temple, but, because many people had been killed in the battles he had fought against Israel's enemies, God did not allow him to go ahead. Instead, Solomon, his son, was given the job.

## A BIRD'S EYE VIEW OF SONG OF SONGS

**Place in the Bible:**
Twenty-second Old Testament book; fifth book of poetry and wisdom.

**Main characters:**
Solomon, Shulammite girl.

**Special features:**
A series of love poems.

**Jesus and the Song of Songs:**
The most famous verse in the Bible states how much God loves everyone: "For God so loved the world that he gave his one and only Son, that whoever believes in him shall not perish but have eternal life" (John 3:16).

**Teaching:**
The beauty and value of love between a woman and a man are joyously depicted. Love and sex within marriage are a gift from the Creator. The Song can also be read as a picture of Christ's love for the Church (God's love for His people is often compared in Scripture with the love of husband and wife).

**A verse to remember:**
"Many waters cannot quench love; rivers cannot wash it away" (Song of Songs 8:7).

---

## SATURDAY Week 20 — Bride and bridegroom

- Love's beginning — *Song of Solomon 2:1–7*
- Love's absence — *Song of Solomon 2:8–17, 3:1–5*
- Love's restoration — *Song of Solomon 3:6–11, 4:1–16, 5:1*
- Love delayed — *Song of Solomon 5:2–16, 6:1–3*
- Love's fulfilment — *Song of Solomon 6:4–13, 7:1–13, 8:1–4*
- Love's triumph — *Song of Solomon 8:5–14*

FOR THOUGHT AND CONTEMPLATION

A popular modern conception of 'love' is "never having to say you are sorry". This implies that where true love exists, asking forgiveness is unnecessary. But is it? Solomon's bride did not think so. Love means *wanting* to say you are sorry — and saying it.

---

"Be kind and compassionate to one another, forgiving each other, just as in Christ God forgave you." (Eph. 4:32, NIV)

---

## SUNDAY Week 21 — Solomon and the Queen of Sheba

- Levy of forced labour — *1 Kings 9:20–23 & 15, 2 Chronicles 8:7–10*
- Building the cities — *1 Kings 9:16–19, 2 Chronicles 8:4–6*
- Burnt offerings — *1 Kings 9:25, 2 Chronicles 8:12–16*
- Solomon's prosperity — *1 Kings 9:26–28, 10:22, 2 Chronicles 8:17–18, 9:21*
- The Queen of Sheba — *1 Kings 10:1–13, 2 Chronicles 9:1–12*
- Solomon's wealth — *1 Kings 10:14–21, 27, 23–25, 2 Chronicles 1:15, 9:13–19*

FOR THOUGHT AND CONTEMPLATION

When the Queen of Sheba saw the magnitude of Solomon's wealth and wisdom, her conclusion was that 'not even half was told me'. Those who come to know God through His Son Jesus Christ arrive at a similar conclusion. Jesus is such a wonder that the combined reports of all the teachers and preachers who have ever lived cannot do Him justice.

---

" ...'No eye has seen, no ear has heard, no mind has conceived what God has prepared for those who love him' — but God has revealed it to us by his Spirit ..." (1 Cor. 2:9–10, NIV)

# Solomon's wealth and wisdom

☑ Solomon's wealth — *2 Chronicles 9:20, 27, 22–24, 1 Kings 4:26, 10:26, 28–29, 2 Chronicles 1:14, 16–17, 9:25, 28*

☑ His kingdom — *1 Kings 4:21, 24, 20, 25, 2 Chronicles 9:26*

☑ His visitors — *1 Kings 4:34*

☑ His wisdom — *1 Kings 4:29–31, 33, 32*

☑ A cry for help — *Psalm 88:1–18*

☑ A hymn in time of national trouble — *Psalm 89:1–52*

☑ Value of proverbs — *Proverbs 1:1–6*

☑ Advice to young men — *Proverbs 1:7–19*

**FOR THOUGHT AND CONTEMPLATION**

If, today, God told you that you could have whatever you wanted — what would you choose? Wealth? Fame? Happiness? Solomon, when faced with that question, chose the greatest of all qualities — *wisdom*. And God was so pleased with his request that He added riches and honour also.

"If any of you lacks wisdom, he should ask God, who gives generously to all without finding fault, and it will be given to him." (Jas. 1:5, NIV)

---

## A BIRD'S EYE VIEW OF PROVERBS

**Place in the Bible:**
Twentieth Old Testament book; third book of poetry and wisdom.

**Special features:**
A collection of about nine hundred short, memorable, pithy sayings, concluding with the famous acrostic poem on the ideal wife in chapter 31.

**Jesus and the book of Proverbs:**
Widsom is personified in chapter 8 and from the New Testament we also know that wisdom became incarnate in Christ "in whom are hidden all the treasures of wisdom and knowledge" (Col. 2:3).

**Teaching:**
Proverbs chapter 1:2–7 explains the purpose of these proverbs. They can provide the reader with widsom, discipline and understanding. The fear of the Lord is the starting point for anybody who seeks to become wise.

**A verse to remember:**
"The fear of the Lord is the beginning of wisdom, and knowledge of the Holy One is understanding" (Prov. 9:10).

---

# The wisdom of moral restraint

☑ Virtue of wisdom — *Proverbs 1:20–33*

☑ Rewards of wisdom — *Proverbs 2:1–22*

☑ Trusting God's wisdom — *Proverbs 3:1–35*

☑ Benefits of wisdom — *Proverbs 4:1–27*

☑ Warning against adultery — *Proverbs 5:1–23*

☑ Caution about putting up security — *Proverbs 6:1–5*

☑ Warning against laziness — *Proverbs 6:6–11*

☑ Things God hates — *Proverbs 6:12–19*

**FOR THOUGHT AND CONTEMPLATION**

Have you ever reflected on what wisdom really is? "Wisdom," said a great man, "is more than knowledge: knowledge is just knowing things, but wisdom is the ability to put knowledge to its best effect." Ask God once again to help you 'wise up'.

"...the wisdom that comes from heaven is first of all pure; then peaceloving, considerate, submissive, full of mercy and good fruit, impartial and sincere." (Jas. 3:17, NIV)

## WEDNESDAY Week 21 The importance of wisdom

☑ Further warning against adultery — *Proverbs 6:20–35*

☑ The importance of learning wisdom — *Proverbs 7:1–5*

☑ The immoral woman — *Proverbs 7:6–27*

☑ The nature and riches of wisdom — *Proverbs 8:1–21*

☑ Wisdom (Christ) at the creation — *Proverbs 8:22–31*

☑ Listen to wisdom (Christ) — *Proverbs 8:32–36*

☑ Wisdom and foolishness — *Proverbs 9:1–18*

☑ Solomon's proverbs — *Proverbs 10:1*

☑ The benefits of righteousness — *Proverbs 10:2–32, 11:1–6*

### FOR THOUGHT AND CONTEMPLATION

One of the greatest definitions of wisdom, and one based on the Scriptures is this: wisdom is "seeing life from God's point of view" (Col. 1:9, J.B. Phillips). The proverbs you are now reading are part of God's plan to make you wise, or, in other words, to help you see life "from God's point of view".

---

"'For my thoughts are not your thoughts, neither are your ways my ways,' declares the Lord. 'As the heavens are higher than the earth, so are my ways higher than your ways and my thoughts than your thoughts.'" (Isa. 55:8–9, NIV)

## THURSDAY Week 21 The benefits of righteousness

☑ The benefits of righteousness — *Proverbs 11:7–11*

☑ The foolishness of quarrelling and wrongdoing — *Proverbs 11:12–31*

☑ The wicked and the righteous — *Proverbs 12:1–11*

☑ The wise and the foolish — *Proverbs 12:12–28*

☑ Watch your words — *Proverbs 13:1–6*

☑ The rich and the poor — *Proverbs 13:7–25*

☑ Contrast between wise and foolish — *Proverbs 14:1–35*

☐ Wisdom, the better way — *Proverbs 15:1–19*

### FOR THOUGHT AND CONTEMPLATION

Words are more powerful than we realise. When God 'spoke', He created a world — a glorious cosmos. And when you speak, you, too, create a world — a world of harmony, or a world of disharmony. Ask yourself now: what kind of world will I create by my words today?

---

"May the words of my mouth and the meditation of my heart be pleasing in your sight, O Lord, my Rock and my Redeemer." (Psa 19:14, NIV)

## THE BOOKS OF WISDOM AND POETRY

Five Old Testament books are grouped together under the heading of poetical books, or books of wisdom: Job, Psalms, Proverbs, Ecclesiastes and Song of Songs. Proverbs, Job and Ecclesiastes are sometimes referred to as 'The Wisdom Literature'. The aim of these three books is to equip us for everyday living as well as to probe and highlight man's deeper questions about life's meaning and suffering. Biblical wisdom is different from other wisdom writing in the ancient world. It stresses that for all right living and understanding a living relationship with God is the essential starting point.

Good conduct

- ☑ Wisdom, the better way — *Proverbs 15:20–33*
- ☑ Warning against pride — *Proverbs 16:1–5*
- ☑ The better way of life — *Proverbs 16:6–26*
- ☑ Warning against violence — *Proverbs 16:27–33*
- ☑ Good conduct — *Proverbs 17:1–28, 18:1–5*
- ☑ A fool's words — *Proverbs 18:6–9*
- ☑ Warnings against pride — *Proverbs 18:10–14*
- ☑ The way of knowledge and justice — *Proverbs 18:15–18*
- ☑ The power of the tongue — *Proverbs 18:19–24*
- ☑ Personal conduct — *Proverbs 19:1–29*

FOR THOUGHT AND CONTEMPLATION

Question: why do so many Christians land up in trouble? Answer: one major reason is pride (see Proverbs 18:12). It was this that made a devil out of an angel and emptied heaven of many of its inhabitants (see Isa. 14:12–14 & Jude 6). Watch out that it doesn't topple you.

"Pride goes before destruction, a haughty spirit before a fall." (Prov. 16:18, NIV)
"'Blessed are the poor in spirit, for theirs is the kingdom of heaven.'" (Matt. 5:3, NIV)

---

Wise sayings

- ☑ Honourable conduct — *Proverbs 20:1–3*
- ☑ Wise counsel — *Proverbs 20:4–21*
- ☑ The way of the Lord — *Proverbs 20:22–30*
- ☑ The importance of justice — *Proverbs 21:1–31*
- ☑ The importance of prudence — *Proverbs 22:1–5*
- ☑ Wise teaching — *Proverbs 22:6–16*
- ☑ The sayings of wise men — *Proverbs 22:17–29, 23:1–14*
- ☑ The blessing of a wise son — *Proverbs 23:15–25*
- ☑ Warnings against vice — *Proverbs 23:26–35*
- ☑ The way of wisdom — *Proverbs 24:1–14*

FOR THOUGHT AND CONTEMPLATION

Are you aware of what God wants to happen to you as you read these proverbs? If not, take a look at Proverbs 22:17–21. He wants you (1) to absorb their truth into your personality, so that (2) your trust in Him might be deepened, and (3) that His truth might be passed on, through you, to others. Are you letting that happen?

"A man finds joy in giving an apt reply — and how good is a timely word!" (Prov. 15:23, NIV)

---

More proverbs

- ☑ More wise sayings — *Proverbs 24:15–34*
- ☑ Solomon's later proverbs — *Proverbs 25:1*
- ☑ Wise conduct — *Proverbs 25:2–28*
- ☑ Other sins — *Proverbs 26:1–28*
- ☑ Other maxims — *Proverbs 27:1–27*
- ☑ Contrast between good and evil — *Proverbs 28:1–18*
- ☑ The way to lasting wealth — *Proverbs 28:19–28*

FOR THOUGHT AND CONTEMPLATION

Ever been hurt by a friend who told you the truth about yourself? Well, according to Proverbs 27:5–6, that's what friends are for! If you don't *have* a friend such as proverbs describes, then *be* such a friend — perhaps today.

"It's better to heed a wise man's rebuke than to listen to the song of fools." (Eccl. 7:5, NIV)

# Solomon's backsliding

- ✓ More wise advice — *Proverbs 29:1–27*
- ✓ The words of Agur — *Proverbs 30:1–6*
- ✓ The way of moderation — *Proverbs 30:7–9*
- ✓ More proverbs — *Proverbs 30:10–33*
- ✓ Solomon's backsliding — *1 Kings 11:1–13*
- ✓ His adversaries: Hadad — *1 Kings 11:14*
- ✓ Rezon — *1 Kings 11:23–25*
- ✓ Jeroboam — *1 Kings 11:26–40*
- ☐ Unhappy condition of backsliders — *Ecclesiastes 1:1–11*

### FOR THOUGHT AND CONTEMPLATION

Wisdom and greatness, although admirable and highly desirable qualities, are insufficient in themselves to guarantee spiritual progress and stability. We must walk in daily dependence upon God — or else, like Solomon, we will fall and fail.

"Trust in the Lord with all your heart and lean not on your own understanding; in all your ways acknowledge him, and he will make your paths straight." (Prov. 3:5–6, NIV)

## A BIRD'S EYE VIEW OF ECCLESIASTES

**Place in the Bible:**
Twenty-first Old Testament book; fourth book of poetry and wisdom.
**Jesus and the book of Ecclesiastes:**
In contrast to the emptiness of a life which has no relation to God, Jesus offers his followers a life that is to be lived with God, "I have come that they may have life, and have it to the full" (John 10:10).
**Teaching:**
The message of Ecclesiastes exposes the meaninglessness of life when it is lived without God.
**A verse to remember:**
"Now all has been heard; here is the conclusion of the matter: Fear God and keep his commandments, for this is the whole duty of man" (Eccles. 12:13).

# The contradictions of life

- ☝ Wisdom is vain — *Ecclesiastes 1:12–18*
- ✓ Emptiness of pleasure — *Ecclesiastes 2:1–3*
- ✓ Vanity of material wealth — *Ecclesiastes 2:4–11*
- ✓ Result of wisdom and folly — *Ecclesiastes 2:12–26*
- ✓ A time for everything — *Ecclesiastes 3:1–8*
- ✓ Weariness of life — *Ecclesiastes 3:9–22*
- ✓ The foolishness of trusting in riches — *Psalm 49:1–20*
- ✓ Oppressions and inequalities of life — *Ecclesiastes 4:1–16*
- ✓ Warning against rash promises — *Ecclesiastes 5:1–7*

### FOR THOUGHT AND CONTEMPLATION

One question Christians frequently ask is this: how can we make sense out of the apparently meaningless events of life? There is only one way. We must endeavour to see life "from God's point of view". You can't make sense out of life, but you can make sense out of God.

"Oh, the depth of the riches of the wisdom and knowledge of God! How unsearchable his judgments, and his paths beyond tracing out! ...For from him and through him and to him are all things. To him be the glory for ever and ever! Amen." (Rom. 11:33 & 36, NIV)

# Thoughts about Life

- ✓ Riches and poverty — *Ecclesiastes 5:8–20*
- ✓ Man's inevitable end — *Ecclesiastes 6:1–12*
- ✓ Incurable evil of man — *Ecclesiastes 7:1–29*
- ✓ Mystery of divine providence — *Ecclesiastes 8:1–17*
- ✓ World's wrong values — *Ecclesiastes 9:1–18*

Faith alone can hold the heart steady in a world where it seems the righteous suffer and the wicked prosper. When we can leave it to the Lord to clear up the difficulties in His own good time, then we are free to absorb the grace that enables us to turn the difficulties into doors of opportunity.

"O righteous God, who searches minds and hearts, bring to an end the violence of the wicked and make the righteous secure. My shield is God Most High, who saves the upright in heart." (Psa. 7:9–10, NIV)

---

## WISE WORDS

*Examples of Biblical wisdom*

### ... in wisdom literature

"Coral and jasper are not worthy of mention; the price of wisdom is beyond rubies."
Job 28:18

"Teach us to number our days aright, that we may gain a heart of wisdom."
Psa. 90:12

"Wisdom is supreme; therefore get wisdom. Though it cost all you have, get understanding."
Prov. 4:7

### ... in other parts of the Bible

"... All this comes from the Lord Almighty, wonderful in counsel and magnificent in wisdom."
Isa. 28:29

"Cursed is the one who trusts in man, ... But blessed is the man who trusts in the Lord."
Jer. 17.5,7

"Who is wise? He will realise these things. Who is discerning? He will understand them. The ways of the Lord are right; the righteous walk in them, but the rebellious stumble in them."
Hosea 14:9

---

## THURSDAY Week 22    Solomon's death

- Anarchy of the world — *Ecclesiastes 10:1–20*
- Wise advice — *Ecclesiastes 11:1–6*
- Advice to young people — *Ecclesiastes 11:7—12:8*
- An optimistic conclusion — *Ecclesiastes 12:9–14*
- Solomon's death — *1 Kings 11:41–43, 2 Chronicles 9:29–31*
- His descendants — *1 Chronicles 3:10–24*
- The 12 tribes — *Genesis 35:23–26, 1 Chronicles 2:1–2*
- Judah and his lineage — *1 Chronicles 4:1–14, 16–23*
- Hezron to David — *Ruth 4:19–22*
- Hezron to David's nephews — *1 Chronicles 2:9–17*

FOR THOUGHT AND CONTEMPLATION

If wealth and honour alone could satisfy the soul, then Solomon would have known complete fulfilment. His disappointment can be summed up in the words, "All is vanity and vexation of spirit." True joy is found not 'under the sun', but above the sun — in God's eternal presence.

"You have made known to me the path of life; you will fill me with joy in your presence, with eternal pleasures at your right hand." (Psa. 16:11, NIV)

---

## FRIDAY Week 22    Genealogies

- Hezron to Elishama — *1 Chronicles 2:21–41*
- Caleb, son of Hezron — *1 Chronicles 2:18–20, 42–49*
- Caleb, son of Hur — *1 Chronicles 2:50–55*
- Caleb, son of Jephunneh — *1 Chronicles 4:15*
- Descendants of Gershon — *Exodus 6:17, Numbers 3:18, 1 Chronicles 6:17, 20–21, 23:7–11*

Descendants of Kohath — *Exodus 6:18, Numbers 3:19, 1 Chronicles 6:2, 18, 23:12, Exodus 6:21–22, 24, 1 Chronicles 6:22–28, 23:18–20*

Aaron's descendants — *1 Chronicles 6:3–15, 50–53, Ezra 7:1–5*

Descendants of Merari — *Exodus 6:19, Numbers 3:20, 1 Chronicles 6:19, 29–30, 23:21–23*

Ancestors of songmasters — *1 Chronicles 6:31–48*

FOR THOUGHT AND CONTEMPLATION

Genealogies may seem boring and irrelevant to some, but they are the evidence of God's interest in individuals. People are not just a part of history — they are part of God's purposes for history. Remember this — you are in the world not simply as part of a family tree, you are here for a purpose.

"'Before I formed you in the womb I knew you, before you were born I set you apart ...'" (Jer. 1:5, NIV)

---

## SATURDAY Week 22  The tribes

Tribe of Reuben — *Exodus 6:14, 1 Chronicles 5:1–9*

Tribe of Gad — *1 Chronicles 5:11–17*

Tribe of Manasseh (east) — *1 Chronicles 5:23–24*

Tribe of Manasseh (west) — *1 Chronicles 7:14–19*

Tribe of Simeon — *Exodus 6:15, 1 Chronicles 4:24–27, 34–38*

Tribe of Issachar — *1 Chronicles 7:1–5*

Tribe of Naphtali — *1 Chronicles 7:13*

Tribe of Ephraim — *1 Chronicles 7:20–29*

Tribe of Asher — *1 Chronicles 7:30–40*

Tribe of Benjamin — *1 Chronicles 7:6–12, 8:1–28*

Summary — *1 Chronicles 9:1*

FOR THOUGHT AND CONTEMPLATION

Have you ever wondered why the family of Israel should be split up into various tribes? One reason is that we need to identify with a small group before we can take our place in a large group. The more easily you relate to your church locally, the more easily you will relate to the church universally.

"'For where two or three come together in my name, there am I with them.'" (Matt. 18:20, NIV)

---

## SUNDAY Week 23  The divided kingdom 945–721 BC

Revolt of the tribes — *2 Chronicles 10:1–19*

Wrong advice causes revolt — *1 Kings 12:1–19*

Jeroboam — *1 Kings 12:20*

Rehoboam — *1 Kings 14:21, 2 Chronicles 12:13*

People led into idolatry — *1 Kings 12:25–33, 2 Chronicles 11:15*

Warning to Rehoboam — *1 Kings 12:21–24, 2 Chronicles 11:1–4*

Prophecy concerning the altar at Bethel — *1 Kings 13:1–10*

FOR THOUGHT AND CONTEMPLATION

Careful words and moderate statements may cost a good deal in terms of self-denial and self-control, but they purchase great things. God's work has often been the casualty of unstudied remarks. Ask the Lord today to make you a peacemaker and not a piece-maker.

"Who is wise and understanding among you? Let him show it by his good life, by deeds done in the humility that comes from wisdom." (Jas. 3:13, NIV)

# THE DIVIDED KINGDOM

**Kings of the Northern Kingdom**

| | |
|---|---|
| Jeroboam | Jehoahaz |
| Nadab | Jehoash |
| Baasha | Jeroboam II |
| Elah | Zechariah |
| Zimri | Shallum |
| Omri | Menahem |
| Ahab | Pekahiah |
| Ahaziah | Pekah |
| Jehoram | Hoshea |
| Jehu | |

Saul, David and Solomon reigned over all Israel for 40 years each. After Solomon's reign and his unfaithfulness to God the united kingdom of Israel was split into two: the Northern Kingdom (which was still known as Israel), and the Southern Kingdom of Judah.

☐ Referred to as Israel and Ephraim
☐ Lasted 224 years: 945–721 B.C.
☐ Nineteen rulers in all – all unrighteous
☐ Composed of ten tribes
☐ Capital was Shechem, then Tirzah. Samaria established as capital from time of Omri onwards.
☐ No return from captivity

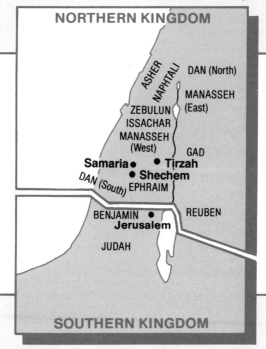

**NORTHERN KINGDOM**

ASHER
NAPHTALI
DAN (North)
MANASSEH (East)
ZEBULUN
ISSACHAR
MANASSEH (West)
GAD
Samaria● ● Tirzah
● Shechem
DAN (South) EPHRAIM
BENJAMIN ● REUBEN
Jerusalem
JUDAH

**SOUTHERN KINGDOM**

**Kings of the Southern Kingdom**

| | |
|---|---|
| Rehoboam | Jotham |
| Abijam | Ahaz |
| Asa | Hezekiah |
| Jehoshaphat | Manasseh |
| Jehoram | Amon |
| Ahaziah | Josiah |
| Athaliah | Jehoahaz |
| Joash | Jehoiakim |
| Amaziah | Jehoichin |
| Uzziah | Zedekiah |

☐ Referred to as Judah
☐ Lasted 359 years: 945–586 B.C.
☐ Twenty rulers in all – eight of them righteous
☐ Composed of two tribes
☐ Capital was Jerusalem
☐ Captured by the Babylonians in 586 B.C.
Three separate returns from captivity

**Jeroboam and Rehoboam**

- Influence of spiritual people — *2 Chronicles 11:13–14, 16–17*
- Rehoboam's kingdom — *2 Chronicles 11:5–12*
- Judgment of a man of God — *1 Kings 13:11–32*
- Rehoboam's family — *2 Chronicles 11:18–23*
- His apostasy — *2 Chronicles 12:1, 14, 1 Kings 14:22–24*
- Shishak invades Jerusalem — *1 Kings 14:25–28, 2 Chronicles 12:2–12*
- Jeroboam's persistence in evil — *1 Kings 13:33–34*
- Ahijah's prediction — *1 Kings 14:1–18*
- Warfare — *1 Kings 14:30, 1 Kings 15:6*
- Rehoboam's death — *1 Kings 14:29, 31, 2 Chronicles 12:15–16*

FOR THOUGHT AND CONTEMPLATION

The reason for Rehoboam's sins and errors is captured in these words, "He hath not set his heart on seeking the Lord" (2 Chron. 12:14). When we fail to *seek* the Lord, then it follows as the night follows the day that we will not *serve* the Lord.

---

"I have set the Lord always before me. Because he is at my right hand, I shall not be shaken, Therefore my heart is glad and my tongue rejoices; my body also will rest secure." (Psa. 16:8–9, NIV)

---

**Evil and good kings**

- Abijah king of Judah — *1 Kings 15:1–2, 2 Chronicles 13:1–2*
- War between Jeroboam and Abijah — *2 Chronicles 13:3–19*
- Abijah's family — *2 Chronicles 13:21*
- His evil life — *1 Kings 15:3–4*
- His death — *2 Chronicles 13:22, 1 Kings 15:7–8*
- Asa king of Judah — *2 Chronicles 14:1, 1 Kings 15:9–11, 2 Chronicles 14:2–5*
- Nadab — *1 Kings 15:25–26*
- Jeroboam's death — *2 Chronicles 13:20, 1 Kings 14:19–20*
- Asa's cities and army — *2 Chronicles 14:6–8*
- Nadab's death — *1 Kings 15:31, 27–28*
- Baasha king of Israel — *1 Kings 15:33–34, 29–30*
- Asa defeats Ethiopians — *2 Chronicles 14:9–15*
- Comfort in distress — *Psalm 77:1–20*

FOR THOUGHT AND CONTEMPLATION

Do you have times when, like Asaph in Psalm 77, you feel God has forgotten to be gracious? (v. 9) In such times, do as Asaph did, and remind yourself of the many blessings He has given you in the past (v. 10). It will help you to keep things in perspective.

---

"Guide me in your truth and teach me, for you are God my Saviour, and my hope is in you all day long. Remember, O Lord, your great mercy and love, for they are from of old." (Psa. 25:5–6, NIV)

---

**Asa's godly reign**

- Azariah's prophecy — *2 Chronicles 15:1–7*
- Reforms in worship — *2 Chronicles 15:8, 17–18, 1 Kings 15:12, 14–15*
- Covenant renewal — *2 Chronicles 15:9–15*
- Asa removes his mother — *1 Kings 15:13, 2 Chronicles 15:16*
- Time of peace — *2 Chronicles 15:19*
- War between Baasha and Asa — *1 Kings 15:16, 32*
- Asa defeats Israel — *2 Chronicles 16:1–6, 1 Kings 15:17–22*
- Jehu's prophecy — *1 Kings 16:1–4, 7*
- Hanani's warning — *2 Chronicles 16:7–10*
- Baasha's death — *1 Kings 16:5–6*
- Elah — *1 Kings 16:8, 14, 9*
- His death — *1 Kings 16:10*
- Zimri — *1 Kings 16:11–13, 20*

His death — *1 Kings 16:15–19*
Omri and Tibni — *1 Kings 16:21–28*
Ahab — *1 Kings 16:29–33, 21:25–26*
Asa's feet diseased — *1 Kings 15:23, 2 Chronicles 16:11–12*

FOR THOUGHT AND CONTEMPLATION

Two years before he died, Asa's feet became diseased. Did God condemn him for seeking the help of physicians? No — God's condemnation was because he sought help *only* from the physicians and not from the Lord. We must never lose sight of the fact that a doctor can only prescribe: it is God who heals.

---

" …'If you listen carefully to the voice of the Lord your God and do what is right in his eyes, if you pay attention to his commands and keep all his decrees, I will not bring on you any of the diseases I brought on the Egyptians, for I am the Lord who heals you.'" (Ex. 15:26, NIV)

---

## THURSDAY Week 23 Elijah's early ministry

Asa's death — *1 Kings 15:24, 2 Chronicles 16:13–14*
Rebuilding of Jericho — *1 Kings 16:34*
Elijah's ministry 882–868 BC
Persecution of prophets — *1 Kings 18:4*
Jehoshaphat — *2 Chronicles 20:31–33, 1 Kings 22:41–43 & 46, 2 Chronicles 17:1–19, 18:1*
Elijah's ministry begins — *1 Kings 17:1–24*
Obadiah and Ahab — *1 Kings 18:1–3, 5–16*

FOR THOUGHT AND CONTEMPLATION

Elijah had to learn to sit quietly before the Lord before he was called upon to engage in activity for Him. Have you learned that lesson yet? Many can work for Him, but are unable to remain quietly before Him. "They also serve who only stand and wait."

---

"I waited patiently for the Lord; he turned to me and heard my cry." (Psa. 40:1, NIV)

---

## ELIJAH

When Israel was sliding into some of its darkest days under Ahab, Elijah's impact was stunning. God's power was dramatically demonstrated to Elijah personally and publicly to the nation.

Elijah is mentioned over 30 times in the New Testament. Both John the Baptist and Jesus were thought to be Elijah come back again. He arrived on the scene of time declaring fiery judgment on the king and nation. He left it in a chariot of fire.

### Elijah's prayers

Elijah's life was characterised by four great prayers:

1. For no more rain to fall: James 5:17
2. For the widow's dead son: 1 Kings 17:19–24
3. For fire to fall from heaven: 1 Kings 18:36–38
4. For rain to fall again: 1 Kings 18:41–46

### There are three marks of Elijah's prayers:

1. He delighted in asking God for the impossible.
2. He believed that he would receive what he prayed for.
3. He didn't give up.

# God's care for Elijah

- ☑ Contest on Mount Carmel — *1 Kings 18:17–39*
- ☑ Prophets of Baal destroyed — *1 Kings 18:40–46, 19:1–2*
- ☑ God's care for Elijah — *1 Kings 19:3–7*
- ☑ God speaks at Horeb — *1 Kings 19:8–18*
- ☑ Elisha joins Elijah — *1 Kings 19:19–21*
- ☑ Benhadad besieges Samaria — *1 Kings 20:1–12*
- ☑ His defeat — *1 Kings 20:13–21*

FOR THOUGHT AND CONTEMPLATION

When God chooses His servants for a special work, He looks for those who are focusing wholeheartedly on the task they have in hand. Elisha was *ploughing* when he received his call, and Peter was *fishing* when he received his. Fulfil your present tasks well, and God will give you even greater things to do.

---

" …'Well done, good and faithful servant! You have been faithful with a few things; I will put you in charge of many things. Come and share your master's happiness!'" (Matt. 25:23, NIV)

---

# Jehoshaphat and Ahab

- ☑ Syrians again defeated — *1 Kings 20:22–30*
- ☑ Ahab makes peace with Benhadad — *1 Kings 20:31–34*
- ☑ Israel's sin — *1 Kings 20:35–43*
- ☑ Three years of peace — *1 Kings 22:1*
- ☑ Ahab and Naboth — *1 Kings 21:1–3*
- ☑ Jezebel causes Naboth's death — *1 Kings 21:4–16*
- ☑ Elijah announces doom — *1 Kings 21:17–24*
- ☑ Ahab's repentance — *1 Kings 21:27–29*
- ☑ Jehoshaphat joins Ahab — *1 Kings 22:2–4, 2 Chronicles 18:2–3*
- ☑ Prophets lie to Ahab — *1 Kings 22:5–6, 10–12, 2 Chronicles 18:4–5, 9–11*

FOR THOUGHT AND CONTEMPLATION

Ahab's desire to possess what didn't belong to him led eventually to discontent, death and destruction. Envy and jealousy are weeds that, if not uprooted the moment they are discovered, will spread like cancer. Is your heart free from these twin evils?

---

"Let us behave decently, as in the daytime, not in orgies and drunkenness, not in sexual immorality and debauchery, not in dissension and jealousy. Rather, clothe yourselves with the Lord Jesus Christ, and do not think about how to gratify the desires of the sinful nature." (Rom. 13:13–14, NIV)

---

# The godly Jehoshaphat

- ☑ Micaiah summoned — *1 Kings 22:7–9, 2 Chronicles 18:6–8*
- ☑ His true prophecy — *1 Kings 22:13–28, 2 Chronicles 18:12–27*
- ☑ Ahab's death — *1 Kings 22:29–40, 2 Chronicles 18:28–34*
- ☑ Jehoshaphat rebuked — *2 Chronicles 19:1–7*
- ☑ God, the supreme Ruler — *Psalm 82:1–8*
- ☑ Jehoshaphat restores order — *2 Chronicles 19:8–11*

FOR THOUGHT AND CONTEMPLATION

When Jehoshaphat was reproved by the prophet over his alliance with the ungodly Ahab, the king searched his heart and set about reforming his ways. How do you respond to the reproofs of God? With repentance — or with rebellion?

---

"'My son, do not make light of the Lord's discipline, and do not lose heart when he rebukes you, because the Lord disciplines those he loves, and he punishes everyone he accepts as a son.'" (Heb. 12:5–6, NIV)

**Jehoshaphat's victory**

☑ Judah invaded — *2 Chronicles 20:1–4*
☑ Jehoshaphat prays — *2 Chronicles 20:5–13*
☑ A prayer for the defeat of enemies — *Psalm 83:1–18*
☑ Jahaziel's prophecy — *2 Chronicles 20:14–19*
☑ God is with us — *Psalm 46:1–11*
☑ Singers appointed — *2 Chronicles 20:20–21*
☑ The enemy destroyed — *2 Chronicles 20:22–26*
☑ Judah rejoices — *2 Chronicles 20:27–28*
☑ The city of God — *Psalm 48:1–14*
☑ Judah's victory causes fear — *2 Chronicles 20:29–30*
☑ Ahaziah and Moab — *1 Kings 22:51–53, 2 Kings 3:4–5, 1:1–2*
☑ A brief alliance — *2 Chronicles 20:35–37, 1 Kings 22:44, 47–49*

FOR THOUGHT AND CONTEMPLATION

Jehoshaphat's strategy of putting his singers at the forefront of his army as they went into battle is full of deep spiritual suggestiveness. Some battles are best approached in the spirit of praise, rather than in the spirit of prayer. This does not mean prayer is unimportant. It simply means that when prayer doesn't seem to bring victory — then try praise.

"Sing to the Lord a new song, for he has done marvellous things, his right hand and his holy arm have worked salvation for him." (Psa. 98:1, NIV)

## A BIRD'S EYE VIEW OF 2 KINGS

**Place in the Bible:**
Twelfth Old Testament book; seventh book of history.
**Main characters:**
Elisha, Naaman, Ahab, Hezekiah, Josiah.
**Special features:**
The story of the two kingdoms continues. Israel is defeated by Assyria, its capital (Samaria) is destroyed, and its people taken into exile.
**Jesus and the book of 2 Kings:**
The phrase "the word of the Lord" (or one very similar to it) comes twenty-four times in this book. Jesus Christ is God's last word to men and women: "In the past God spoke to our forefathers through the prophets at many times and in various ways, but in these last days he has spoken to us by his Son ..." (Heb. 1:2).
**Teaching:**
1 and 2 Kings teach that rebellion against God is always a recipe for disaster. Yet the power and faithfulness of God shine out through the lives of prophets and kings who are true to Him.
**A verse to remember:**
"O Lord, God of Israel ... you alone are God over all the kingdoms of the earth. You have made heaven and earth" (2 Kings 19:15).

**Elisha's ministry begins**

☑ Elijah calls down fire — *2 Kings 1:3–16*
☑ Ahaziah's death — *2 Kings 1:18, 17*
  Elisha's ministry 868–808 BC
☑ Jehoram — *2 Kings 3:1–3*
☑ Elijah divides Jordan — *2 Kings 2:1–8*
☑ Elijah is taken to heaven — *2 Kings 2:9–11*
☑ Elisha gains mantle — *2 Kings 2:12–18*
☑ The miracle of fresh water — *2 Kings 2:19–22*
☑ Children destroyed — *2 Kings 2:23–25*
☑ Jehoshaphat joins Jehoram — *2 Kings 3:6–9*
☑ Elisha's promise — *2 Kings 3:10–20*

FOR THOUGHT AND CONTEMPLATION

For Elisha to receive the coveted mantle of power the condition was quite simple — he had to keep his eyes fixed on Elijah as his Master was translated to heaven. The same principle applies in relation to the receiving of power in today's Church. You have to keep your eyes on Jesus.

"My heart is steadfast, O God; I will sing and make music with all my soul." (Psa. 108:1, NIV)

# Elisha and the Shunammite woman

- Defeat of the Moabites — *2 Kings 3:21–27*
- The widow's oil — *2 Kings 4:1–7*
- The Shunammite woman — *2 Kings 4:8–17*
- Her son restored — *2 Kings 4:18–37*
- Elisha predicts famine — *2 Kings 8:1–2*
- Jehoram — *2 Kings 8:16–17, 2 Chronicles 21:5*
- Jehoshaphat's death — *2 Chronicles 20:34, 1 Kings 22:45, 50, 2 Chronicles 21:1–4*
- Jehoram's evil life — *2 Kings 8:18–19, 2 Chronicles 21:6–7, 11*
- Edom judged — *Obadiah 1:1–9*
- Edom's great sin — *Obadiah 1:10–14*

FOR THOUGHT AND CONTEMPLATION

Some disciples might have responded to Elijah's request, "What would you like me to do for you?" by saying, "Master — if only I could do half as many miracles as you." But not Elisha. His request was not for half as much, but twice as much. He asked big things — and got big things. How big is your asking?

"'And I will do whatever you ask in my name, so that the Son may bring glory to the Father. You may ask me for anything in my name, and I will do it.'" (Jn. 14:13–14, NIV)

## A BIRD'S EYE VIEW OF OBADIAH and NAHUM

**Place in the Bible:**
Thirty-first and thirty-fourth Old Testament books; ninth and twelfth books of prophecy.

**Jesus and the prophecy of Obadiah:**
Like the good news the messenger brought in verse 17 Jesus Christ came to tell people about the gospel of salvation.

**Jesus and the prophecy of Nahum:**
After the celebrated verse from Nahum 1:15, "Look, there on the mountains, the feet of one who brings good news, who proclaims peace!" the next mention of 'good news' is in Matthew 4:23. There Matthew describes the supreme bearer of good news: Jesus.

**Teaching:**
In common with Israel's other enemies, Obadiah prophesied that Edom would be punished. Nahum's poems reflect the delight the Jews felt when Nineveh, the capital of their sworn enemy Assyria, fell.

**A verse to remember:**
"The Lord is good, a refuge in times of trouble. He cares for those who trust in him ..." (Nahum 1:7).

# Elisha's other miracles

- Elisha's other miracles — *2 Kings 4:38–44*
- Condemnation of nations — *Obadiah 1:15–16*
- Future kingdom — *Obadiah 1:17–21*
- Revolt of Edom and Libnah — *2 Kings 8:20–22, 2 Chronicles 21:8–10*
- Elijah's prophecy — *2 Chronicles 21:12–15*
- The invasion — *2 Chronicles 21:16–17*
- Healing of Naaman — *2 Kings 5:1–19*
- Gehazi's punishment — *2 Kings 5:20–27*
- Recovery of axe head — *2 Kings 6:1–7*

FOR THOUGHT AND CONTEMPLATION

When the axe head was lost, no futher work could be done as the tool had lost its cutting edge. But miraculously, and in response to a desperate cry, the axe head returned from the deep. Have you lost the cutting edge in your Christian experience? Then cry out in repentance and desperation, and God will return it to you — today.

"Yet I hold this against you: You have forsaken your first love. Remember the height from which you have fallen! Repent and do the things you did at first ..." (Rev. 2:4–5, NIV)

# The siege of Samaria

☑ The Syrians' defeat — *2 Kings 6:8–23*
☑ Jehoram's sickness — *2 Chronicles 21:18*
☑ Ahaziah — *2 Kings 9:29, 8:25*
☑ Jehoram's death — *2 Chronicles 21:19–20, 2 Kings 8:23–24*
☑ Siege of Samaria — *2 Kings 6:24–33, 7:1–20*
☑ Shunammite land restored — *2 Kings 8:3–6*
☑ Ahaziah's evil reign — *2 Kings 8:26–27, 2 Chronicles 22:1–4*
☐ Benhadad's death — *2 Kings 8:7–15*

**FOR THOUGHT AND CONTEMPLATION**

The four lepers of Samaria who came upon the abandoned food and supplies of the Syrian army knew instinctively that what they had discovered must be shared. "This is a day of good news and we are keeping it to ourselves." Do you long to share what you have miraculously received?

---

"Heal the sick, raise the dead, cleanse those who have leprosy, drive out demons. Freely you have received, freely give." (Matt. 10:8, NIV)

## ELISHA'S MIRACLES

Elisha's prayer was that when Elijah was taken up to heaven, he would receive a double portion of his spirit (2 Kings 2:9). His life was characterised by miracles:

1. Dividing of the Jordan    *2 Kings 2:14*
2. The healing of the waters  *2 Kings 2:21–22*
3. The judgement of irreverence    *2 Kings 2:23–24*
4. Valleys filled with water, and defeat of the Moabite army    *2 Kings 3:9–24*
5. Multiplying the widow's oil  *2 Kings 4:1–7*
6. Raising of the Shunammite's son    *2 Kings 4:32–36*
7. Poisonous stew made wholesome    *2 Kings 4:38–41*
8. Feeding of the multitude  *2 Kings 4:42–44*
9. Healing of Naaman    *2 Kings 5:1–14*
10. Gehazi struck with leprosy  *2 Kings 5:26–27*
11. The lost axe-head    *2 Kings 6:5–7*
12. Syrians struck with blindness    *2 Kings 6:15–23*
13. Prophecy of the Syrians' defeat and the death of the king's officer  *2 Kings Ch. 7*
14. Resurrection life even after death    *2 Kings 13:20–21*

---

# Royal killings

☑ Ahaziah and Jehoram — *2 Kings 8:28–29, 2 Chronicles 22:5–6*
☑ Jehu anointed king — *2 Kings 9:1–13*
☑ Jehu slays Jehoram — *2 Kings 9:14–26, 2 Chronicles 22:7*
☑ Princes slain — *2 Kings 10:12–14, 2 Chronicles 22:8*
☑ Ahaziah's death — *2 Kings 9:27–28, 2 Chronicles 22:9*
☑ Royal family slain — *2 Kings 11:1, 2 Chronicles 22:10*
☑ Joash spared — *2 Kings 11:2–3, 2 Chronicles 22:11–12*
☑ Jezebel — *2 Kings 9:30–37*

**FOR THOUGHT AND CONTEMPLATION**

It's sad, of course, when anyone is killed, but when a royal family is wiped out in this way, then it is very tragic. When did you last pray for the protection and safety of the royal family? Remember that, for a Christian, prayer for the royal family is not an option: it's a command.

---

"I urge, then, first of all, that requests, prayers, intercession and thanksgiving be made for everyone — for kings and all those in authority, that we may live peaceful and quiet lives in all godliness and holiness." (1 Tim. 2:1–2, NIV)

---

# Jehu and Joash

☑ Judgment on Ahab — *2 Kings 10:1–11*
☑ Jehonadab spared — *2 Kings 10:15–17*

☑ Jehu destroys Baal worship — *2 Kings 10:18–28, 30*

☑ Joash becomes king — *2 Kings 11:4–12, 2 Chronicles 23:1–11*

☑ Jehu's backsliding — *2 Kings 10:29, 31–33*

☑ Athaliah executed — *2 Kings 11:13–16, 2 Chronicles 23:12–15*

☑ Joash's good life — *2 Chronicles 24:1–2, 2 Kings 11:21, 12:1–3*

**FOR THOUGHT AND CONTEMPLATION**

Joash's concern to restore the temple of the Lord was highly commendable; the Lord's house must be kept in good repair (2 Chron. 24:4). Your body, too, is a temple of the Lord. How good a caretaker are you of the Lord's property?

---

"Do you not know that your body is a temple of the Holy Spirit, who is in you, whom you have received from God? You are not your own." (1 Cor. 6:19, NIV)

---

## MONDAY Week 25 — Joash's godly reign

☑ Revival under Jehoiada — *2 Kings 11:17–20, 2 Chronicles 23:16–21*

☑ Joash's family — *2 Chronicles 24:3*

☑ Jehu's death — *2 Kings 10:34–36*

☑ Faithless priests — *2 Chronicles 24:4–7, 2 Kings 12:4–8*

☑ Jehoahaz — *2 Kings 13:1–2*

☑ Syria's oppression — *2 Kings 13:22, 3–7*

☑ Joash repairs temple — *2 Kings 12:9–16, 2 Chronicles 24:8–14*

☑ Plague of insects — *Joel 1:1–20*

**FOR THOUGHT AND CONTEMPLATION**

Jehoiada's idea of placing an offering chest at the side of the altar was an inspired one (2 Kings 12:9); it underlined the fact that worship and giving are inseparably linked. You cannot worship God and money, but you can worship God with money.

---

" ...No man should appear before the Lord empty-handed: Each of you must bring a gift in proportion to the way the Lord your God has blessed you." (Deut. 16:16–17, NIV)

### A BIRD'S EYE VIEW OF JOEL

**Place in the Bible:**
Twenty-ninth Old Testament book; seventh book of prophecy.

**Special feature:**
A recent event, a devastating plague of locusts, is used by Joel for illustration.

**Jesus and the prophecy of Joel:**
Jesus Christ enlarged on Joel's wonderful promises about the Holy Spirit in John 16:13, "But when he, the Spirit of truth, comes, he will guide you into all truth...."

**Teaching:**
God will intervene decisively in human history. God will then be seen to be who he is — King.

**A verse to remember:**
"And afterwards, I will pour out my Spirit on all people. Your sons and daughters will prophecy, your old men will dream dreams, your young men will see visions." (Joel 2:28–29)

---

## TUESDAY Week 25 — Joel's prophecy

☑ God's judgments — *Joel 2:1–11*

☑ Exhortation to repent — *Joel 2:12–17*

☑ Results of repentance — *Joel 2:18–27*

☑ The great promise — *Joel 2:28–32*

☑ Nations judged — *Joel 3:1–17*

☑ Judah's restoration — *Joel 3:18–21*

☑ Jehoiada's death — *2 Chronicles 24:15–16*

☑ Princes backslide — *2 Chronicles 24:17–19*

☑ Joash bribes Hazael — *2 Kings 12:17–18*

☑ Jehoash — *2 Kings 13:10*

☑ Jehoahaz's death — *2 Kings 13:8–9*

☑ Jehoash's evil life — *2 Kings 13:11*

☑ Zechariah slain — *2 Chronicles 24:20–22*

☑ Judah defeated — *2 Chronicles 24:23–24*

☑ Joash slain — *2 Chronicles 24:25–27, 2 Kings 12:19–21*

Joel saw that one day the Spirit would come, not at special times and on special occasions, but that He would dwell in the hearts of His people permanently and perpetually. The day of which Joel spoke is here! Aren't you glad?

" …this is what was spoken by the prophet Joel: 'In the last days, God says, I will pour out my Spirit on all people. Your sons and daughters will prophesy, your young men will see visions, and your old men will dream dreams.'" (Acts 2:16–17, NIV)

## WEDNESDAY Week 25 Judah and Israel

☑ Jehoash visits Elisha — *2 Kings 13:14–19*
☑ Miracle in tomb — *2 Kings 13:20–21*
☑ Amaziah — *2 Chronicles 25:1–4, 2 Kings 14:1–6*
☑ Army ready — *2 Chronicles 25:5*
☑ Syria's defeat — *2 Kings 13:23–25*
☑ Judah hires Israelites — *2 Chronicles 25:6–10*
☑ Amaziah's victory — *2 Kings 14:7, 2 Chronicles 25:11–12*
☑ Cities plundered — *2 Chronicles 25:13*
☑ Amaziah's idolatry — *2 Chronicles 25:14–16*
☑ Jerusalem plundered — *2 Kings 14:8–14, 2 Chronicles 25:17–24*
☑ Uzziah (Azariah) — *2 Kings 14:21, 15:1–4, 2 Chronicles 26:1, 3–5*
☑ Jehoash's death — *2 Kings 13:12–13, 14:15–16*

☑ Amaziah's last years — *2 Kings 14:17, 22, 2 Chronicles 25:25, 26:2*

FOR THOUGHT AND CONTEMPLATION

Such was the power of God that rested on Elisha that it remained in his bones even after his death (2 Kings 13:21). Seems like there was more power in Elisha after he was dead than in many Christians when they are alive!

"And if the Spirit of him who raised Jesus from the dead is living in you, he who raised Christ from the dead will also give life to your mortal bodies through his Spirit, who lives in you." (Rom. 8:11, NIV)

## THE MINOR PROPHETS

There are twelve prophetic books in the Old Testament which are commonly known as 'The Minor Prophets'. They are Hosea, Joel, Amos, Obadiah, Jonah, Micah, Nahum, Habakkuk, Zephaniah, Haggai, Zechariah, Malachi. These prophetic books are only 'minor' in the sense that they are very much shorter in length than the 'major' Old Testament prophetic books. Once joined in a single scroll known as 'The Twelve', all the minor prophets together are roughly equal to the length of Isaiah.

The Israelites had been rescued from slavery, had been given a land to live in, and God's law to live by, but very often they needed to hear the voice of the prophets to bring them back to their God in humility and repentance.

## THURSDAY Week 25 Hosea's message

☑ Jeroboam — *2 Kings 14:23–27*
☑ Amaziah's death — *2 Kings 14:18–20, 2 Chronicles 25:26–28*
☑ Philistines defeated — *2 Chronicles 26:6–15*

☑ Israel's future restoration — *Amos 9:11–15*
☑ Israel rebuked — *Hosea 1:1—2:5*
☑ God's judgments — *Hosea 2:6–13*

☑ His promises — *Hosea 2:14–23*
☑ Israel restored — *Hosea 3:1–5*
☑ Jonah's disobedience — *Jonah 1:1–11*

FOR THOUGHT AND CONTEMPLATION

Hosea may have been a minor prophet, but he was given a major task by God of demonstrating to Israel the kind of love that goes on loving even in the face of unfaithfulness. Is God asking the same of you at this moment? Then do as Hosea did — lean hard on the Lord. He will never fail.

---

"Love is patient, love is kind. It does not envy, it does not boast, it is not proud ... It always protects, always trusts, always hopes, always perseveres. Love never fails ..." (1 Cor. 13:4, 7 & 8, NIV)

---

## A BIRD'S EYE VIEW OF HOSEA

**Place in the Bible:**
Twenty-eighth Old Testament book; sixth book of prophecy.
**Main characters:**
Hosea and Gomer.
**Special feature:**
Hosea uses the adultery of his wife to illustrate the theme of this book.
**Jesus and the prophecy of Hosea:**
Jesus Christ quotes from Hosea 6:6: "It is not the healthy who need a doctor, but the sick. But go and learn what this means: 'I desire mercy, not sacrifice.' But I have not come to call the righteous, but sinners." (Matt. 9:12–13)
**Teaching:**
Hosea depicts God's yearning and overflowing love for his people in the book, reaching breath-taking heights in chapter 14. Hosea shows how, despite Israel's unfaithfulness to God, God continually loves his people and desires them to return to him.
**A verse to remember:**
"I will heal their waywardness and love them freely, for my anger has turned away from them. I will be like the dew to Israel; he will blossom like a lily" (Hos. 14:4–5).

---

**FRIDAY Week 25** Jonah

☑ Jonah in the fish — *Jonah 1:12–17*
☑ Jonah's prayer — *Jonah 2:1–9*
☑ His deliverance — *Jonah 2:10*
☑ Jonah at Nineveh — *Jonah 3:1–10*
☑ His strange reaction — *Jonah 4:1–11*
☑ Judgments against nations — *Amos 1:1–15, 2:1–3*
☑ Judgments against Israel and Judah — *Amos 2:4—3:15*

FOR THOUGHT AND CONTEMPLATION

Jonah's greatest problem was his fear of being proved wrong (see Jonah 4:2). He thought more of himself than he did of God, or of the message he had been given by God. If you want to be used by God then you must be willing to put His message first, and your feelings second. Otherwise, like Jonah, you're heading for trouble.

---

"Yet when I preach the gospel, I cannot boast, for I am compelled to preach. Woe to me if I do not preach the gospel!" (1 Cor. 9:16, NIV)

---

**SATURDAY Week 25** Amos' message

☑ Israel is reproved — *Amos 4:1–5*
☑ Their impenitence shown — *Amos 4:6–13*
☑ The call to seek the Lord — *Amos 5:1–6*
☑ Exhortations to repentance — *Amos 5:7–17*

☑ Warnings of judgment — *Amos 5:18–27*
☑ The danger of luxury — *Amos 6:1–7*
☑ Punishments for sins — *Amos 6:8–14*
☑ Amos' visions — *Amos 7:1–9*

☑ Amos and Amaziah — *Amos 7:10–17*

When Amos placed God's plumbline against Israel, the nation was found greatly wanting. What would happen if Amos was to pay you a visit today and set your life against God's plumbline? Would it measure up — or would it be found wanting?

"Blessed is the man who perseveres under trial, because when he has stood the test, he will receive the crown of life that God has promised to those who love him." (Jas. 1:12, NIV)

## A BIRD'S EYE VIEW OF JONAH

**Place in the Bible:**
Thirty-second Old Testament book; tenth book of prophecy.
**Jesus and the prophecy of Jonah:**
Jesus Christ took Jonah's experience as an illustration of his own (death and) resurrection to life (Matt. 12:39–41).
**Teaching:**
Nineveh, the capital of the hated Assyrians, a byword for evil and cruelty, was the last place in the world Jonah would have chosen to go to, hence Jonah's reluctance to obey God's call and go there. Throughout this book God's great love for non-Israelites is portrayed.
**A verse to remember:**
"... I knew that you are a gracious and compassionate God, slow to anger and abounding in love" (Jon. 4:2).

---

SUNDAY Week 26 **Evil kings**

---

☑ Another vision — *Amos 8:1–3*
☑ Israel's doom — *Amos 8:4–14*
☑ The Lord's judgments — *Amos 9:1–10*
☑ Jeroboam's death — *2 Kings 14:28–29*
☑ The Lord's accusation — *Hosea 4:1–11*
☑ Pagan worship condemned — *Hosea 4:12–19*
☑ Zachariah — *2 Kings 15:8–12*
☑ Shallum — *2 Kings 15:13–15*
☑ Menahem — *2 Kings 15:16–18*
☑ Assyrian invasion — *2 Kings 15:19–20*
☑ Uzziah's intrusion — *2 Chronicles 26:16–18*
☑ Uzziah's leprosy — *2 Chronicles 26:19–21, 2 Kings 15:5*
☑ Menahem's death — *2 Kings 15:21–22*

☑ Pekahiah — *2 Kings 15:23–24*

Uzziah's sin was that he intruded upon the work of the priests by burning incense on God's altar — a task assigned only to the descendants of Aaron. As a result he was punished by becoming a leper and had to live in isolation. Those who covet forbidden honours often find they forfeit legitimate ones.

---

"For it is not the one who commends himself who is approved, but the one whom the Lord commends." (2 Cor. 10:18, NIV)

## A BIRD'S EYE VIEW OF AMOS

**Place in the Bible:**
Thirtieth Old Testament book; eighth book of prophecy.
**Jesus and the prophecy of Amos:**
Like Amos, Jesus Christ set his face implacably against all religious hypocrisy and spiritual humbug: see, for example, Matthew 23:23.
**Teaching:**
Amos's hard hitting message starts by roundly condemning Israel's sinful neighbours, but then he homes in on Israel itself and teaches them about God's basic demands — social justice, and faithful worship.
**A verse to remember:**
"But let justice roll on like a river, righteousness like a never-failing stream!" (Amos 5:24)

## Isaiah's message

☑ Pekahiah killed — *2 Kings 15:25–26*
☑ Pekah — *2 Kings 15:27–28*
☑ Uzziah's death — *2 Kings 15:6–7, 2 Chronicles 26:22–23*
☑ Isaiah's vision — *Isaiah 6:1–13*
☑ Jotham — *2 Chronicles 27:1, 8, 2, 2 Kings 15:32–35*
☑ Isaiah's vision — *Isaiah 1:1*
☑ The promise — *Isaiah 2:1–6*
☑ Chastisement before blessing — *Isaiah 2:7—3:26*

### FOR THOUGHT AND CONTEMPLATION

Isaiah said, "In the year that King Uzziah died, I saw the Lord." It was only when the prophet saw the earthly king in his coffin that he was able to see the heavenly King on His throne. How sad that God sometimes has to take something from us in order to focus our gaze on Himself.

"But as for me, I watch in hope for the Lord, I wait for God my Saviour, my God will hear me." (Mic. 7:7, NIV)

## A BIRD'S EYE VIEW OF ISAIAH

**Place in the Bible:**
Twenty-third Old Testament book; first book of prophecy.
**Jesus and the prophecy of Isaiah:**
Isaiah 52:13 to 53:12 ranks as the perfect commentary on the sacrificial death of Jesus for sinful men and women. As many as eighty-five quotes and allusions to Isaiah 53 have been counted in the New Testament.
**Teaching:**
Isaiah, a colossus among the prophets, has a message which is unsurpassed in its depth and breadth. His central theme is that God's wonderful salvation has come to his people the Israelites, and beyond them, to all nations. Isaiah has abundant teaching about God, His righteousness, His holiness, His sovereignty, His Day (the Day of the Lord), His servant, His judgement and His comfort.
**A verse to remember:**
"We all, like sheep, have gone astray, each of us has turned to his own way; and the Lord has laid on him the iniquity of us all" (Isa. 53:6).

## Micah's message

☑ Restoration of Jerusalem — *Isaiah 4:1–6*
☑ Parable of vineyard — *Isaiah 5:1–7*
☑ Six woes — *Isaiah 5:8–30*
☑ Micah's message — *Micah 1:1*
☑ The wrath of God — *Micah 1:2–16*
☑ Israel's sins — *Micah 2:1–5*
☑ Their evil practices — *Micah 2:6–11*
☑ A promise — *Micah 2:12–13*
☑ Jotham's strength — *2 Chronicles 27:3–6*
☐ Rezin joins Pekah — *2 Kings 15:37*
☐ Jotham's death — *2 Kings 15:36 & 38, 2 Chronicles 27:7 & 9*

### FOR THOUGHT AND CONTEMPLATION

Micah shows that the game, 'follow my leader', can be fine when the leaders are following the Lord. Who leads you spiritually? Are they people whose lives radiate the love of Christ? If not, then you need to re-examine your spiritual commitments.

"Be imitators of God, therefore, as dearly loved children and live a life of love, just as Christ lived us and gave himself up for us as a fragrant offering and sacrifice to God." (Eph. 5:1–2, NIV)

## The coming Messiah

☑ Ahaz — *2 Kings 16:1–4, 2 Chronicles 28:1–4*
☑ Pekah's victory — *2 Chronicles 28:5–8*

☑ Future hope — *Isaiah 7:10–16*
☑ The future King — *Isaiah 9:1–7*

☑ Judah will be invaded — *Isaiah 7:17–25, 8:5–22*

☑ The coming chastisement — *Isaiah 9:8—10:4*

☑ Obed's intercession — *2 Chronicles 28:9–15*

**FOR THOUGHT AND CONTEMPLATION**

It is only in recent times that it has become possible to determine the sex of a child in advance. Yet Isaiah, hundreds of years before Christ was born, predicts that a virgin would conceive and bear a son. You need have no worries about the accuracy of Scripture when it contains such unerring predictions.

"And we have the word of the prophets made more certain, and you will do well to pay attention to it, as to a light shining in a dark place ... For prophecy never had its origin in the will of man, but men spoke from God as they were carried along by the Holy Spirit." (2 Pet. 1:19 & 21, NIV)

---

**THURSDAY Week 26** ## Assyria's victories

☑ The conspiracy — *2 Kings 16:5–6, Isaiah 7:1–2*

☑ Israel to be broken — *Isaiah 7:3–9*

☑ Judah invaded — *2 Chronicles 28:17–19*

☑ True worship — *Psalm 50:1–23*

☑ Damascus to be judged — *Isaiah 8:1–4, 17:1–14*

☑ Assyria defeats Syria — *2 Chronicles 28:16 & 21, 2 Kings 16:7–9*

☑ Eastern tribes deported — *2 Kings 15:29, 1 Chronicles 5:25–26*

☑ Warning to Judah — *Isaiah 1:2–20*

**FOR THOUGHT AND CONTEMPLATION**

God will prune and purify His people even if He has to use an ungodly nation like Assyria to achieve it. Are you being plagued or harassed by a non-Christian source at the moment? Then ask the Lord to show you why. This may be the only way He can bring you into line with His will and purposes!

"These have come so that your faith — of greater worth than gold, which perishes even though refined by fire — may be proved genuine and may result in praise, glory and honour when Jesus Christ is revealed." (1 Pet. 1:7, NIV)

---

**FRIDAY Week 26** ## Hezekiah's godly reign

☑ The sinful city — *Isaiah 1:21–31*

☑ Jerusalem plundered — *2 Kings 16:10–18, 2 Chronicles 28:20, 22–25*

☑ Pekah killed — *2 Kings 15:31 & 30*

☑ Hoshea — *2 Kings 17:1–2*

☑ Hezekiah — *2 Kings 18:1–3, 5–6, 2 Chronicles 29:1–2*

☑ Temple reconsecrated and cleansed — *2 Chronicles 29:3–19*

☑ Temple worship restored — *2 Chronicles 29:20–36*

As soon as Hezekiah heard that the temple was ready for worship, he lost no time in making an atonement — and, as the offering was laid on the altar, the Levites broke out in song. Be sure that your sorrow over sin does not prevent you, in due course, from praising God.

"We will shout for joy when you are victorious and will lift up our banners in the name of our God. May the Lord grant all your requests." (Psa. 20:5, NIV)

## SATURDAY Week 26 — The Passover renewed

☑ A warning — *Isaiah 28:1–6*
☑ The drunken prophets of Judah — *Isaiah 28:7–13*
☑ A cornerstone for Zion — *Isaiah 28:14–22*
☑ God's wisdom — *Isaiah 28:23–29*
☐ A warning against idolatry — *Hosea 5:1–7*
☑ Judgment on Judah and Israel — *Hosea 5:8–15*
☑ The people's insincere repentance — *Hosea 6:1–11*
☑ Preparations for the Passover — *2 Chronicles 30:1–12*
☑ The Passover is celebrated — *2 Chronicles 30:13–22*
☑ A second celebration — *2 Chronicles 30:23–27*

FOR THOUGHT AND CONTEMPLATION

We ought never to think lightly of sin. Those who view the Passover as God simply overlooking human faults and errors are quite mistaken. God does not overlook sin; He 'looks over' it to focus His gaze, not on the sinner and his sins, but on the substitutionary sacrifice. Forgiveness may be free, but it is never cheap.

"If we claim to be without sin, we deceive ourselves and the truth is not in us. If we confess our sins, he is faithful and just and will forgive us our sins and purify us from all unrighteousness." (1 Jn. 1:8–9, NIV)

## SUNDAY Week 27 — Hezekiah's reforms

☑ A festival song — *Psalm 81:1–16*
☑ Idols destroyed — *2 Chronicles 31:1, 2 Kings 18:4*
☑ Hezekiah's further reforms — *2 Chronicles 31:2–21*
☑ Israel's leaders denounced — *Micah 3:1–12*
☑ Hoshea taken prisoner — *2 Kings 17:3–4*
☑ Israel's wickedness — *Hosea 7:1–2*
☑ Conspiracy in the palace — *Hosea 7:3–7*
☑ Israel and the nations — *Hosea 7:8–16*

FOR THOUGHT AND CONTEMPLATION

Following the celebration of the Passover, great spiritual reforms took place in Israel. This is how it ought always to be. The benefits we receive through prayer, Holy Communion and the ministry of the Word in the house of God on Sundays ought to be worked out in our own house on Mondays. And Tuesdays. And Wednesdays ...

" ...continue to work out your salvation with fear and trembling, for it is God who works in you to will and to act according to his good purpose." (Phil. 2:12–13, NIV)

## MONDAY Week 27 — Israel's punishment

☑ The Lord condemns Israel — *Hosea 8:1–14*
☑ Hosea's announcement — *Hosea 9:1–9*
☑ The consequences of Israel's sin — *Hosea 9:10–14*

☑ The Lord's judgment — *Hosea 9:15–16*
☑ The prophet speaks — *Hosea 9:17, 10:1–8*
☑ The Lord pronounces judgment — *Hosea 10:9–15*

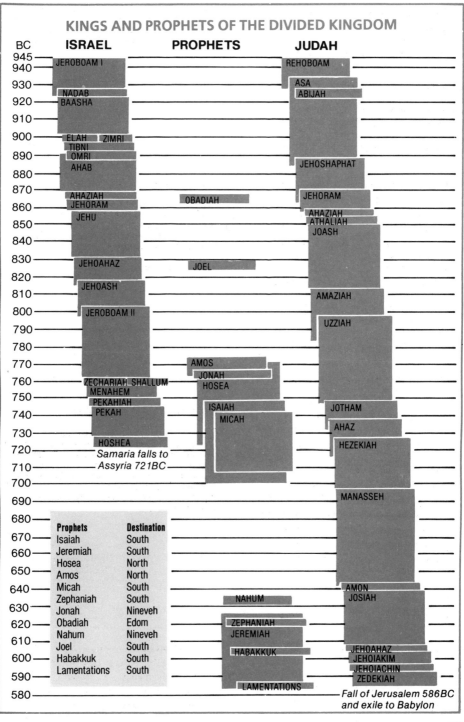

# KINGS AND PROPHETS OF THE DIVIDED KINGDOM

| BC | ISRAEL | PROPHETS | JUDAH |
|---|---|---|---|

945
940 — JEROBOAM I — REHOBOAM
930 — ASA
— NADAB — ABIJAH
920 — BAASHA
910
900 — ELAH  ZIMRI
— TIBNI
890 — OMRI
— AHAB — JEHOSHAPHAT
880
870 — AHAZIAH — JEHORAM
860 — JEHORAM — OBADIAH
— JEHU — AHAZIAH
850 — ATHALIAH
— JOASH
840
830 — JEHOAHAZ — JOEL
820
810 — JEHOASH — AMAZIAH
800 — JEROBOAM II
790 — UZZIAH
780
770 — AMOS
— JONAH
760 — ZECHARIAH SHALLUM — HOSEA
— MENAHEM
750 — PEKAHIAH
— PEKAH — ISAIAH — JOTHAM
740 — MICAH
730 — AHAZ
— HOSHEA — HEZEKIAH
720 — *Samaria falls to*
710 — *Assyria 721BC*
700
690 — MANASSEH
680

| Prophets | Destination |
|---|---|
| Isaiah | South |
| Jeremiah | South |
| Hosea | North |
| Amos | North |
| Micah | South |
| Zephaniah | South |
| Jonah | Nineveh |
| Obadiah | Edom |
| Nahum | Nineveh |
| Joel | South |
| Habakkuk | South |
| Lamentations | South |

670
660
650
640 — AMON
— NAHUM — JOSIAH
630
— ZEPHANIAH
620 — JEREMIAH
610
— HABAKKUK — JEHOAHAZ
600 — JEHOIAKIM
— JEHOIACHIN
590 — ZEDEKIAH
— LAMENTATIONS
580 — *Fall of Jerusalem 586BC and exile to Babylon*

- ☑ God's love — *Hosea 11:1–11*
- ☑ Israel and Judah are condemned — *Hosea 11:12, 12:1–6*
- ☑ Further words of judgment — *Hosea 12:7–14*
- ☑ Final judgment on Israel — *Hosea 13:1–8*

FOR THOUGHT AND CONTEMPLATION

It is important to remember that God's judgment of His people's sins is not merely retributive, but remedial. He isn't against us for our sin, but for us against our sin. Think about it. It's a thought worth holding in our minds throughout the whole of this day.

---

"But God demonstrates his own love for us in this: While we were still sinners, Christ died for us." (Rom. 5:8, NIV)

---

## TUESDAY Week 27   Israel taken captive

- ☑ Final judgment on Israel — *Hosea 13:9–16*
- ☑ Hosea's plea — *Hosea 14:1–3*
- ☑ Israel's restoration — *Hosea 14:4–9*
- ☑ Samaria besieged — *2 Kings 17:5, 18:9*
- ☑ Israel taken captive — *2 Kings 17:6, 18:10–11*
- ☑ Reasons for Israel's downfall — *2 Kings 17:7–23, 18:12*
- ☑ Prayer for Israel's restoration — *Psalm 80:1–19*
- ☑ Death of Ahaz — *2 Kings 16:19–20, 2 Chronicles 28:26–27*
- The Fall of Israel 721 BC
- ☑ A vision of Babylon's fall — *Isaiah 21:1–10*

FOR THOUGHT AND CONTEMPLATION

One of the greatest mysteries of life is why God uses ungodly people or nations to chastise His own children. Surely one answer must be that if we fail to examine our own hearts, then God must do it for us. And the 'examination board' He uses may not always be to our liking!

---

" ...the Lord disciplines those he loves, and he punishes everyone he accepts as a son." (Heb. 12:6, NIV)

---

## WEDNESDAY Week 27   The nations judged

- ☑ A message about Edom — *Isaiah 21:11–12*
- ☑ A message about Arabia — *Isaiah 21:13–17*
- ☑ Judgment upon the Philistines — *Isaiah 14:28–32*
- ☑ Judgment upon Moab — *Isaiah 15:1–9*
- ☑ Moab's hopeless situation — *Isaiah 16:1–14*
- ☑ Hezekiah defies Assyria — *2 Kings 18:7–8*
- ☑ The Amalekites slain — *1 Chronicles 4:39–43*
- ☑ Judgment against Ethiopia — *Isaiah 18:1–7*
- ☑ Judgment against Egypt — *Isaiah 19:1–15*
- ☑ Egypt will worship the Lord — *Isaiah 19:16–25*

FOR THOUGHT AND CONTEMPLATION

The theme of judgment, although very conspicuous in Old Testament times, is often missing from modern Christian thought. Yet make no mistake about it — judgment will come. As someone has said: "If God will not judge the nations for their sins, then He will surely have to apologise to Sodom and Gomorrah."

---

" ...the Lord ... comes to judge the earth. He will judge the world in righteousness and the peoples in his truth." (Psa. 96:13, NIV)

---

## THURSDAY Week 27   Assyria's coming destruction

- ☑ The sign to Egypt and Ethiopia — *Isaiah 20:1–6*
- ☑ Judgment against Tyre — *Isaiah 23:1–18*
- ☑ Assyria, God's instrument — *Isaiah 10:5–19*
- ☑ Remnant of Israel to be saved — *Isaiah 10:20–23*
- ☑ Judgment against Assyria — *Isaiah 10:24–27*
- ☑ The invader attacks — *Isaiah 10:28–34*
- ☑ The peaceful kingdom — *Isaiah 11:1–9*
- ☑ The exiles will return — *Isaiah 11:10–16*
- ☑ Hymns of thanksgiving — *Isaiah 12:1–6*

This point must never be forgotten: when God allows His people to fall into trouble, it is to humble them and bring their sin to remembrance. The ultimate end of all God's judgments, as they relate to His people, is the putting away of sin. He upsets us in order to set us up.

"The eyes of the arrogant man will be humbled and the pride of men brought low; the Lord alone will be exalted in that day." (Isa. 2:11, NIV)

## FRIDAY Week 27 — The Lord's judgments

☑ Judgment upon Babylon — *Isaiah 13:1–16*
☐ The return from exile — *Isaiah 14:1–3*
☑ The king of Babylon's fall — *Isaiah 14:4–11, 18–21*
☑ God will destroy Babylon — *Isaiah 14:22–23*
☑ God will destroy the Assyrians — *Isaiah 14:24–27*
☑ Judgment upon the world — *Isaiah 24:1–23*
☑ A hymn of praise — *Isaiah 25:1–5*
☑ God prepares a banquet — *Isaiah 25:6–9*
☑ God will punish Moab — *Isaiah 25:10–12*
☑ God's victorious people — *Isaiah 26:1–11*

FOR THOUGHT AND CONTEMPLATION

More and more judgment! When will God stop? The answer surely is — when men turn from their sin and follow the path of righteousness. And those who obey the divine command to cease from sin discover this encouraging truth — the Almighty is as great in mercy as He is in judgment. Hallelujah!

"...unless you repent, you too will all perish." (Lk. 13:3, NIV)

## SATURDAY Week 27 — The way of holiness

☑ God's victorious people — *Isaiah 26:12–19*
☑ Judgment and restoration — *Isaiah 26:20–21, 27:1–13*
☑ The coming siege — *Isaiah 22:1–14*
☑ God will punish His enemies — *Isaiah 34:1–17*
☑ The coming victory — *Isaiah 35:1–10*
☑ Hezekiah's divine healing — *2 Kings 20:1–11*
☑ Hezekiah's pride — *2 Chronicles 32:24–26*

FOR THOUGHT AND CONTEMPLATION

Never let it be forgotten that God's way is a way of holiness. Did you know that the root meaning of 'holiness' is 'healthiness'? Perhaps this is a good moment to check your spiritual health. When we are unholy, we are unhealthy. How 'healthy' are you at this present moment?

"Consecrate yourselves and be holy, because I am the Lord your God." (Lev. 20:7, NIV)

## SUNDAY Week 28 — The incomparable God

☑ Hezekiah's illness and healing — *Isaiah 38:1–8, 21–22*
☑ Hezekiah is thankful — *Isaiah 38:9–20*
☑ Words of hope — *Isaiah 40:1–9*
☑ God's care and protection — *Isaiah 40:10–11*
☑ Israel's incomparable God — *Isaiah 40:12–26*
☑ God reassures His people — *Isaiah 40:27–31*
☑ God's promise to Israel — *Isaiah 41:1–20*
☑ The Lord's challenge — *Isaiah 41:21–29*

FOR THOUGHT AND CONTEMPLATION

It's worth reflecting on the fact that our spiritual progress is largely determined by our view of God. If we hold in our hearts a limited or inadequate picture of Him, this will mirror itself in how we live, and what we ask of Him. Isaiah saw God as not just mighty but *almighty*. Do you?

"For by him all things were created: things in heaven and on earth, visible and invisible, whether thrones or powers or rulers or authorities; all things were created by him and for him." (Col. 1:16, NIV)

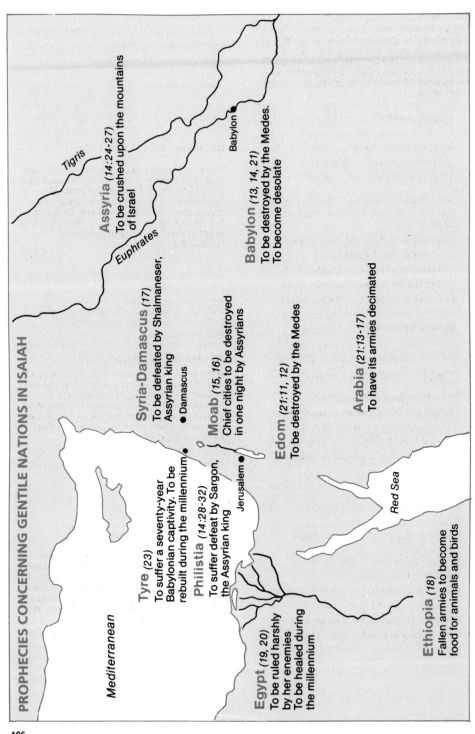

PROPHECIES CONCERNING GENTILE NATIONS IN ISAIAH

Mediterranean

Tigris

Euphrates

Assyria *(14:24-27)*
To be crushed upon the mountains
of Israel

Babylon *(13, 14, 21)*
To be destroyed by the Medes.
To become desolate

● Babylon

Syria-Damascus *(17)*
To be defeated by Shalmaneser,
Assyrian king
● Damascus

Moab *(15, 16)*
Chief cities to be destroyed
in one night by Assyrians

Edom *(21:11, 12)*
To be destroyed by the Medes

Arabia *(21:13-17)*
To have its armies decimated

Tyre *(23)*
To suffer a seventy-year
Babylonian captivity. To be
rebuilt during the millennium

Philistia *(14:28-32)*
To suffer defeat by Sargon,
the Assyrian king

● Jerusalem

Red Sea

Egypt *(19, 20)*
To be ruled harshly
by her enemies
To be healed during
the millennium

Ethiopia *(18)*
Fallen armies to become
food for animals and birds

106

## MONDAY Week 28 — Israel: God's witness

- ☑ The Lord's servant — *Isaiah 42:1–9*
- ☑ A song of praise — *Isaiah 42:10–13*
- ☑ God promises His help — *Isaiah 42:14–17*
- ☑ Israel's failure to learn — *Isaiah 42:18–25*
- ☑ God's promised rescue — *Isaiah 43:1–7*
- ☑ Israel is God's witness — *Isaiah 43:8–13*
- ☑ Escape from Babylon — *Isaiah 43:14–21*
- ☑ Israel's sin — *Isaiah Isaiah 43:22–28*
- ☑ The only God — *Isaiah 44:1–8*
- ☑ Idolatry ridiculed — *Isaiah 44:9–20*
- ☑ The Creator and Saviour — *Isaiah 44:21–27*

FOR THOUGHT AND CONTEMPLATION

Throughout time, God has always sought to maintain in His creation a witness to His honour and to His Name. In the Old Testament age, God's chief witness was Israel. In the New Testament age, His chief witness is the Church. Israel failed miserably. Do we?

"But you will receive power when the Holy Spirit comes on you; and you will be my witnesses in Jerusalem, and in all Judea and Samaria, and to the ends of the earth." (Acts 1:8, NIV)

## TUESDAY Week 28 — Lord of all

- ☑ Cyrus, a chosen vessel — *Isaiah 45:1–8*
- ☑ The Lord of creation and history — *Isaiah 45:9–17, 19*
- ☑ Lord of all — *Isaiah 45:20–25*
- ☑ Deliverance from Babylon — *Isaiah 46:1–13*
- ☑ Judgment on Babylon — *Isaiah 47:1–15*
- ☑ God is Lord of the future — *Isaiah 48:1–11*
- ☑ Cyrus, the Lord's chosen leader — *Isaiah 48:12–16*
- ☑ The Lord's plan for His people — *Isaiah 48:17–22*

FOR THOUGHT AND CONTEMPLATION

History, as someone has pointed out, is really His-story. Men, though unaware of it, are girded and guided by the divine hand. So remember this — behind every nation is a leader, and behind every leader is God. And God, not men, will have the last word in the nations' affairs. It's God, our God, who *reigns*!

"Everyone must submit himself to the governing authorities, for there is no authority except that which God has established. The authorities that exist have been established by God." (Rom. 13:1, NIV)

## WEDNESDAY Week 28 — The restoration of Jerusalem

- ☑ Israel, a light to the nations — *Isaiah 49:1–7*
- ☑ Restoration of Jerusalem — *Isaiah 49:8–26, 50:1–3*
- ☑ Obedience of the Lord's servant — *Isaiah 50:4–11*
- ☑ The faithful encouraged — *Isaiah 51:1–16*
- ☑ The end of Jerusalem's suffering — *Isaiah 51:17–23*
- ☑ God will rescue Jerusalem — *Isaiah 52:1–12*
- ☑ The suffering servant — *Isaiah 52:13–15*

FOR THOUGHT AND CONTEMPLATION

When God's people repent and confess their sins, the inevitable consequence is restoration and revival. Can you imagine what would happen if God's people throughout the world would seek His face in earnest confession and repentance? The restoration of Jerusalem would be as nothing compared to the glory and power that would flow through His Church.

"If my people, who are called by my name, will humble themselves and pray and seek my face and turn from their wicked ways, then will I hear from heaven and will forgive their sin and will heal their land." (2 Chron. 7:14, NIV)

God's people comforted

- [x] Christ, the sinbearer — *Isaiah 53:1–12*
- [x] The Lord's never-ending love — *Isaiah 54:1–10*
- [x] The future Jerusalem — *Isaiah 54:11–17*
- [x] God's offer of mercy — *Isaiah 55:1–13*
- [x] God's worldwide invitation — *Isaiah 56:1–8*
- [x] Israel's leaders condemned — *Isaiah 56:9–12*
- [x] Israel's idolatry condemned — *Isaiah 57:1–13*
- [x] God's promise of help and healing — *Isaiah 57:14–21*

**FOR THOUGHT AND CONTEMPLATION**

Let your thoughts linger today on Isaiah 53:5

— what someone has called the greatest verse of the Old Testament. It will only have meaning for you, however, if you have personalised it by faith. Can you say, 'He was wounded for *my* transgressions ... bruised for *my* iniquities"? If you have not yet done so, receive the Lord Jesus Christ into your heart and life right now.

"For Christ died for sins once for all, the righteous for the unrighteous, to bring you to God. He was put to death in the body but made alive by the Spirit." (1 Pet. 3:18, NIV)

---

Jerusalem's future greatness

- [x] True worship — *Isaiah 58:1–12*
- [x] Reward for keeping the Sabbath — *Isaiah 58:13–14*
- [x] The people's sins condemned — *Isaiah 59:1–8*
- [x] The people's confession — *Isaiah 59:9–15*
- [x] The coming of Christ — *Isaiah 59:16–21*
- [x] Jerusalem's future glory — *Isaiah 60:1–5*
- [x] All nations to honour God's people — *Isaiah 60:6–9*
- [x] God's favour and mercy — *Isaiah 60:10–22*
- [x] Good news of deliverance — *Isaiah 61:1–11*

**FOR THOUGHT AND CONTEMPLATION**

When God's people forsake their evil ways and turn back to Him, the future is bright indeed! That applies not only to the people of 'natural' Jerusalem — the Jews — but also to those who belong to the 'spiritual' Jerusalem — the Church. For all people, repentance before God is the key to everlasting joy.

"Repent, then, and turn to God, so that your sins may be wiped out, that times of refreshing may come from the Lord." (Acts 3:19, NIV)

---

The Lord's mercy

- [x] God's care — *Isaiah 62:1–5*
- [x] The faithful watchmen — *Isaiah 62:6–9*
- [x] Announcement of salvation — *Isaiah 62:10–12*
- [x] Christ's victory — *Isaiah 63:1–6*
- [x] His mercy to Israel — *Isaiah 63:7–14*
- [x] Prayer of intercession — *Isaiah 63:15–19, 64:1–5*
- [x] A confession of sin — *Isaiah 64:6–12*
- [x] The calling of the Gentiles — *Isaiah 65:1–7*
- [x] Remnant preserved — *Isaiah 65:8–10*
- [x] Judgments on the wicked — *Isaiah 65:11–16*
- [x] The new Jerusalem — *Isaiah 65:17–25*

**FOR THOUGHT AND CONTEMPLATION**

Here's a threefold truth that ought to stimulate your spiritual digestive system! Think about it every spare moment of this day: When the Messiah, the light of Jerusalem, comes (60:1) then righteousness will shine forth to the nations of the world (62:1) and Jerusalem shall be "a praise in the earth" (62:7).

"You are the light of the world. A city on a hill cannot be hidden." (Matt. 5:14, NIV)

# Micah's prophecies

- Vengeance is threatened — *Isaiah 66:1–4*
- Jerusalem's future glory — *Isaiah 66:5–14*
- Final ruin of the ungodly — *Isaiah 66:15–24*
- The millennial kingdom — *Micah 4:1–8*
- Final triumph of Israel — *Micah 4:9–13*
- Christ's birth prophesied — *Micah 5:1–6*
- Deliverance and punishment — *Micah 5:7–15*
- God's controversy with Israel — *Micah 6:1–5*
- The duties God requires — *Micah 6:6–8*
- The wickedness of Israel — *Micah 6:9–16*

**FOR THOUGHT AND CONTEMPLATION**

The Old Testament prophets lived in eager anticipation of their coming Messiah. Do you? Someone has said: 'The degree to which we desire Christ's coming is the degree to which we are experiencing His presence in our lives." The one is the natural outcome of the other.

"He who testifies to these things says, 'Yes, I am coming soon.' Amen. Come, Lord Jesus." (Rev. 22:20, NIV)

# Jerusalem threatened

- Israel's moral corruption — *Micah 7:1–7*
- The Lord brings salvation — *Micah 7:8–13*
- The Lord's compassion — *Micah 7:14–20*
- Sennacherib and Hezekiah — *2 Chronicles 32:1, Isaiah 36:1, 2 Kings 18:13–16*
- Jerusalem's defence prepared — *2 Chronicles 32:2–8*
- Sennacherib threatens Jerusalem — *2 Kings 18:17–26, 2 Chronicles 32:9–14, Isaiah 36:2–11*
- Rabshakeh's defiance — *2 Kings 18:27–35, 2 Chronicles 32:15–16, 18–19*

**FOR THOUGHT AND CONTEMPLATION**

The history of Israel is a series of ups and downs. One day repentant — the next day recalcitrant. Yet God loved them too much to let them get away with anything. Never forget that love is the reason for His discipline, not His discipline the reason for His love.

"Keep yourselves in God's love as you wait for the mercy of our Lord Jesus Christ to bring you to eternal life." (Jude 21, NIV)

# Israel seeks help

- Rabshakeh's defiance — *Isaiah 36:12–20*
- Siege of Jerusalem prophesied — *Isaiah 29:1–8*
- The Jews' hypocrisy — *Isaiah 29:9–16*
- Future blessings — *Isaiah 29:17–24*
- The Jews reproved — *Isaiah 30:1–7*
- The disobedient people — *Isaiah 30:8–17*
- God's mercies — *Isaiah 30:18–26*
- Final ruin of the Assyrians — *Isaiah 30:27–33*
- The folly of seeking help — *Isaiah 31:1–3*
- God's care for Jerusalem — *Isaiah 31:4–9*

**FOR THOUGHT AND CONTEMPLATION**

The leaders of Judah were upset that Isaiah lectured them like children: 'precept upon precept, line upon line ...' (Isa. 28:9–11), and they completely ignored his warnings. Instead they had to listen to the stronger voice of their Assyrian conquerors. Beware of failing to heed the gentle reproofs of the Spirit, or else you may well be forced to heed the stronger voice of circumstances.

"You stiff-necked people, with uncircumcised hearts and ears! You are just like your fathers: You always resist the Holy Spirit!" (Acts 7:51, NIV)

# SEASONS IN ISRAEL

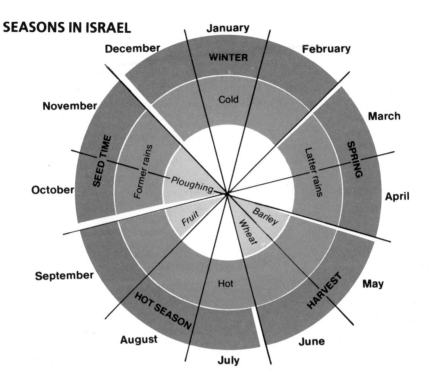

Hezekiah's consultation

☑ Time of peace — *Isaiah 32:1–8*
☑ Time of trouble — *Isaiah 32:9–14*
☑ Time of blessing — *Isaiah 32:15–20*
☑ A prayer for help — *Isaiah 33:1–9*
☑ The Lord's warning — *Isaiah 33:10–16*
☑ The glorious future — *Isaiah 33:17–24*
☑ Hezekiah humbles himself — *2 Kings 18:36–37, 19:1, Isaiah 36:21–22, 37:1*
☑ Hezekiah consults Isaiah — *2 Kings 19:2–7, Isaiah 37:2–7*
☑ A prayer for protection — *Psalm 44:1–26*

FOR THOUGHT AND CONTEMPLATION

How extremely comforting it must have been for Hezekiah when, concerned about the dishonour done to God by Rabshakeh's blasphemy, he was able to share his burden with the godly Isaiah. Do you have a prayer partner in whom you can confide? If not, ask God today to give you one.

"For where two or three come together in my name, there am I with them." (Matt. 18:20, NIV)

## THURSDAY Week 29 Hezekiah's prayer answered

☑ Sennacherib's letters — *2 Chronicles 32:17*
☑ He defies God — *2 Kings 19:8–13, Isaiah 37:8–13*
☑ Hezekiah's prayer — *2 Chronicles 32:20, 2 Kings 19:14–19, Isaiah 37:14–20*

☑ The psalmist's temptation — *Psalm 73:1–14*
☑ How he gained victory — *Psalm 73:15–20*
☑ How he profited by it — *Psalm 73:21–28*
☑ Isaiah's response to Hezekiah — *2 Kings 19:20–34, Isaiah 37:21–35*

Hezekiah's plea to God through Isaiah was not only heard, but answered. God not only listened but responded. Some think that prayer is merely talking to God. It's much more than that. Prayer is *conversation*; you talking to God and God talking to you. Is that the way it is in your prayer life?

"come near to God and he will come near to you ..." (Jas. 4:8, NIV)

---

## FRIDAY Week 29 — Hezekiah's last days

☑ Assyrian army destroyed — *2 Kings 19:35–36, 2 Chronicles 32:21–22, Isaiah 37:36–37*

☑ God the Judge — *Psalm 75:1–10*

☑ God the Victor — *Psalm 76:1–12*

☑ Hezekiah's prosperity — *2 Chronicles 32:23, 27–30, 2 Kings 20:20*

☑ The Babylonian ambassadors — *2 Kings 20:12–19, Isaiah 39:1–8, 2 Chronicles 32:31*

☑ Hezekiah's death — *2 Kings 20:21, 2 Chronicles 32:32–33*

☑ Assyrians settle in Samaria — *2 Kings 17:24–41*

### FOR THOUGHT AND CONTEMPLATION

God extended Hezekiah's life by fifteen years but, regrettably, Hezekiah used those years for his own selfish endeavours rather than for God's glory. How sad when divine favour is prostituted and used for self-centred ends.

"When you ask, you do not receive, because you ask with wrong motives, that you may spend what you get on your pleasures." (Jas. 4:3, NIV)

---

## SATURDAY Week 29 — Manasseh turns to God

☑ Manasseh's sinful ways — *2 Kings 21:1–9, 2 Chronicles 33:1–9*

☑ God's displeasure — *2 Kings 21:10–15, 2 Chronicles 33:10*

☑ Warning to Shebna — *Isaiah 22:15–25*

☑ Sennacherib's death — *2 Kings 19:37, Isaiah 37:38*

☑ Manasseh's sin and repentance — *2 Kings 21:16, 2 Chronicles 33:11–13*

☑ His reforms — *2 Chronicles 33:14–17*

☑ His death — *2 Kings 21:17–18, 2 Chronicles 33:18–20*

☑ Amon's evil life and death — *2 Kings 21:19–22, 2 Chronicles 33:21–23, 2 Kings 21:25, 23, 26, 2 Chronicles 33:24*

☑ Josiah becomes king — *2 Kings 21:24, 2 Chronicles 33:25*

### FOR THOUGHT AND CONTEMPLATION

Manasseh and Amon were two of the most evil men who ever lived. One wonders why God allowed such rulers to hold sway over His people. One thing, however, is sure — all will ultimately perish who refuse to walk in God's ways.

"Therefore the wicked will not stand in the judgment, nor sinners in the assembly of the righteous. For the Lord watches over the way of the righteous, but the way of the wicked will perish." (Psa. 1:5–6, NIV)

---

## SUNDAY Week 30 — The fall of Nineveh

☑ Josiah's godly character — *2 Chronicles 34:1–2, 2 Kings 22:1–2, 23:25*

☑ God's justice and power — *Nahum 1:1–8*

☑ The Assyrians overthrown — *Nahum 1:9–15*

☑ Nineveh's destruction foretold — *Nahum 2:1–10*

☑ The cause — *Nahum 2:11–13*

☑ The fall of Nineveh — *Nahum 3:1–19*

- ☑ Josiah's early reforms — *2 Chronicles 34:3–7*
- Jeremiah's ministry begins 628 BC
- ☑ Jeremiah's call and early vision — *Jeremiah 1:1–19*

FOR THOUGHT AND CONTEMPLATION

When a nation comes under the judgment of God then the mightiest defences are of no avail. It's a sobering thought that one day God will judge the nations of the world for their disobedience to His commands. And when He does, the most powerful nuclear defence strategy will be powerless to stand against His wrath.

"But they will have to give account to him who is ready to judge the living and the dead." (1 Pet. 4:5, NIV)

---

## MAJOR PROPHETS

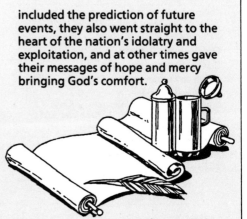

The five Old Testament books Isaiah, Jeremiah, Lamentations, Ezekiel and Daniel are usually known as the "Major Prophets".

The main mission of the prophets was to call God's people back to Himself. The Lord had especially appointed them for the task. They were to deliver God's message faithfully no matter what the cost. While their prophecies included the prediction of future events, they also went straight to the heart of the nation's idolatry and exploitation, and at other times gave their messages of hope and mercy bringing God's comfort.

---

## MONDAY Week 30 — Jeremiah's first message

- ☑ Israel's early love for God — *Jeremiah 2:1–3*
- ☑ The sin of Israel's leaders — *Jeremiah 2:4–8*
- ☑ The Lord's plea — *Jeremiah 2:9–13*
- ☑ The results of unfaithfulness — *Jeremiah 2:14–19*
- ☑ The sins of Judah — *Jeremiah 2:20–28*
- ☑ Their false confidence — *Jeremiah 2:29–37*
- ☑ Exhortations to repentance — *Jeremiah 3:1–5*
- ☑ The coming judgment — *Zephaniah 1:1–18*
- ☑ A plea for repentance — *Zephaniah 2:1–3*
- ☑ Judgment against the nations — *Zephaniah 2:4–15*

FOR THOUGHT AND CONTEMPLATION

"I'll do it if I feel like it." Unfortunately many Christians adopt this attitude to God's commands. If Jeremiah had done that, then it would have changed a whole section of Old Testament history. Are you fighting the 'God-said-it-but-I-don't-feel-like-it' battle? Then decide right now to do what God asks — *whether you feel like it or not.*

"If you love me, you will obey what I command." (Jn. 14:15, NIV)

---

## TUESDAY Week 30 — Josiah's godly reign

- ☑ Further reproofs for sin — *Zephaniah 3:1–7*
- ☑ God's mercy — *Zephaniah 3:8–13*
- ☑ Restoration of Israel and Jerusalem — *Zephaniah 3:14–20*
- ☑ Josiah repairs the temple — *2 Kings 22:3–7, 2 Chronicles 34:8–13*
- ☑ The book of the Law is found — *2 Kings 22:8–10, 2 Chronicles 34:14–18*
- ☑ Josiah consults Huldah — *2 Kings 22:11–20, 2 Chronicles 34:19–28*
- ☑ The king's covenant — *2 Kings 23:1–3, 2 Chronicles 34:29–32*

**Question**: Why did some of Israel's kings turn out to be evil and wicked men while others were righteous? **Answer**: It depended not merely on their upbringing, their temperament or their view of life, but on their *willingness* to obey the word of the Lord. The will is a crucial issue in the battle between sin and evil. So ask yourself at this moment: How willing am I to obey the divine will?

"Whether it is favourable or unfavourable, we will obey the Lord our God, to whom we are sending you, so that it will go well with us, for we will obey the Lord our God." (Jer. 42:6, NIV)

---

## WEDNESDAY Week 30 Jeremiah's second message

- ☑ Israel better than Judah — *Jeremiah 3:6–11*
- ☑ Pardon is promised — *Jeremiah 3:12–20*
- ☑ Israel's repentance — *Jeremiah 3:21–25*
- ☑ A call to repentance — *Jeremiah 4:1–4*
- ☐ Judah is threatened — *Jeremiah 4:5–12*
- ☐ Judah is surrounded — *Jeremiah 4:13–18*
- ☑ Jeremiah's sorrow — *Jeremiah 4:19–22*
- ☑ His vision — *Jeremiah 4:23–31*
- ☑ Jerusalem's sin — *Jeremiah 5:1–11*
- ☑ Israel's enemies — *Jeremiah 5:12–19*
- ☐ God's warning — *Jeremiah 5:20–31*

FOR THOUGHT AND CONTEMPLATION

Many of God's people are spiritually shipwrecked because they believe that God will not be as strict as His Word suggests. Adam and Eve failed because of this. And, as our present reading shows, so did the people of Israel. Ask yourself right now: is this same attitude to be found in me?

"'Is not my word like fire,' declares the Lord, 'and like a hammer that breaks a rock in pieces?'" (Jer. 23:29, NIV)

---

## A BIRD'S EYE VIEW OF ZEPHANIAH

**Place in the Bible:**
Thirty-sixth Old Testament book; fourteenth book of prophecy.

**Special feature:**
The prominence of "The Day of the Lord".

**Jesus and the prophecy of Zephaniah:**
Jesus Christ often spoke about his second coming, which is closely linked in the Bible to Zephaniah's message of the Day of the Lord: see Matthew 24:42, "Therefore keep watch because you do not know on what day your Lord will come."

**Teaching:**
Zephaniah's message is similar to many other prophets: punishment for sin because of idol worship will come before God's blessing. The prophet insists that the Day of the Lord, God's day of judgement, will come to Jerusalem. But for those who trust in God there will be mercy and rejoicing.

**A verse to remember:**
"Seek the Lord, all you humble of the land, you who do what he commands. Seek righteousness, seek humility ..." (Zeph. 2:3).

---

## THURSDAY Week 30 The Passover is kept

- ☑ The invasion of Jerusalem — *Jeremiah 6:1–8*
- ☑ Rebellious Israel — *Jeremiah 6:9–15*
- ☑ Israel's rejection of God's way — *Jeremiah 6:16–21*
- ☑ Invasion from the north — *Jeremiah 6:22–30*
- ☑ Josiah celebrates the Passover — *2 Kings 23:21–23, 26–27, 2 Chronicles 35:1–19*
- ☐ Josiah's further reforms — *2 Kings 23:4–14*

Josiah's decision to celebrate the Passover — an ordinance that had been neglected in previous reigns — brought joy to God and delight to the people. The Almighty rewarded their commitment with evidences of His approval and favour. When we draw near to Him, He never fails to draw near to us.

"Let us draw near to God with a sincere heart in full assurance of faith, having our hearts sprinkled to cleanse us from a guilty conscience and having our bodies washed with pure water." (Heb. 10:22, NIV)

---

**FRIDAY Week 30**    ## Jeremiah's third message

✓ Josiah's reforms — *2 Kings 23:15–20, 2 Chronicles 34:33*

✓ Jeremiah preaches in the temple — *Jeremiah 7:1–15*

Birth of Ezekiel 622 BC

✓ The people's disobedience — *Jeremiah 7:16–28*

✓ Vengeance threatened — *Jeremiah 7:29–34*

✓ Bones to remain unburied — *Jeremiah 8:1–3*

✓ The people's stupidity — *Jeremiah 8:4–13*

✓ The alarm of invasion — *Jeremiah 8:14–17*

✓ Jeremiah's lamentation — *Jeremiah 8:18–22*

FOR THOUGHT AND CONTEMPLATION

Israel's greatest sin was that of idolatry — replacing the true object of worship with one which made lesser demands. But God will brook no rival in His universe, and therefore idolatry *must* be removed. If we don't get rid of the idols in our lives by our own volition, then we give God no other option than to topple them Himself.

"The acts of the sinful nature are obvious ... idolatry and witchcraft ..." (Gal. 5:19–20, NIV)

---

**A BIRD'S EYE VIEW OF JEREMIAH**

Place in the Bible:
Twenty-fourth Old Testament book; second book of prophecy.
Special features:
Autobiographical style.
Jesus and the prophecy of Jeremiah:
Jeremiah speaks about a "new covenant" (Jer. 31:31–34) and this is precisely what Jesus says he is ushering in when he held the Last Supper with his twelve disciples: "Then he [Jesus] took the cup, gave thanks and offered it to them, saying, 'Drink from it, all of you. This is my blood of the covenant, which is poured out for many for the forgiveness of sins" (Matt. 26:27–28).
Teaching:
Far from being negative, Jeremiah's prescription for Israel's sins of immorality and idolatry was positive because he told the Israelites to return to God in repentance. He insisted that this was much more important than relying on a foreign army to deliver them from the seige of Jerusalem.
A verse to remember:
"This is the covenant that I will make with the house of Israel ... I will put my law in their minds and write it on their hearts. I will be their God, and they will be my people" (Jer. 31:33).

---

**SATURDAY Week 30**    ## A further message

✓ The people are corrected — *Jeremiah 9:1–11*

✓ The captives suffer — *Jeremiah 9:12–22*

✓ God's loving-kindness — *Jeremiah 9:23–24*

✓ Punishment of the unrighteous — *Jeremiah 9:25–26*

✓ Idolatry and true worship — *Jeremiah 10:1–11*

✓ A hymn of praise — *Jeremiah 10:12–16*

✓ The coming exile — *Jeremiah 10:17–25*

✓ Disobedient Jews reproved — *Jeremiah 11:1–10*

✓ Their utter ruin — *Jeremiah 11:11–17*

✓ A plot against Jeremiah's life — *Jeremiah 11:18–23*

FOR THOUGHT AND CONTEMPLATION

How do you feel when you see God's hand of discipline on someone you know and love? Do you ignore it or do you 'weep' over it as did Jeremiah? Pause for a moment to see if God wants you to intercede on behalf of an erring brother or sister. Let Jeremiah's deep concern be your example.

"Brothers, if someone is caught in a sin, you who are spiritual should restore him gently. But watch yourself, or you also may be tempted." (Gal. 6:1, NIV)

## PROPHECIES OF JEREMIAH

1. Fall of Jerusalem (1:14–16, 4:5–9, 5:15–17, 6:1–6, 32:2–3, 38:17–18)
2. Destruction of the Temple (7:11–15, 26:6–9)
3. Death of deposed King Jehoahaz in Egypt (22:10–12)
4. Unlamented death of King Jehoiakim (36:27–30)
5. Cutting of the royal line of King Jehoiachin (22:24–30)
6. Death of two false prophets and punishment of another – all three living in Babylon (29:20–32)
7. Death of a false Jerusalem prophet (28:13–17)
8. Capture and exile of a friend named Seraiah (51:59)
9. Failure of the Egyptian-Judean military alliance against Babylon (37:5–10)
10. Defeat of Egypt by Babylon at Carchemish (46:1–12)
11. Babylonian occupation of Egypt (43:9–13)
12. Seventy-year captivity of Judah in Babylon (25:11, 29:10)
13. Restoration to Jerusalem after the seventy years (27:19–22; 30:3, 10–11, 18–21; 31:9, 12, 38–39; 33:3–9)
14. Defeat of Babylon after the seventy years (25:12, 27:7)
15. Capture of Zedekiah (21:3–7, 34:1–5, 37:17)
16. Kindly treatment of the godly exiles in Babylon (24:1–7)
17. Final regathering of people of Israel (30:3, 10; 31:8–12)
18. Final rebuilding of the land of Israel (30:18–21, 31:38–39, 33:7–9)

---

**SUNDAY Week 31**  ## The sign of the ox yoke

Jeremiah's questions and God's answer — *Jeremiah 12:1–6*

The Lord's sorrow — *Jeremiah 12:7–13*
Babylon: the world power 612–539 BC

His promise — *Jeremiah 12:14–17*

Josiah slain — *2 Kings 23:28–30, 2 Chronicles 35:20–24*

Lamentation for Josiah — *2 Chronicles 35:25–27*

Jehoahaz' evil life — *2 Kings 23:31–32, 2 Chronicles 36:1–2*

Judah pays tribute — *2 Kings 23:33, 2 Chronicles 36:3*

Jehoahaz' death — *2 Kings 23:34, Jeremiah 22:10–12*

Jehoiakim made king — *2 Kings 23:36–37 & 35, 2 Chronicles 36:5*

The sign of the yoke — *Jeremiah 27:1–11*

Jeremiah in the temple court — *Jeremiah 26:1–7*

Jeremiah's sign of the ox alerted the people to the fact that soon they would become subservient to the king of Babylon. He urges them to submit with meekness to this hard and humbling turn of providence in the sure knowledge that, in the lives of His people, God only allows what He can use.

"And we know that in all things God works for the good of those who love him, who have been called according to his purpose." (Rom. 8:28, NIV)

## MONDAY Week 31 — Habakkuk's message

- ☑ Jeremiah proclaimed a traitor — *Jeremiah 26:8–19*
- ☑ Habakkuk complains of injustice — *Habakkuk 1:1–4*
- ☑ The Lord's reply — *Habakkuk 1:5–11*
- ☑ Habakkuk's further complaint — *Habakkuk 1:12–17*
- ☑ Habakkuk must wait — *Habakkuk 2:1–4*
- ☑ Judgments on the unrighteous — *Habakkuk 2:5–20*
- ☑ Habakkuk's plea — *Habakkuk 3:1–2*
- ☑ His prayer and praise — *Habakkuk 3:3–19*

FOR THOUGHT AND CONTEMPLATION

Almost all of God's prophets confessed to being confused by the ways and designs of God in the Old Testament. But as they waited before Him, the confusion gave way to confidence. The secret of understanding God's ways is to 'wait'. Finally, the answer always comes.

"'For my thoughts are not your thoughts, neither are your ways my ways,' declares the Lord.' As the heavens are higher than the earth, so are my ways higher than your ways and my thoughts than your thoughts.'" (Isa. 55:8–9, NIV)

---

## A BIRD'S EYE VIEW OF HABAKKUK

**Place in the Bible:**
Thirty-fifth Old Testament book; thirteenth book of prophecy.

**Special features:**
Two rounds of questions and answers.

**Jesus and the prophecy of Habakkuk:**
Habakkuk states that God is his Saviour (3:18), which is the same word given to Jesus in Matthew 1:21, "... you are to give him the name Jesus, because he will save his people from their sins." Jesus is the Greek for Joshua, which means 'The Lord saves'. Jesus is the Saviour of the world.

**Teaching:**
Habakkuk observes unjust suffering, and God reveals that something even worse is in store for Judah — being crushed by the Babylonians. In all this perplexity and turmoil God shows Habakkuk that the only way a righteous person can survive is by being faithful to God.

**A verse to remember:**
"I will rejoice ... in God my Saviour" (Hab. 3:18).

---

## TUESDAY Week 31 — The first deportation

- ☑ Obedience of the Rechabites — *Jeremiah 35:1–11*
- ☑ The Jews' disobedience — *Jeremiah 35:12–19*
  Jerusalem's 20-year siege begins 606 BC
- ☑ The wine cup of wrath — *Jeremiah 25:15–38*
- ☑ Nebuchadnezzar beseiges Jerusalem — *Daniel 1:1*
- ☑ Some Israelites deported — *Daniel 1:2–3*

☑ Prophecy concerning Israel's captivity — *Jeremiah 25:1–11*

☑ Prophecies to be written — *Jeremiah 36:1–8*

☑ God's promise to Baruch — *Jeremiah 45:1–5*

FOR THOUGHT AND CONTEMPLATION

Why would God allow His people to be deported and sent into exile? There could be only one reason: if they would not heed God's tender disciplines as given through the word of His prophets, then they must submit to His terrible disciplines as brought about through difficult circumstances. Got the point?

---

"These things happened to them as examples and were written down as warnings for us, on whom the fulfilment of the ages has come." (1 Cor. 10:11, NIV)

---

## A BIRD'S EYE VIEW OF DANIEL

**Place in the Bible:**
Twenty-seventh Old Testament book; fifth book of prophecy.
**Main characters:**
Daniel, Nebuchadnezzar.
**Special features:**
Dreams and visions.
**Jesus and the prophecy of Daniel:**
Both Daniel and Jesus Christ concentrate on the end times. (See Mark chapter 13:26–27.)

**Teaching:**
Daniel, a prisoner-of-war, shows his faith in God — as seen in the well known lion's den incident and in his interpreting dreams — and so taught his captors, and teaches us today, that true widsom and ultimate power belong only to God.
**A verse to remember:**
"Praise be to the name of God for ever and ever; wisdom and power are his. He changes times and seasons; he sets up kings and deposes them. He gives wisdom to the wise and knowledge to the discerning" (Dan. 2:20–22).

---

**WEDNESDAY Week 31** Daniel's ministry in Babylon

☑ Egypt's defeat — *Jeremiah 46:1–12*

☑ Nebuchadnezzar's conquests — *2 Kings 24:7*

☑ Daniel, Hananiah, Mishael and Azariah — *Daniel 1:4–7*

☑ Their refusal — *Daniel 1:8–16*

☑ Their improvement in wisdom — *Daniel 1:17–20*

☑ Urijah martyred — *Jeremiah 26:20–24*

☑ Jeremiah's lament — *Jeremiah 22:13–19*

☑ A fast proclaimed — *Jeremiah 36:9*

☑ Nebuchadnezzar's dream — *Daniel 2:1–13*

☑ The dream revealed to Daniel — *Daniel 2:14–35*

FOR THOUGHT AND CONTEMPLATION

Daniel endured three great tests in Babylon: (1) The test of *food*, proving his obedience to God's law. (2) The test of the *dream*, proving his willingness to trust God's provision. (3) The test of the *lions' den*, proving his allegiance to God's Word. Could you have passed those three tests?

---

"These have come so that your faith — of greater worth than gold, which perishes even though refined by fire — may be proved genuine and may result in praise, glory and honour when Jesus Christ is revealed." (1 Pet. 1:7, NIV)

---

**THURSDAY Week 31** The sign of the linen girdle

☑ Daniel's interpretation — *Daniel 2:36–45*

☑ The king rewards Daniel — *Daniel 2:46–49*

☑ The Word of God is read — *Jeremiah 36:10–19*

☑ The king destroys the roll — *Jeremiah 36:20–26*

☑ Jeremiah replaces it — *Jeremiah 36:27–32*

- ☑ The sign of the linen girdle — *Jeremiah 13:1–11*
- ☑ The wine jar — *Jeremiah 13:12–14*
- ☑ Jeremiah's warning — *Jeremiah 13:15–27*
- ☑ The drought — *Jeremiah 14:1–12*

**FOR THOUGHT AND CONTEMPLATION**

Jeremiah's sign of the linen girdle was meant to show that Israel had corrupted themselves by their idolatry, so much that they were good for nothing. What an indictment!

What sign, do you think, would Jeremiah give us if he were alive today, and wanted to indicate the true condition of the contemporary Christian Church?

_____

"For it is time for judgment to begin with the family of God; and if it begins with us, what will the outcome be for those who do not obey the gospel of God?" (1 Pet. 4:17, NIV)

_____

---

**FRIDAY Week 31**     # Punishment for sin

- ☑ False prophets — *Jeremiah 14:13–18*
- ☑ The people's plea — *Jeremiah 14:19–22*
- ☑ The destruction of the wicked — *Jeremiah 15:1–9*
- ☑ Jeremiah's complaint — *Jeremiah 15:10–18*
- ☑ The Lord's reply — *Jeremiah 15:19–21*
- ☑ The Lord's will for Jeremiah — *Jeremiah 16:1–9*
- ☑ Return from exile prophesied — *Jeremiah 16:10–15*
- ☑ The coming punishment — *Jeremiah 16:16–18*
- ☑ Jeremiah's prayer — *Jeremiah 16:19–21*
- ☑ The sin and punishment of Judah — *Jeremiah 17:1–13*

**FOR THOUGHT AND CONTEMPLATION**

We are indebted to Jeremiah for reminding us that the heart of human problems is the problem of the heart (17:9). And what is the solution? This: "I the Lord search the heart" (17:10). Let God apply the searchlight of His Spirit today to those areas of your life where you have trouble trusting Him.

_____

"Create in me a pure heart, O God, and renew a steadfast spirit within me." (Psa. 51:10, NIV)

_____

## BABYLON

The Assyrian empire was replaced by the Babylonian. Nebuchadnezzar, its most famous king, conquered Judah in 597 BC, when Judah's king and skilled artisans were deported to Babylon. The city of Babylon was described by Herodotus as occupying about 200 square miles. It had eight ornamental gates, magnificent buildings and wide, tree-lined streets and double defensive walls. Its 'hanging gardens', built by Nebuchadnezzar for his wife, were one of the wonders of the ancient world. The prophecy concerning Babylon in Isaiah 13 has been literally fulfilled. Its ruins are uninhabited except by wild animals. The region, once fertile, is now mostly barren marshland. There have been many excavations, and a few buildings have been reconstructed, but it has never been rebuilt.

Further signs

Jeremiah's prayer — *Jeremiah 17:14–18*

The Sabbath — *Jeremiah 17:19–27*

The sign of the potter's vessel — *Jeremiah 18:1–10*

The people's rejection — *Jeremiah 18:11–17*

A plot against Jeremiah — *Jeremiah 18:18–23*

The broken jar — *Jeremiah 19:1–13*

Jeremiah's conflict with Pashhur — *Jeremiah 19:14–15, 20:1–6*

His complaint — *Jeremiah 20:7–18*

Jehoiakim's rebellion — *2 Kings 24:1*

Message against Philistia — *Jeremiah 47:1–7*

FOR THOUGHT AND CONTEMPLATION

Do you feel a failure in your Christian life? A broken and defiled vessel? Then take note of what Jeremiah learned in the potter's house — namely, that God can refashion you into a new and glorious vessel. Ask Him to make you anew right now, and stay still under His touch as He puts you back on to the wheel of His purpose this very day.

"He restores my soul. He guides me in paths of righteousness for his name's sake." (Psa. 23:3, NIV)

The Lord's judgments

The destruction of Moab — *Jeremiah 48:1–10*

Cities of Moab destroyed — *Jeremiah 48:11–25*

Moab will be humbled — *Jeremiah 48:26–39*

No escape for Moab — *Jeremiah 48:40–47*

The Lord's judgment on Ammon — *Jeremiah 49:1–6*

His judgment of Edom — *Jeremiah 49:7–22*

His judgment on Damascus — *Jeremiah 49:23–27*

His judgment on Kedar and Hazor — *Jeremiah 49:28–33*

His judgment of Elam — *Jeremiah 49:34–39*

FOR THOUGHT AND CONTEMPLATION

Just as the New Testament shows how marvellous is God's mercy, so the Old Testament shows how terrible He is in judgment. Without judgment, grace would be sickly and sentimental, and without mercy, judgment would be terrifying and overwhelming. God needs to be seen in both aspects if He is really to be properly served and understood.

"It does not, therefore, depend on man's desire or effort, but on God's mercy." (Rom. 9:16, NIV)

Second and third deportations: 598 BC

Jehoiakim's enemies — *2 Kings 24:2–4*

Second deportation: 3023 captives — *2 Chronicles 36:6–7, Jeremiah 52:28*

Jehoiakim's death — *2 Kings 24:5–6, 2 Chronicles 36:8*

Jehoiachin — *2 Kings 24:8–9, 2 Chronicles 36:9*

His captivity foretold — *Jeremiah 22:24–30*

Third deportation: 10,000 captives — *2 Kings 24:10–16, 2 Chronicles 36:10, Esther 2:6*

Zedekiah — *2 Kings 24:17–20, 2 Chronicles 36:11–16, Jeremiah 37:1–2, 52:1–2*

Israel's captivity foretold — *Jeremiah 21:1–14*

Jeremiah's message to the king — *Jeremiah 22:1–9, 20–23*

FOR THOUGHT AND CONTEMPLATION

Ancient Israel is seen by many as being haughty in times of peace, fearful in time of trouble, downcast under the yoke of oppression, and unwilling to break with sin and idolatry until the last possible moment. Sounds a bit like many in today's Church, don't you agree?

"See to it, brothers, that none of you has a sinful, unbelieving heart that turns away from the living God." (Heb. 3:12, NIV)

# Good and bad figs

☑ Faithless shepherds rebuked — *Jeremiah 23:1–4*

☑ Israel's future restoration — *Jeremiah 23:5–8*

☑ Message to prophets — *Jeremiah 23:9–32*

☑ The Lord's burden — *Jeremiah 23:33–40*

☑ Two baskets of figs — *Jeremiah 24:1–10*

☑ Jeremiah's advice to Zedekiah — *Jeremiah 27:12–22*

☑ Jeremiah's letter to the exiles — *Jeremiah 29:1–14*

☑ Message to those who remained — *Jeremiah 29:16–19*

FOR THOUGHT AND CONTEMPLATION

Just as in Israel, so in today's Church there are 'good and bad figs'. The 'good figs' are those who learn from corrective discipline, and the 'bad figs' are those who continue in their wilfulness. In which basket do you think God might place you?

---

"Endure hardship as discipline; God is treating you as sons. For what son is not disciplined by his father?" (Heb. 12:7, NIV)

---

# Israel's bright future

☑ Jeremiah's letter to the exiles — *Jeremiah 29:20, 15, 21–23*

☑ Message to Shemaiah — *Jeremiah 29:24–28*

☑ Shemaiah's punishment — *Jeremiah 29:30–32*

☑ Coming trouble — *Jeremiah 30:1–7*

☑ The Lord's promises — *Jeremiah 30:8–17*

☑ Future restoration — *Jeremiah 30:18–24*

☑ Israel's return home — *Jeremiah 31:1–14*

☑ The Lord's mercy — *Jeremiah 31:15–22*

☑ Future prosperity — *Jeremiah 31:23–30*

☑ God's new covenant with Israel — *Jeremiah 31:31–34*

☑ His everlasting mercy — *Jeremiah 31:35–40*

FOR THOUGHT AND CONTEMPLATION

It is characteristic of the Almighty that once His people are purified by oppression and exile, He acts at once to re-establish them and bring about their restoration. What would happen, do you think, if God's Church broke with all forms of idolatry, lukewarmness and indolence, and sought His face? There can only be one answer — *revival.*

---

"Restore to me the joy of your salvation and grant me a willing spirit, to sustain me. Then I will teach transgressors your ways, and sinners will turn back to you." (Psa. 51:12–13, NIV)

---

## A BIRD'S EYE VIEW OF EZEKIEL

**Place in the Bible:**
Twenty-sixth Old Testament book; fourth book of prophecy.

**Special features:**
Visions are the characteristic feature of this book.

**Jesus and the prophecy of Ezekiel:**
In chapter 34 Ezekiel contrasts faithful shepherds with uncaring shepherds, and in John 10:11 Jesus described himself as the "good shepherd" caring, leading and giving life to His followers.

**Teaching:**
Through the six visions, six parables and ten signs Ezekiel comforted the down-cast Jews, in their exile in Babylon. The prophet of the exile taught the Israelites how God had to punish sin, and also how God promised a new life through the activity of His Spirit.

**A verse to remember:**
"For I will take you out of the nations; I will gather you from all the countries and bring you back into your own land. I will sprinkle clean water on you, and you will be clean; I will cleanse you from all your impurities and from all your idols. I will give you a new heart and put a new spirit in you; I will remove from you your heart of stone and give you a heart of flesh. And I will put my Spirit in you ... " (Ezek. 36:24–27).

**Ezekiel's vision**

☑ Hananiah's false prophecy — *Jeremiah 28:1–16*
☑ His death — *Jeremiah 28:17*
☑ Seraiah and Zedekiah visit Babylon — *Jeremiah 51:59*
☑ Ezekiel's preparation — *Ezekiel 1:1*
☑ His vision of God — *Ezekiel 1:2–14*
☑ The four wheels — *Ezekiel 1:15–21*
☑ God's throne — *Ezekiel 1:22–28*
☑ Filled with the Spirit — *Ezekiel 2:1–2*
☑ Ezekiel's commission as prophet — *Ezekiel 2:3–10, 3:1–9*

FOR THOUGHT AND CONTEMPLATION

Jeremiah prophesied to the remaining Jews in Jerusalem, while Ezekiel prophesied to the exiles in Babylon. Although God has one message, He uses many different messengers. If you run from the word of the Lord in your own church, then you will find the same message facing you in another. Worth pondering — don't you think?

"Where can I go from your Spirit? Where can I flee from your presence?" (Psa. 139:7, NIV)

---

**Ezekiel portrays the siege**

☑ Ezekiel appointed watchman — *Ezekiel 3:10–21*
☑ God's glory — *Ezekiel 3:22–23*
☑ Filled with the Spirit again — *Ezekiel 3:24–27*
☑ The sign of the tile — *Ezekiel 4:1–17*
☑ The sign of the sharp knife — *Ezekiel 5:1–17*
☑ Idolatry condemned *Ezekiel 6:1–7*
☑ Remnant to be spared — *Ezekiel 6:8–10*
☑ Desolation to come — *Ezekiel 6:11–14*

FOR THOUGHT AND CONTEMPLATION

There are two essential prerequisites to an effective ministry for God. They are: (1) an overwhelming vision of God's power and greatness and (2) an understanding of where one fits into God's programme for the world. Ezekiel knew something of both these factors. Do you?

"Brothers, think of what you were when you were called. Not many of you were wise by human standards; not many were influential; not many were of noble birth. But God chose the foolish things of the world to shame the wise; God chose the weak things of the world to shame the strong." (1 Cor. 1:26–27, NIV)

---

**Ezekiel's second vision**

☑ The desolation of the land — *Ezekiel 7:1–15*
☑ The distress of the few — *Ezekiel 7:16–22*
☑ The captivity — *Ezekiel 7:23–27*
☑ Idolatry in Jerusalem — *Ezekiel 8:1–6*
☑ The hole in the wall — *Ezekiel 8:7–12*
☑ Mourning for Tammuz — *Ezekiel 8:13–14*
☑ The sun worshippers — *Ezekiel 8:15–16*
☑ The Lord's response — *Ezekiel 8:17–18*
☑ Marked men — *Ezekiel 9:1–11*
☑ The Lord's departure — *Ezekiel 10:1–15*

FOR THOUGHT AND CONTEMPLATION

What foolishness was manifested by the elders of Israel in thinking that what they did in the dark could not be seen by the Lord. Someone has said that sin is the greatest of detectives. "Be sure your sin will find you out."

"Therefore judge nothing before the appointed time; wait till the Lord comes. He will bring to light what is hidden in darkness and will expose the motives of men's hearts. At that time each will receive his praise from God." (1 Cor. 4:5, NIV)

**The Lord's condemnation**

- ☑ The Lord's departure — *Ezekiel 10:16–22*
- ☑ Jerusalem is condemned — *Ezekiel 11:1–13*
- ☑ God's promise to the exiles — *Ezekiel 11:14–21*
- ☑ God's glory leaves Jerusalem — *Ezekiel 11:22–25*
- ☑ Ezekiel the refugee — *Ezekiel 12:1–7*
- ☑ The approaching captivity — *Ezekiel 12:8–12, 15–16*
- ☑ The sign of the trembling prophet — *Ezekiel 12:17–20*
- ☑ Objections answered — *Ezekiel 12:21–28*
- ☑ False male prophets condemned — *Ezekiel 13:1–16*
- ☑ False female prophets condemned — *Ezekiel 13:17–23*

FOR THOUGHT AND CONTEMPLATION

Much of Israel's downfall was due to the failure of her shepherds — those who *plundered* rather than *protected* the flock. How true is the saying that it takes dedicated leaders to produce dedicated followers. Pray for your spiritual shepherd today.

"Obey your leaders and submit to their authority. They keep watch over you as men who must give an account. Obey them so that their work will be a joy, not a burden, for that would be of no advantage to you." (Heb. 13:17, NIV)

---

**Jerusalem's adultery**

- ☑ Hypocrites threatened — *Ezekiel 14:1–11*
- ☑ God's punishment — *Ezekiel 14:12–23*
- ☑ Parable of the vine — *Ezekiel 15:1–8*
- ☑ The Lord's covenant — *Ezekiel 16:1–8*
- ☑ God's blessings — *Ezekiel 16:9–14*
- ☑ Jerusalem's unfaithfulness — *Ezekiel 16:15–22*
- ☑ Her adultery — *Ezekiel 16:23–34*
- ☑ God's judgment on Jerusalem — *Ezekiel 16:35–43*

FOR THOUGHT AND CONTEMPLATION

Spend a few moments comparing the vine in Ezekiel with the vine in John 15. Remember that, in both cases, the only value of a vine is in the fruit it produces; its wood is quite useless (Ezek. 15:3). How much fruit is growing on your vine?

"I am the vine; you are the branches. If a man remains in me and I in him, he will bear much fruit; apart from me you can do nothing." (Jn. 15:5, NIV)

---

**A parable explained**

- ☑ Like mother, like daughter — *Ezekiel 16:44–45*
- ☑ Judah worse than Sodom and Samaria — *Ezekiel 16:46–52*
- ☑ Sodom and Samaria's future prosperity — *Ezekiel 16:53–58*
- ☑ The renewed covenant — *Ezekiel 16:59–63*
- ☑ Parable of the eagles and the vine — *Ezekiel 17:1–10*
- ☑ The parable explained — *Ezekiel 17:11–21*
- ☑ God's promise — *Ezekiel 17:22–24*
- ☑ No respecter of persons — *Ezekiel 18:1–20*
- ☑ The Lord's vindication — *Ezekiel 18:21–29*

- ☑ Invitation to repent — *Ezekiel 18:30–32*

FOR THOUGHT AND CONTEMPLATION

There is only one word to describe the act of playing fast and loose with spiritual things — *prostitution*. It's a grim and horrifying word, but how else can God view the condition of those who pledge their fidelity to Him and then renege on their commitment?

"Now it is required that those who have been given a trust must prove faithful" (1 Cor. 4:2, NIV)

☑ A lament for Israel's princes — *Ezekiel 19:1–9*
☑ Another lament — *Ezekiel 19:10–14*
☑ A reminder to the leaders — *Ezekiel 20:1–9*
☑ In the wilderness — *Ezekiel 20:10–26*
☑ In Canaan — *Ezekiel 20:27–32*
☑ Pardon and restoration — *Ezekiel 20:33–44*
☑ Prophecy against Jerusalem — *Ezekiel 20:45–49*
☑ The Lord's sword — *Ezekiel 21:1–7*

FOR THOUGHT AND CONTEMPLATION

Why is it that we have to learn things the *hard* way? Israel had received so many warnings from God, yet they persisted in following their own stubborn and wilful ways. Know anyone else like that?

"We must pay more careful attention, therefore, to what we have heard, so that we do not drift away." (Heb. 2:1, NIV)

☑ Judgment by the sword — *Ezekiel 21:8–17*
☑ The king of Babylon's approach — *Ezekiel 21:18–27*
☑ The Ammonites' destruction — *Ezekiel 21:28–32*
☑ The sins of Jerusalem — *Ezekiel 22:1–16*
☑ God's furnace — *Ezekiel 22:17–22*
☑ The sins of Israel's leaders — *Ezekiel 22:23–31*
☑ The lustful sisters — *Ezekiel 23:1–21*

FOR THOUGHT AND CONTEMPLATION

Israel spent much of their time in God's refinery. This was because, as we have seen, they failed to heed His Word. Ever been in God's refinery? Perhaps you are there right now. The heat is intense and the pressure is relentless, but the results are well worth the cost. You'll see.

"For you, O God, tested us; you refined us like silver." (Psa. 66:10, NIV)

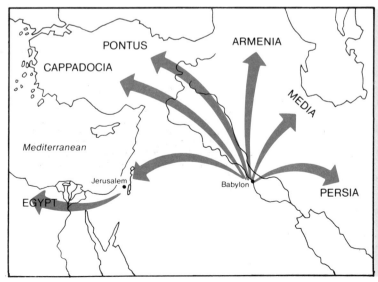

**THE DIASPORA**

The term 'diaspora' refers to Jews who live outside of Palestine (now Israel). Moses had warned the Israelites that they would be scattered among the Gentiles if they deserted the true God and worshipped idols. This scattering began through the Assyrian and Babylonian captivities, and became worldwide after the destruction of Jerusalem and the Temple in AD 70.

# The fourth deportation: 588 BC

☑ God's judgment on Oholibah — *Ezekiel 23:22–35*

☑ God's judgment on Oholah and Oholibah — *Ezekiel 23:36–49*

☑ The boiling cauldron — *Ezekiel 24:1–14, 19–27*

☑ City's capture approaches — *Jeremiah 52:3–5, 39:1, 2 Kings 25:1–2*

☑ Ezekiel's wife dies — *Ezekiel 24:15–18*

☑ 832 captives taken — *Jeremiah 52:29*

☑ Jeremiah's first imprisonment — *Jeremiah 32:1–5*

☑ Deceitful treatment of slaves — *Jeremiah 34:8–11*

**FOR THOUGHT AND CONTEMPLATION**

By now the message that we either "take God's way or take the consequences" will undoubtedly have got home to you. Isolate one area of your life where you are going your own way, and draw up an alternative plan — God's plan. Then keep a diary of your progress and watch how things work out.

---

"In all your ways acknowledge him, and he will make your paths straight. Do not be wise in your own eyes; fear the Lord and shun evil." (Prov. 3:6–7, NIV)

---

# The overthrow of Tyre

☑ Dishonourable treatment punished — *Jeremiah 34:12–22*

☑ Prophecy against Egypt — *Ezekiel 29:1–7*

☑ The desolation of Egypt — *Ezekiel 29:8–16*

☐ Tyre's rejoicing — *Ezekiel 26:1–2*

☑ Tyre's enemy — *Ezekiel 26:3–6*

☐ Tyre's attacker — *Ezekiel 26:7–8*

☐ Tyre's destruction — *Ezekiel 26:9–14*

☐ A terrifying example — *Ezekiel 26:15–21*

☐ Tyre's funeral song — *Ezekiel 27:1–25*

**FOR THOUGHT AND CONTEMPLATION**

One of the greatest dangers we face in life is prosperity — whether it be financial, social or spiritual. It's the successful person who is in danger of forgetting their dependency on God. Self-sufficiency brought Tyre down to ruins. Watch that it doesn't do the same to you.

---

"So, if you think you are standing firm, be careful that you don't fall!" (1 Cor. 10:12, NIV)

---

# Further prophecies

☑ Tyre's funeral song — *Ezekiel 27:26–36*

☑ The fall of the king of Tyre — *Ezekiel 28:1–12, 19*

☑ Prophecy against Pharaoh — *Ezekiel 30:20–26*

☑ Further prophecy against Egypt — *Ezekiel 31:1–18*

☑ Jeremiah's advice sought — *Jeremiah 37:3–4*

☑ Egyptian intervention — *Jeremiah 37:5*

☑ Egyptian army to return home — *Jeremiah 37:6–10*

☑ Jeremiah arrested, then released — *Jeremiah 37:11–21*

**FOR THOUGHT AND CONTEMPLATION**

Ever heard the statement: Cheer up, things could be worse. So you cheered up, and sure enough — things got worse! Jeremiah could have identified with that. How did he cope? By living above his circumstances rather than under them! Have you learned that secret yet?

---

"But he said to me, 'My grace is sufficient for you, for my power is made perfect in weakness.' Therefore I will boast all the more gladly about my weaknesses, so that Christ's power may rest on me." (2 Cor. 12:9, NIV)

---

# The promised Messiah

☑ Jeremiah buys a field — *Jeremiah 32:6–15*
☑ Jeremiah's prayer — *Jeremiah 32:16–25*
☑ The Lord's answer — *Jeremiah 32:26–35*
☑ The Lord's promise — *Jeremiah 32:36–44*
☑ The restoration of the Jews — *Jeremiah 33:1–13*
☑ The promised Messiah — *Jeremiah 33:14–26*
☑ A message for Zedekiah — *Jeremiah 34:1–7*
☑ Jeremiah in the well — *Jeremiah 38:1–13*

FOR THOUGHT AND CONTEMPLATION

Has life's circumstances cast you, like

Jeremiah, into a well? Figuratively, we mean. Well, look up, for we are told that even in the daytime one can see the stars shining from the bottom of a well. And what do they say? "God's in His heaven — all's right with the world."

"Consider it pure joy, my brothers, whenever you face trials of many kinds, because you know that the testing of your faith develops perseverance. Perseverance must finish its work so that you may be mature and complete, not lacking anything." (Jas. 1:2–4, NIV)

## FAMOUS SAYINGS OF JEREMIAH

"Is there no balm in Gilead? Is there no physician there? Why then is there no healing for the wound of my people?" (8:22)

"Can the Ethiopian change his skin or the leopard his spots? Neither can you do good who are accustomed to doing evil." (13:23)

"The heart is deceitful above all things and beyond cure. Who can understand it?" (17:9)

"Is not my word like fire ... and like a hammer that breaks a rock in pieces?" (23:29)

"Call to me and I will answer you and tell you great and unsearchable things you do not know." (33:3)

---

# The fall of Jerusalem

☐ Zedekiah seeks advice — *Jeremiah 38:14–27*
☑ Message to Ebedmelech — *Jeremiah 39:15–18*
☑ The fall of Jerusalem — *Jeremiah 38:28*
☑ The famine — *2 Kings 25:3, Jeremiah 52:6*
  Fall of Judah 586 BC
☑ The Babylonian princes — *Jeremiah 39:2–3*
☑ Zedekiah's flight and capture — *2 Kings 25:4–5, Jeremiah 39:4–5, 52:7–8*
☑ The slaughter — *2 Chronicles 36:17*
☑ Zedekiah's sons slain — *Jeremiah 52:9–10, 39:6*
☑ His blindness — *Ezekiel 12:13–14, 2 Kings 25:6–7, Jeremiah 39:7, 52:11*
☑ Temple and walls destroyed — *2 Kings 25:8–10, 2 Chronicles 36:19, Jeremiah 39:8, 52:12–14*

FOR THOUGHT AND CONTEMPLATION

Sad though the fall of Jerusalem was, it is important to remember that from God's point of view, those walls were ever upright before Him (Isa. 49:16). God sees with a double vision. He sees things, not only as they are, but as they will be. Our hope must be His hope.

"Remember the former things, those of long ago; I am God, and there is no other; I am God, and there is none like me. I make known the end from the beginning, from ancient times, what is still to come. I say: My purpose will stand, and I will do all that I please." (Isa. 46:9–10, NIV)

☑ Fifth deportation: the poor left behind — *2 Kings 25:11–12, 2 Chronicles 36:20–21, Jeremiah 39:9–10, 52:15–16*

☑ God the judge of all — *Psalm 94:1–23*

☑ The Temple looted — *2 Kings 25:13–17, 2 Chronicles 36:18, Jeremiah 52:17–23*

☑ Priests deported — *2 Kings 25:18, Jeremiah 52:24*

☑ Prayer for nation's deliverance — *Psalm 74:1–23, 79:1–13*

☑ Important men killed — *2 Kings 25:19–21, Jeremiah 52:25–27*

FOR THOUGHT AND CONTEMPLATION

In the midst of desolation and catastrophe, where can one turn? Thankfully, those who know the Lord can lean hard upon His breast (Psalm 74). The old adage, though a cliché, is still reassuring: when the outlook is dark and depressing, try the uplook!

---

"God is our refuge and strength, an ever present help in trouble. Therefore we will not fear, though the earth give way and the mountains fall into the heart of the sea." (Psa. 46:1–2, NIV)

## A BIRD'S EYE VIEW OF LAMENTATIONS

**Place in the Bible:**
Twenty-fifth Old Testament book; third book of prophecy.

**Special features:**
Laments.

**Jesus and the book of Lamentations:**
"How deserted lies the city, once so full of people! How like a widow...." This opening verse of the five poems of Lamentations describes Jerusalem in mourning, as it laments the destruction of its city and its temple. Jesus also wept over Jerusalem, reflecting his heartfelt love for the rebellious people of

Jerusalem (Matt. 23:37–38).
**Teaching:**
For the Jews the capture of Jerusalem in BC 586 was the ultimate disaster. They no longer had their land, their city or their temple. It was as if they no longer had God! Lamentations poignantly relfects this situation but also has a bright ray of hope in its well known verses in chapter 3:22–24.
**A verse to remember:**
"Because of the Lord's great love we are not consumed, for his compassions never fail. They are new every morning; great is your faithfulness" (Lam. 3:22–23).

---

☐ Jerusalem's miserable state — *Lamentations 1:1–11*

☑ Jerusalem's sorrow — *Lamentations 1:12–22*

☐ The Lord's terrible punishment — *Lamentations 2:1–10*

☑ Jeremiah's deep sorrow — *Lamentations 2:11–22*

☑ His suffering — *Lamentations 3:1–20*

☑ His hope — *Lamentations 3:21–30*

☑ The Lord's mercy — *Lamentations 3:31–36*

FOR THOUGHT AND CONTEMPLATION

The more Jeremiah looked at the troubles of Israel, the more he was grieved. The more he looked on God's mercy, however, the more his spirit revived. It's not wrong to look at your difficulties and your problems, but it is wrong to look *only* at them. Do as one great saint said: "I glance at my difficulties, but I *gaze* at God."

---

"What, then, shall we say in response to this? If God is for us, who can be against us?" (Rom. 8:31, NIV)

# Unexpected kindness

☑ Jeremiah's plea — *Lamentations 3:37–66*
☑ Jerusalem after the fall — *Lamentations 4:1–22*
☑ A prayer for mercy — *Lamentations 5:1–22*
☑ Gedaliah becomes governor — *2 Kings 25:22–24*
☑ Kindness shown to Jeremiah — *Jeremiah 39:11–13*
☑ Jeremiah stays with Gedaliah — *Jeremiah 39:14, 40:1–5*
The captivity 586–516 BC
☑ Gedaliah's care for the poor — *Jeremiah 40:6–12*

**FOR THOUGHT AND CONTEMPLATION**

When Jeremiah was in need of help he found it, not through his own people, but through Nebuzaradan, one of the oppressors of his people. It's a sad and sobering thought, that often God's people meet with more kindness from unbelievers than they do from their Christian brothers and sisters. Ought not this to be a matter of great prayer and concern?

"Carry each other's burdens, and in this way you will fulfil the law of Christ." (Gal. 6:2, NIV)

---

# No help in Egypt

☑ Gedaliah killed — *Jeremiah 40:13–16, 41:1, 2 Kings 25:25, Jeremiah 41:2–9*
☑ Ishmael's escape — *Jeremiah 41:10–15*
☑ The exodus to Egypt — *2 Kings 25:26, Jeremiah 41:16–18*
☑ Jeremiah's assistance requested — *Jeremiah 42:1–6*
☑ Safety in Judah — *Jeremiah 42:7–12*
☑ Destruction in Egypt — *Jeremiah 42:13–22*
☑ Jeremiah taken to Egypt — *Jeremiah 43:1–7*
☑ Conquest of Egypt foretold — *Jeremiah 43:8–13*

**FOR THOUGHT AND CONTEMPLATION**

Jeremiah's message could be summed up in these words: "Don't flee to Egypt. Stand your ground against the Babylonians, face them with the truth and you will be spared." Are you running from something at this moment? Then STOP. Face your problem in God's strength. Jer. 42:11 is God's special word to you today.

"He gives strength to the weary and increases the power of the weak. Even youths grow tired and weary, and young men stumble and fall; but those who hope in the Lord will renew their strength. They will soar on wings like eagles; they will run and not grow weary, they will walk and not be faint." (Isa. 40:29–31, NIV)

---

# The Jews in Egypt

☑ The coming of Nebuchadnezzar — *Jeremiah 46:13*
☑ The Lord's message to Jeremiah — *Jeremiah 46:14–18*
☑ Egypt's overthrow — *Jeremiah 46:19–26*
☑ God's promise to the Jews — *Jeremiah 46:27–28*

☑ Their idolatry in Egypt — *Jeremiah 44:1–14*
☑ Their refusal to reform — *Jeremiah 44:15–19*
☑ Jeremiah's denouncement — *Jeremiah 44:20–30*
☑ Ezekiel hears of Jerusalem's fall — *Ezekiel 33:21–33*

Israel was plagued with 'rabbititis'. It is a condition that affects many people and makes them believe that there is no problem so big or complicated that it can't be run away from. We learned yesterday that running away from problems never solves them. Look again at Jer. 44:1–14 and you'll see why.

"No temptation has seized you except what is common to man. And God is faithful; he will not let you be tempted beyond what you can bear. But when you are tempted, he will also provide a way out so that you can stand up under it." (1 Cor. 10:13, NIV)

---

## MONDAY Week 35 — The seventh deportation: 582 BC

☑ Prophecy against Ammon — *Ezekiel 25:1–7*
☑ Prophecy against Moab — *Ezekiel 25:8–11*
☑ Prophecy against Edom — *Ezekiel 25:12–14*
☑ Prophecy against Philistia — *Ezekiel 25:15–17*
☑ Prophecy against Sidon — *Ezekiel 28:20–23*
☑ Blessing for Israel — *Ezekiel 28:24–26*
☑ The fall of Egypt — *Ezekiel 32:1–16*
☑ The world of the dead — *Ezekiel 32:17–32*
☑ 745 more captives taken — *Jeremiah 52:30*
☑ Nebuchadnezzar's golden image — *Daniel 3:1–7*

FOR THOUGHT AND CONTEMPLATION

Have you noticed how, in every setting of human failure, God breaks through with a heartening promise? Can you spot it in the list above? (It's the sixth reading.) But what is more to the point, have you learned to look for God's promises in the midst of your own failures and circumstances? They're always there — just keep on looking.

---

"Through these he has given us his very great and precious promises, so that through them you may participate in the divine nature and escape the corruption in the world caused by evil desires." (2 Pet. 1:4, NIV)

---

## THE BAD AND THE GOOD SHEPHERD

### THE MANY FALSE SHEPHERDS

They fed themselves instead of the flock (34:2, 3)

They had not taken care of the weak, tended the sick, bound up the broken bones, nor sought the lost (34:4)

The sheep were then scattered, having no shepherd (34:5)

Therefore, the shepherds would be punished (34:10)

They would be removed from their position as shepherds (34:10)

They would not themselves be fed by the Great Shepherd (34:10)

### THE GOOD SHEPHERD IN EZEKIEL

He would search out the lost sheep (34:11)

He would deliver them from their enemies (34:12)

He would gather them from all nations (34:13)

He would feed them upon the mountains of Israel (34:14)

He would give them rest in green pastures (34:15)

He would put splints and bandages upon their broken limbs (34:16)

He would heal the sick (34:16)

He would make an eternal pact with them (34:25)

He would guarantee their safety and place them in a perfect paradise (34:25–28)

# The fiery furnace

☑ Shadrach, Meshach and Abednego — *Daniel 3:8–18*
☑ The fiery furnace — *Daniel 3:19–25*
☑ Nebuchadnezzar acknowledges God — *Daniel 3:26–30*
☑ His proclamation — *Daniel 4:1–3*
☑ The watchman — *Ezekiel 33:1–9*
☑ Individual responsibility — *Ezekiel 33:10–20*
☑ Message to faithless shepherds — *Ezekiel 34:1–10*
☑ The Good Shepherd — *Ezekiel 34:11–16*
☑ The flock judged — *Ezekiel 34:17–19*

### FOR THOUGHT AND CONTEMPLATION

The faith of Daniel and his friends was of a special quality. It has been called "the 'if not' faith". They said: "Our God is able to deliver us … BUT IF NOT … we will still refuse to bow." They believed in the rightness of their stand, irrespective of whether God delivered them or not. Ask God to give you that kind of faith. There is nothing higher.

"Now faith is being sure of what we hope for and certain of what we do not see." (Heb. 11:1, NIV)

---

# New life

☑ The Lord's flock — *Ezekiel 34:20–31*
☑ Prophecy against Edom — *Ezekiel 35:1–15*
☑ God's blessing on Israel — *Ezekiel 36:1–15*
☑ Israel's former sins — *Ezekiel 36:16–23*
☑ Israel's new life — *Ezekiel 36:24–32*
☑ A witness to neighbouring nations — *Ezekiel 36:33–38*
☑ The valley of dry bones — *Ezekiel 37:1–14*

### FOR THOUGHT AND CONTEMPLATION

When God's people are in right standing before the Lord, the blessings that flow from this are innumerable. Some of them can be seen in Ezek. 36:24–31. How many can you find? There are at least ten.

"The blessing of the Lord brings wealth, and he adds no trouble to it." (Prov. 10:22, NIV)

---

# The destruction of Gog

☑ The sign of the two sticks — *Ezekiel 37:15–19*
☑ Judah and Israel to be one nation — *Ezekiel 37:20–28*
☑ The malice of Gog — *Ezekiel 38:1–13*
☑ God's punishment of Gog — *Ezekiel 38:14–23*
☑ The defeat of Gog — *Ezekiel 39:1–10*
☑ The burial of Gog — *Ezekiel 39:11–20*
☑ Israel's restoration — *Ezekiel 39:21–29*

### FOR THOUGHT AND CONTEMPLATION

Many believe that the restoring of the nation of Israel, as predicted by Ezekiel, is taking place right before our eyes. What will happen next? Keep your finger on Ezekiel 38. This chapter may bear more relation to the events of this generation than we think.

"Pray for the peace of Jerusalem: 'May those who love you be secure. May there be peace within your walls and security within your citadels.'" (Psa. 122:6–7, NIV)

Vision of future Temple

☑ Ezekiel's vision — *Ezekiel 40:1–5*
☑ The East Gate — *Ezekiel 40:6–16*
☑ The Outer Courtyard — *Ezekiel 40:17–19*
☑ The North and South Gates — *Ezekiel 40:20–27*
☑ The Inner Courtyard — *Ezekiel 40:28–37*
☑ Buildings near the North Gate — *Ezekiel 40:38–47*
☑ The Temple Porch — *Ezekiel 40:48–49*
☑ The Most Holy Place — *Ezekiel 41:1–4*
☑ The rooms — *Ezekiel 41:5–12*
☑ The total measurements and details of the Temple building — *Ezekiel 41:13–26*

FOR THOUGHT AND CONTEMPLATION

The attention to detail which God displays in relation to His mighty works is just as evident, if you could but see it, in His personal plan for your life. Remember that the next time you are tempted to think that God might not be interested in the 'little' things that go on in your life.

"Are not two sparrows sold for a penny? Yet not one of them will fall to the ground apart from the will of your Father. And even the very hairs of your head are all numbered. So don't be afraid; you are worth more than many sparrows." (Matt. 10:29–31, NIV)

The Lord's return

☑ Two buildings near the Temple — *Ezekiel 42:1–14*
☑ Measurements of the Temple area — *Ezekiel 42:15–20*
☑ The Lord returns to the Temple — *Ezekiel 43:1–12*
☑ The Altar — *Ezekiel 43:13–17*
☑ Consecration of Altar — *Ezekiel 43:18–27*
☑ Use of the East Gate — *Ezekiel 44:1–3*
☑ Rules for admission to Temple — *Ezekiel 44:4–9*
☑ The Levites are excluded — *Ezekiel 44:10–14*
☑ The priests — *Ezekiel 44:15–31*

FOR THOUGHT AND CONTEMPLATION

Make a point today of reflecting that, in these New Testament times, God's glory does not dwell in temples made with hands, but in the hearts of those who truly own Him as Lord. Are you one of them?

"Do you not know that your body is a temple of the Holy Spirit, who is in you, whom you have received from God? You are not your own; you were bought at a price. Therefore honour God with your body." (1 Cor. 6:19–20, NIV)

Temple worship

☑ The Lord's portion of the land — *Ezekiel 45:1–6*
☑ The prince's portion — *Ezekiel 45:7–8*
☑ Weights and measures — *Ezekiel 45:9–15*
☑ The prince's duty — *Ezekiel 45:16–17*
☑ The Festivals — *Ezekiel 45:18–25*
☑ Rules regarding worship — *Ezekiel 46:1–12*
☑ The daily offering — *Ezekiel 46:13–15*
☑ The prince's land — *Ezekiel 46:16–18*
☑ Place for boiling the offerings — *Ezekiel 46:19–24*
☑ The stream flowing from the Temple — *Ezekiel 47:1–12*

FOR THOUGHT AND CONTEMPLATION

"Where do you worship?" asked one Christian of another. The reply he got quite startled him. "I worship in Woolworth's, in the High Street, in the bus, in the train, in the office, in my house ... anywhere and everywhere." If you can't worship God everywhere, then you won't worship Him anywhere.

"God is spirit, and his worshippers must worship in spirit and in truth." (Jn 4:24, NIV)

# Division of land

- [x] The land's boundaries — *Ezekiel 47:13–23*
- [x] Division of land among the tribes — *Ezekiel 48:1–9*
- [x] The priests' and Levites' section — *Ezekiel 48:10–20*
- [x] The prince's section — *Ezekiel 48:21–22*
- [x] Land for the other tribes — *Ezekiel 48:23–29*
- [x] The gates of Jerusalem — *Ezekiel 48:30–35*
- [x] More prophecy against Egypt — *Ezekiel 29:17–21, 30:1–19*

**FOR THOUGHT AND CONTEMPLATION**

In the divine order of things, worship must always precede work. First comes God's command to worship, then the command to divide and resettle the land. Which takes precedence in your life? Work, or worship? We are worshippers first and workers second. Reverse the order and you will end up spiritually bankrupt.

---

"Therefore, I urge you, brothers, in view of God's mercy, to offer your bodies as living sacrifices, holy and pleasing to God — which is your spiritual worship." (Rom. 12:1, NIV)

---

# God's dealings with Nebuchadnezzar

- [x] Nebuchadnezzar's second dream — *Daniel 4:4–18*
- [x] Daniel's explanation — *Daniel 4:19–27*
- [x] Nebuchadnezzar's seven years of madness — *Daniel 4:28–33*
- Death of Jeremiah 570 BC
- [x] He is restored and praises God — *Daniel 4:34–37*
- [x] Release of Jehoiachin — *2 Kings 25:27–30, Jeremiah 52:31–34*
- [x] Daniel's vision of the four beasts — *Daniel 7:1–8*
- [x] His vision of the eternal God — *Daniel 7:9–14*

**FOR THOUGHT AND CONTEMPLATION**

How true is the Scripture that says: "Pride goes before destruction, a haughty spirit before a fall" (Proverbs 16:18, NIV). Lucifer's pride cost him his place in heaven, and the prospect of eternal judgment. Nebuchadnezzar's pride cost him his throne for seven years. How much is pride costing you?

---

" ...That is why Scripture says: 'God opposes the proud but gives grace to the humble.' Submit yourselves, then, to God. Resist the devil, and he will flee from you." (Jas. 4:6–7, NIV)

---

# Psalms of the captivity

- [x] The meaning of the visions — *Daniel 7:15–28*
- [x] Captivity psalms: A song of thanksgiving — *Psalm 67:1–7*
- [x] A prayer for mercy — *Psalm 123:1–4*
- [x] A prayer for help — *Psalm 130:1–8*
- [x] The Israelites' lament — *Psalm 137:1–9*
- [x] Daniel's vision of a ram and a goat — *Daniel 8:1–14*
- [x] The vision explained — *Daniel 8:15–27*
- [x] Fall of Babylon prophesied — *Isaiah 13:17–22, Jeremiah 25:12–14, 50:1–8*

**FOR THOUGHT AND CONTEMPLATION**

Some of the greatest psalms came out of the greatest distresses. Are you in distress at this moment. Then follow the example of the psalmists who, though they began by focusing on their problems, finished by focusing on God. This will help you, too, to turn your pain into a paean of praise.

---

"God is our refuge and strength, an ever present help in trouble. The Lord Almighty is with us; the God of Jacob is our fortress." (Psa. 46:1 & 11, NIV)

# The judgment of Babylon

☑ Babylon's fall prophesied — *Jeremiah 50:9–16*
☑ Israel's return prophesied — *Jeremiah 50:17–20*
☑ God's judgment on Babylon — *Jeremiah 50:21–46*
☑ Further judgment on Babylon — *Jeremiah 51:1–14*
☑ A hymn of praise to God — *Jeremiah 51:15–19*
☑ The Lord's hammer — *Jeremiah 51:20–23*
☑ Babylon's punishment — *Jeremiah 51:24–35*

**FOR THOUGHT AND CONTEMPLATION**

Ever found yourself wondering why God allows sin and godlessness such freedom? Then remind yourself also of this — that every nation that rises up against God will one day fall. What happened to Babylon will happen to the godless nations of our own day. Learn to be patient with the patience of God.

---

"Blessed is the man who does not walk in the counsel of the wicked or stand in the way of sinners or sit in the seat of mockers. But his delight is in the law of the Lord, and on his law he meditates day and night." (Psa. 1:1–2, NIV)

---

# Belshazzar's feast

☑ Help for Israel — *Jeremiah 51:36–40*
☑ Babylon's fate — *Jeremiah 51:41–49*
☑ God's message — *Jeremiah 51:50–53*
☑ Complete destruction of Babylon — *Jeremiah 51:54–58, 60–64*
   Persia the world power—539–333 BC
☑ Belshazzar's feast — *Daniel 5:1–4*
☑ The handwriting on the wall — *Daniel 5:5–12*
☑ Belshazzar calls for Daniel — *Daniel 5:13–16*
☑ Daniel's interpretation — *Daniel 5:17–29*
☑ Darius takes over — *Daniel 5:30–31*
☑ Reigns of Cyrus and Darius — *Isaiah 44:28, Daniel 1:21, 11:1*

**FOR THOUGHT AND CONTEMPLATION**

There are three occasions in Scripture when God wrote with His finger a special message to men. Can you think of them? One, of course, is found here in the story of Belshazzar's feast. The other two can be found in Exodus 31:18 and John 8:6. Look them up right now.

---

"'This is the covenant I will make with them after that time, says the Lord. I will put my laws in their hearts, and I will write them on their minds.' Then he adds: 'Their sins and lawless acts I will remember no more.'" (Heb. 10:16–17, NIV)

---

# The command to rebuild the Temple

☑ Daniel's prayer — *Daniel 9:1–19*
☑ Gabriel's explanation — *Daniel 9:20–27*
☑ The prayer of a troubled young man — *Psalm 102:1–28*
☑ People challenged to rebuild the Temple — *Ezra 5:13, 2 Chronicles 36:22–23, Ezra 1:1–4*
☑ A prayer for deliverance — *Psalm 126:1–6*
☑ A prayer for the nation's welfare — *Psalm 85:1–13*
☑ The people's response to the challenge — *Ezra 1:5–6*

**FOR THOUGHT AND CONTEMPLATION**

If there is one truth that is underlined in reading through the Old Testament, it is the truth of God's great patience and everlasting mercy. Though time and time again He is disappointed with His people, He does not cast them off. And what He was He is, and always will be. Hallelujah!

---

"But because of his great love for us, God, who is rich in mercy, made us alive with Christ even when we were dead in transgressions — it is by grace you have been saved." (Eph. 2:4–5, NIV)

## A BIRD'S EYE VIEW OF EZRA and NEHEMIAH

**Place in the Bible:**
Fifteenth and sixteenth Old Testament books; tenth and eleventh books of history.

**Main characters:**
Ezra, Nehemiah.

**Special features:**
God's promise of release from Babylon is fulfilled. Some of the Jews return to Jerusalem to rebuild the temple. A later return under Ezra calls the community to wholehearted obedience to God's laws, and Nehemiah, 14 years afterward, leads the reconstruction of the devastated city walls.

**Jesus and the books of Ezra and Nehemiah:**
Nehemiah and the Israelites faced ridicule and great opposition as they set about rebuilding Jerusalem. Jesus warned His followers to expect the same treatment: "blessed are you when people insult you, persecute you and falsely say all kinds of evil against you because of me" (Matt. 5:11).

**Teaching:**
Ezra and Nehemiah are two books about building for God. Ezra the priest teaches the returned exiles about true worship, holiness and entire obedience to God; while Nehemiah himself is a good example of how diligent work and constant prayer go hand in hand in God's service.

**A verse to remember:**
"'Blessed be your glorious name, and may it be exalted above all blessing and praise. You alone are the Lord. You made the heavens, and all their starry host, the earth and all that is on it, the seas and all that is in them. You give life to everything, and the multitudes of heaven worship you.'" (Neh. 9:5–6)

---

**SUNDAY Week 37** ## Daniel in the lions' den

☑ The Temple's vessels returned — *Ezra 1:7–11, 5:14–16*

☑ Cyrus' decree — *Ezra 6:3–5*

☑ Daniel thrown to the lions — *Daniel 6:1–18*

☐ His deliverance and its result — *Daniel 6:19–28*

☑ Daniel's three weeks of mourning — *Daniel 10:1–3*

☑ His vision by the River Tigris — *Daniel 10:4–20*

☑ Revelation promised — *Daniel 10:21*

☑ Revelation of future kingdom — *Daniel 11:2–4*

FOR THOUGHT AND CONTEMPLATION

You may not have to face the prospect of spending a night in a lions' den, but no doubt you have encountered that 'roaring lion' who goes about "looking for someone to devour" (1 Pet. 5:8, NIV). Take heart — what God did for Daniel, He will do for you.

" ...in all these things we are more than conquerors through him who loved us." (Rom. 8:37, NIV)

---

**MONDAY Week 37** ## The end times

☐ The kingdoms of Egypt and Syria — *Daniel 11:5-20*

☑ The evil king of Syria — *Daniel 11:21–24*

☑ He will invade Egypt — *Daniel 11:25–30*
    **Remnant returns (49,897) — 536 BC**

☑ The abomination that causes desolation — *Daniel 11:31–35*

☑ Prophecy of the Antichrist — *Daniel 11:36–39*

☑ His final hour — *Daniel 11:40–45*

☐ The end times — *Daniel 12:1–13*

☐ The list of the returning exiles: the men of Israel — *Ezra 2:1–20*

☑ Those from various towns — *Ezra 2:21–35*

☑ The priests — *Ezra 2:36–39*

Someone has pointed out that Daniel is one of the few people in the Bible about whom nothing negative is written. What was the secret of his wonderful life? There are many reasons, not the least being his prowess in prayer. Are you satisfied with your prayer life? If not, then decide now to do something positive about it.

"This is the assurance we have in approaching God: that if we ask anything according to his will, he hears us. And if we know that he hears us — whatever we ask — we know that we have what we asked of him." (1 Jn 5:14–15, NIV)

## TUESDAY Week 37 — Nehemiah checks the list

- The Levites, singers and gatekeepers — *Ezra 2:40–42*
- The Temple servants and children of Solomon's servants — *Ezra 2:43–58*
- No proof of ancestry — *Ezra 2:59–63*
- The exiles' arrival at the Temple — *Ezra 2:64–70*
- Nehemiah checks the family records — *Nehemiah 7:5–7*
- Another list of the exiles — *Nehemiah 7:8–69*
- Many contribute to the cost of restoring the Temple — *Nehemiah 7:70–72*
- List of priests and Levites — *Nehemiah 12:1–23*
- Assignment of duties — *Nehemiah 12:24–26*

FOR THOUGHT AND CONTEMPLATION

Nehemiah made certain that all who came to live in Jerusalem were there by divine right — hence the painstaking procedure of checking every name. How will it be with you when the time comes for you to enter the 'New Jerusalem'? Is your name written there?

" ...do not rejoice that the spirits submit to you, but rejoice that your names are written in heaven." (Lk. 10:20, NIV)

## THE RETURN

During the first year of Cyrus' reign in Babylon (539 BC), he issued the decree which permitted the Jews to return and rebuild the temple at Jerusalem.

Jeremiah had predicted the length of the captivity (see 25:11, 12; 29:10).

Isaiah had prophesied, 170 years before, that Cyrus would act in this way. (See Isa. 44:28; 45:1.)

There were three separate returns by the Jewish remnant: Zerubbabel led the first in 536 BC; Ezra led the second in 458 BC; and Nehemiah led the third in 445 BC.

In 535 BC the construction on the temple began but it faced bitter opposition and so the prophets Haggai and Zechariah ministered to the discouraged remnant.

# Rebuilding programme begins

☑ The exiles rebuild the altar — *Ezra 3:1–7*
☑ In praise of Jerusalem — *Psalm 87:1–7*
☑ Rebuilding of the Temple begins — *Ezra 3:8–9*
☑ The priests and Levites praise the Lord — *Ezra 3:10–13*
☑ Longing for God's house — *Psalm 84:1–12*
☑ In praise of God's goodness — *Psalm 107:1–43*
☑ A song of praise and thanksgiving — *Psalm 66:1–20*

**FOR THOUGHT AND CONTEMPLATION**

The first thing the children of Israel did when they returned to Jerusalem was to build an altar. Worship, they realised, must come before work. Make a list of the things you have to do today, and before you do them, commit each item to God. You will find life runs better this way.

"Come, let us bow down in worship, let us kneel before the Lord our Maker; for he is our God and we are the people of his pasture, the flock under his care." (Psa. 95:6–7, NIV)

---

# Opposition to the work

☑ Samaritan interference — *Ezra 4:1–5*
☑ The security of God's people — *Psalm 125:1–5*
☑ Letters of accusation — *Ezra 4:6–16*
☑ Artaxerxes' answer — *Ezra 4:17–22*
☑ Work suspended for seven years — *Ezra 4:23–24*
☑ A prayer against Israel's enemies — *Psalm 129:1–8*
☑ Haggai and Zechariah — *Ezra 5:1*
☑ People reproached for neglect of Temple — *Haggai 1:1–10*
☑ Zerubbabel and Joshua — *Ezra 5:2, Haggai 1:11–15*
☑ The splendour of the future Temple — *Haggai 2:1–9*
☑ Zechariah's plea — *Zechariah 1:1–6*

**FOR THOUGHT AND CONTEMPLATION**

No work of God is ever established without opposition. Perhaps you are finding this to be true in your own life at this very moment. Be encouraged; opposition may seem to work against you — but it really works *for* you. It makes you less dependent on yourself and more dependent on God.

"What, then, shall we say in response to this? If God is for us, who can be against us?" (Rom. 8:31, NIV)

---

## A BIRD'S EYE VIEW OF HAGGAI and ZECHARIAH

**Place in the Bible:**
Thirty-seventh and thirty-eighth Old Testament books; fifteenth and sixteenth books of prophecy.

**Jesus and the prophecies of Haggai and Zechariah:**
Haggai was clear that the Lord had chosen the Jews to be His people, just as Christ called and chose people to be His followers: "You did not choose me, but I chose you ..." (John 15:16).

Zechariah has numerous references pointing to Jesus, the coming Messiah: the 'Branch' (3:8), the King Priest (6:13), the humble King, mounted on a donkey (9:9–10), the good shepherd who is sold for thirty pieces of silver (11:4–13) and the one who is pierced (12:10).

**Teaching:**
Haggai aimed to galvanise the Jews into action and complete rebuilding the temple. Zechariah also reminds the Jews to finish this task and spells out the necessity for God's people to be pure. Zechariah concludes with a vision about the coming Messiah.

**A verse to remember:**
"On that day ... I will take you my servant Zerubbabel ... and I will make you like my signet ring, for I have chosen you ..." (Hagg. 2:23).

# Zechariah's visions

- ☑ Haggai confronts the priests — *Haggai 2:10–14*
- ☑ The Lord promises blessing — *Haggai 2:15–23*
- ☑ Zechariah's vision of the horses — *Zechariah 1:7–17*
- ☑ God's promise to Zerubbabel — *Zechariah 4:6–10*
- ☑ Zechariah's vision of the horns — *Zechariah 1:18–21*
- ☑ His vision of the measuring line — *Zechariah 2:1–13*
- ☑ His vision of the High Priest — *Zechariah 3:1–10*
- ☑ His vision of the golden candlestick — *Zechariah 4:1–5, 11–14*
- ☑ His vision of the flying scroll — *Zechariah 5:1–4*
- ☑ His vision of the woman in the basket — *Zechariah 5:5–11*

FOR THOUGHT AND CONTEMPLATION

Although the phrase, "Thus saith the Lord", is found 1,904 times in the Old Testament, Zechariah uses it, or its equivalent, close on 90 times. How sad that so many modern pulpits lack this kind of authority. Pray today that God will restore the Old Testament note of authority to the present-day Church.

---

"When Jesus had finished saying these things, the crowds were amazed at his teaching, because he taught as one who had authority, and not as their teachers of the law." (Matt. 7:28–29, NIV)

---

## THE TWO COVENANTS

**The old covenant**

a. It was mediated by Moses *(Ex. 19; Jn.1:17; Gal. 3:19)*
b. It was conditional *Deut. 28)*
c. It could not produce righteousness *(Heb. 8:8)*
d. It was written on stone tablets *(Ex. 32:15)*

**The new covenant**

a. Mediated by Christ *(Heb. 9:15; Jn. 1:17)*
b. It is unconditional *(Heb. 8:9)*
c. It can produce the necessary righteousness *(Heb. 8:11)*
d. It is written on living hearts *(Heb. 8:10)*

---

# The decree discovered

- ☑ The vision of the four chariots — *Zechariah 6:1–8*
- ☑ Symbolic crowning of Joshua — *Zechariah 6:9–15*
- ☑ Tattenai and Shethar-Bozenai's question — *Ezra 5:3–4*
- ☑ They appeal to Darius — *Ezra 5:5–12, 17*
- ☑ Cyrus' decree is discovered — *Ezra 6:1–2*

- ☑ Darius adds to it — *Ezra 6:6–12*
- ☑ Co-operation of Tattenai and Shethar-Bozenai — *Ezra 6:13–14*
- ☑ Insincere fasting condemned — *Zechariah 7:1–7*
- ☑ The cause of exile — *Zechariah 7:8–14*
- ☑ The Lord's promise — *Zechariah 8:1–15*

An effective father, it has been said, needs two outstanding qualifications: firmness in discipline and a readiness to encourage. Some think God has just one of these characteristics — firmness in discipline — but look again at Zech. 8:15 and remind yourself that God is a Father who not only disciplines, but encourages and cares.

"As a father has compassion on his children, so the Lord has compassion on those who fear him … from everlasting to everlasting the Lord's love is with those who fear him, and his righteousenss with their children's children." (Psa. 103:13 & 17, NIV)

## SUNDAY Week 38 — The completion of the Temple

☑ The Lord promises to restore Israel — *Zechariah 8:16–23*

Temple completed 516 BC

☑ The Temple is completed — *Ezra 6:15*

☑ Dedication of the Temple — *Ezra 6:16–18*

☑ The Passover celebration — *Ezra 6:19–22*

The Restoration 516–400 BC

☑ In praise of God the Saviour — *Psalm 146:1–10*

☑ In praise of the Lord — *Psalm 111:1–10*

☑ The happiness of a good person — *Psalm 112:1–10*

☑ In praise of the Lord's goodness — *Psalm 113:1–9*

☑ A man saved from death praises God — *Psalm 116:1–19*

☑ In praise of the Lord — *Psalm 117:1–2*

☑ Judgment on neighbouring cities — *Zechariah 9:1–8*

☑ A divine deliverer — *Zechariah 9:9–17*

FOR THOUGHT AND CONTEMPLATION

The Temple project is at last complete — a full twenty-three years after it was begun. God's plans and purposes may be hindered or postponed, but they will ultimately be fulfilled. Has there been a hindering of the divine purpose in your life? Then hold on — the day of its fulfilment will most certainly come.

"Being confident of this, that he who began a good work in you will carry it on to completion until the day of Christ Jesus." (Phil. 1:6, NIV)

## MONDAY Week 38 — Israel's deliverance

☑ The Lord promises deliverance — *Zechariah 10:1–12*

☑ Destruction to come — *Zechariah 11:1–3*

☑ The two shepherds — *Zechariah 11:4–17*

☑ Punishment of Israel's enemies — *Zechariah 12:1–8*

☑ Israel's repentance and sorrow — *Zechariah 12:9–14*

☑ Israel's cleansing — *Zechariah 13:1–6*

☑ The command to kill God's shepherd — *Zechariah 13:7–9*

☑ Jerusalem and the nations — *Zechariah 14:1–15*

☑ Israel's restoration — *Zechariah 14:16–21*

FOR THOUGHT AND CONTEMPLATION

Men predict that history will reach its climax through a nuclear holocaust. God predicts that it will reach its climax at the coming of His Son. Whom do you believe — men or God? Keep Zechariah 14:1–9 before you, and it will hold you fast in the midst of the greatest nuclear threat.

"For the Lord himself will come down from heaven, with a loud command, with the voice of the archangel and with the trumpet call of God, and the dead in Christ will rise first. After that, we who are still alive and are left will be caught up with them in the clouds to meet the Lord in the air …" (1 Thess. 4:16–17, NIV)

## A BIRD'S EYE VIEW OF ESTHER

**Place in the Bible:**
Seventeenth Old Testament book; twelfth book of history.

**Main characters:**
King Xerxes, Queen Vashti, Esther, Mordecai, Haman.

**Special features:**
There is no mention of God anywhere in this book, but from beginning to end God's hand is seen in action.

**Jesus and the book of Esther:**
Esther knew that she was risking her life. Jesus voluntarily gave up his life to rescue us from the stranglehold of sin, as John chapter 10:15 says: "... I lay down my life for the sheep."

**Teaching:**
This book explains the origin of the Jewish Feast of Purim and how, had it not been for Mordecai's astuteness and Esther's courage, the Jews would have been slaughtered. The Jews believed that God was their deliverer.

**A verse to remember:**
"'If you remain silent at this time, relief and deliverance for the Jews will arise from another place, but you and your father's family will perish'" (Esth. 4:14).

---

**TUESDAY Week 38**  A beauty contest

- ☑ Ahasuerus' feast — *Esther 1:1–8*
- ☑ Vashti's rebellion — *Esther 1:9–12*
- ☑ Her dethronement — *Esther 1:13–22*
- ☑ New queen sought — *Esther 2:1–4*
- ☑ Esther brought to Shushan — *Esther 2:5, 7–11*
- ☑ Esther made queen — *Esther 2:12–17*
- ☑ Feast in honour of Esther — *Esther 2:18–20*
- ☑ Mordecai saves the king's life — *Esther 2:21–23*
- ☑ Haman's plot — *Esther 3:1–7*
- ☑ Haman gains the king's support — *Esther 3:8–11*

FOR THOUGHT AND CONTEMPLATION

Esther won the first-ever "Miss World" beauty contest hands down. Yet her real beauty lay, not in her appearance, but in her character. Men judge the outward appearance, but God judges the heart (1 Sam. 16:7).

"Your beauty should not come from outward adornment ... Instead, it should be that of your inner self, the unfading beauty of a gentle and quiet spirit, which is of great worth in God's sight." (1 Pet. 3:3–4, NIV)

---

**WEDNESDAY Week 38**  The tables are turned

- ☑ The command to annihilate all Jews — *Esther 3:12–15*
- ☑ Mordecai enlists Esther's help — *Esther 4:1–17*
- ☑ Esther's invitation — *Esther 5:1–8*
- ☑ Haman's rage against Mordecai — *Esther 5:9–14*
- ☑ The king's sleepless night — *Esther 6:1–3*
- ☑ Mordecai honoured — *Esther 6:4–14*
- ☑ Haman accused — *Esther 7:1–6*
- ☑ Haman hanged — *Esther 7:7–10*

FOR THOUGHT AND CONTEMPLATION

Do you believe in prayer? *Really* believe?

Esther believed in prayer enough to go to the king at an unappointed time with an unlikely request. Underline Esther 5:1–8 in your Bible as a constant reminder that faith sees the invisible, believes the incredible and receives the impossible.

"Ask and it will be given to you; seek and you will find; knock and the door will be opened to you. For everyone who asks receives; he who seeks finds; and to him who knocks, the door will be opened." (Matt. 7:7–8, NIV)

**The Jews triumph**

☑ The king's edict — *Esther 8:1–14*
☑ The Jews rejoice — *Esther 8:15–17*
☑ Their revenge and triumph — *Esther 9:1–15*
☑ Days of rejoicing — *Esther 9:16–19*
☑ The Feast of Purim — *Esther 9:20–27*
☑ Its perpetual celebration — *Esther 9:28–32*
☑ Mordecai's promotion — *Esther 10:1–3*
☑ Ezra's commission — *Ezra 7:11–20*

FOR THOUGHT AND CONTEMPLATION

When you are next tempted to think that

God is not working because He does not show Himself to you, read again the story of Esther and realise that He is a God who often works behind the scenes. After all, as this book so wonderfully shows, history is really His-story.

———

"And we know that in all things God works for the good of those who love him, who have been called according to his purpose." (Rom. 8:28, NIV)

---

**The return to Jerusalem**

☑ Artaxerxes' decree — *Ezra 7:21–26*
☑ Ezra's thanksgiving — *Ezra 7:27–28*
☑ The exiles who returned with Ezra — *Ezra 8:1–14*

Ezra returns to Jerusalem 458 BC

☑ The camp site — *Ezra 7:9, 8:15*
☑ Ezra finds Levites — *Ezra 8:16–20*
☑ Prayer and fasting — *Ezra 8:21–23*
☑ The Temple treasures — *Ezra 8:24–30*
☑ Journey begins — *Ezra 8:31*
☑ Ezra's arrival at Jerusalem — *Ezra 7:6–8, 10, 8:32–36*
☑ Ezra's grief — *Ezra 9:1–4*
☑ His prayer — *Ezra 9:5–15*

FOR THOUGHT AND CONTEMPLATION

The secret of Ezra's successful ministry is found in Ezra 7:10. He not only knew what he had to do, but he also did it. As someone has said, "It is of no benefit to know more, unless you first do something with what you know already."

———

"What good is it, my brothers, if a man claims to have faith but has no deeds? Can such faith save him? In the same way, faith by itself, if it is not accompanied by action, is dead." (Jas. 2:14 & 17, NIV)

---

**Ezra and Nehemiah**

☑ Ezra plans national gathering — *Ezra 10:1–8*
☑ He preaches and the people repent — *Ezra 10:9–15*
☑ Foreign wives divorced — *Ezra 10:16–44*
☑ Nehemiah's grief — *Nehemiah 1:1–4*
☑ His prayer — *Nehemiah 1:5–11*

Nehemiah goes to Jerusalem 444BC

☑ His request — *Nehemiah 2:1–6*
☑ Nehemiah appointed governor — *Nehemiah 5:14*
☑ Letters and escort provided — *Nehemiah 2:7–9*
☑ Sanballat and Tobiah's indignation — *Nehemiah 2:10*
☑ Nehemiah's arrival in Jerusalem — *Nehemiah 2:11–16*

FOR THOUGHT AND CONTEMPLATION

Although the centre of Israel's prayer life, the Temple, was established, there was still a need to build the walls. Prayer is important, but so is work. As someone once put it: "We must pray as if it all depended on God, and work as though it all depended on us."

———

"Therefore, my dear friends, as you have always obeyed — not only in my presence, but now much more in my absence — continue to work out your salvation with fear and trembling, for it is God who works in you to will and to act according to his good purpose." (Phil. 2:12–13, NIV)

## BUILDING FOR GOD

"So the wall was completed ... with the help of our God." (Neh. 6:15,16) In December 446 BC, Nehemiah learns from his brother Hanani of the pitiful state of Jerusalem. Broken-hearted, Nehemiah begins a time of confession and intercession to God on His people's behalf (1:6–11).

Nehemiah returns to Judah and despite intimidation his confidence in the Lord never wavers. In 53 days the walls are finished. The returning Jewish exiles make a binding covenant to dedicate themselves and the city to the Lord.

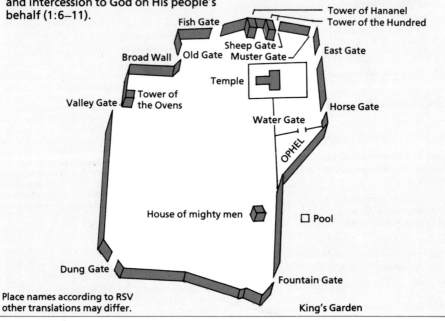

Place names according to RSV other translations may differ.

---

**Rebuilding the walls**

☑ Nehemiah's encouragement to rebuild — *Nehemiah 2:17–18*

☑ The contempt of Sanballat and others — *Nehemiah 2:19–20*

☑ List of builders — *Nehemiah 3:1–16*

☑ The Levites — *Nehemiah 3:17–21*

☑ The priests — *Nehemiah 3:22–26*

☑ Other builders — *Nehemiah 3:27–32*

☑ Nehemiah overcomes ridicule — *Nehemiah 4:1–6*

☑ The conspiracy — *Nehemiah 4:7–15*

☑ Nehemiah's precautions — *Nehemiah 4:16–23*

☑ The people's complaint — *Nehemiah 5:1–5*

☑ Nehemiah's rebuke — *Nehemiah 5:6–11*

☑ The restitution — *Nehemiah 5:12–13*

FOR THOUGHT AND CONTEMPLATION

One of the characteristics of God's people, in the New Testament as well as the Old, is that sometimes, instead of fighting the enemy, they turn to fighting each other. How Satan must enjoy these lapses! Pray that Christians might come to see the stupidity of this.

---

"How good and pleasant it is when brothers live together in unity! It is as if the dew of Hermon were falling on Mount Zion. For there the Lord bestows his blessing, even life for evermore." (Psa. 133:1 & 3, NIV)

140

# Rebuilding programme completed

☑ Nehemiah's unselfishness — *Nehemiah 5:15–19*

☑ Plots against Nehemiah — *Nehemiah 6:1–14*

☑ Rebuilding completed — *Nehemiah 6:15–19*

☑ Hanani and Hananiah to protect Jerusalem — *Nehemiah 7:1–4*

☑ The first to return — *1 Chronicles 9:2–9*

☑ The priests — *1 Chronicles 9:10–13*

☑ The Levites — *1 Chronicles 9:14–16*

☑ The Temple guards — *1 Chronicles 9:17–27*

☑ Other tasks of the Levites — *1 Chronicles 9:28–34*

☑ The inhabitants of Jerusalem — *Nehemiah 11:1–9*

**FOR THOUGHT AND CONTEMPLATION**

Ever heard of the "Nehemiah Management Principles"? Then read this book carefully, and you will see how expertly he got God's task done, *through people*. Good supervision, it has been said, is "the art of getting ordinary people to do extraordinary work." Is God saying something to you in all this?

---

"Just as each of us has one body with many members, and these members do not all have the same function, so in Christ we who are many form one body, and each member belongs to all the others. We have different gifts, according to the grace given us ..." (Rom. 12:4–6, NIV)

---

# The Law is read

☑ The priests — *Nehemiah 11:10–14*

☑ The Levites — *Nehemiah 11:15–18*

☑ The Temple guards — *Nehemiah 11:19*

☑ Further distribution of the people — *Nehemiah 11:20–36*

☑ Ezra reads the Law — *Nehemiah 7:73, 8:1–12*

☑ Feast of Tabernacles — *Nehemiah 8:13–18*

☑ The people confess their sins — *Nehemiah 9:1–4*

☑ God's goodness remembered — *Nehemiah 9:5–31*

**FOR THOUGHT AND CONTEMPLATION**

One of the great principles of Old Testament worship was the way in which they reminded themselves of God's goodness to them in the past. Take a lesson from their example today. Recite at lest ten instance of how God has blessed your life in the past year.

---

"These things happened to them as examples and were written down as warnings for us, on whom the fulfilment of the ages has come. So, if you think you are standing firm, be careful that you don't fall!" (1 Cor. 10:11–12, NIV)

## RESTORATION OF ISRAEL

| | |
|---|---|
| **Rebuilt walls** *ch. 1–7* | — plans received<br>— building commences<br>— work is completed |
| **Renewed worship** *ch. 8–10* | — the law is read<br>— repentance follows<br>— a celebration of worship |
| **Restored nation** *ch. 11–13* | — people placed in cities<br>— walls are dedicated<br>— Temple is cleansed |

**about 25 years' duration**

**The covenant**

☑ God's goodness and mercy remembered —
Nehemiah 9:32–37

☑ Covenant made — Nehemiah 9:38

☑ The people sign the covenant — Nehemiah
10:1–27

☑ The covenant — Nehemiah 10:28–39

☑ The dedication of the wall — Nehemiah
12:27–43

☑ In praise of God the Almighty — Psalm
147:1–20

FOR THOUGHT AND CONTEMPLATION

In the light of what you have read today, this

would be an excellent time to renew any
promises or vows you have made to the Lord.
Are you married? Then spend some quiet
moments re-affirming your commitment.
Are you single? Then commit yourself to
serving Him with undivided attention (1 Cor.
7:32–34).

"May the God of peace, who through the blood
of the eternal covenant brought back from the
dead our Lord Jesus, that great Shepherd of
the sheep, equip you with everything good for
doing his will, and may he work in us what is
pleasing to him, through Jesus Christ, to
whom be glory for ever and ever. Amen." (Heb.
13:20–21, NIV)

---

**The law of the Lord**

☑ A call to praise God — Psalm 148:1–14

☑ Hymns of praise — Psalm 149:1–9, 150:1–6

☑ Tobiah in the storeroom — Nehemiah 13:4–5

☑ Temple order restored — Nehemiah 12:44–47

☑ Separation from foreigners — Nehemiah
13:1–3

☑ The law of the Lord — Palm 119:1–8

☑ Obedience to it — Psalm 119:9–24

☑ Determination to obey — Psalm 119:25–32

☑ A prayer for understanding — Psalm
119:33–40

☑ Trusting God's law — Psalm 119:41–56

☑ Devotion to it — Psalm 119:57–64

☑ The value and justice of it — Psalm 119:65–80

☑ Prayer for deliverance — Psalm 119:81–88

FOR THOUGHT AND CONTEMPLATION

Revival could not come to Israel while Tobiah
was living in the Temple. A Tobiah in God's
House is like having the devil living in the
church vestry. Would to God we had men in
the Church today who would follow
Nehemiah's example, and expel from the
midst of God's people all those things which
are not of Him.

"Jesus ... overturned the tables of the money
changers and the benches of those selling
doves. 'It is written,' he said to them, '"My
house will be called a house of prayer," but you
are making it a "den of robbers".'" (Matt.
21:12–13, NIV)

---

**Nehemiah's reforms**

☑ Faith in God's law — Psalm 119:89–96

☑ Love for it — Psalm 119:97–112

☑ Safety in it — Psalm 119:113–128

☑ Desire to obey it — Psalm 119:129–136

☑ Its justice — Psalm 119:137–144

☑ A plea for help — Psalm 119:145–176

☑ True happiness — Psalm 1:1–6

Cleansing of Temple 432 BC

☑ Nehemiah cleanses the Temple — Nehemiah
13:6–9

☑ Tithing and worship re-established —
Nehemiah 13:10–14

☑ Sabbath keeping violated — Nehemiah
13:15–22

One of Nehemiah's great reforms was to re-establish the principle of tithing for the support of the priests. The work of God was neglected because the workmen were not properly rewarded. Could this be a reform that is needed in your church? If so, then ask the Lord just what He would have you do about it.

"Each man should give what he has decided in his heart to give, not reluctantly or under compulsion, for God loves a cheerful giver." (2 Cor. 9:7, NIV)

## A BIRD'S EYE VIEW OF MALACHI

**Place in the Bible:**
Thirty-ninth Old Testament book; seventeenth book of prophecy.

**Jesus and the prophecy of Malachi:**
Malachi predicts that the prophet Elijah would come before the Messiah, and Jesus identified John the Baptist as this person (Matt. 11:10–11).

**Teaching:**
Hard hearts, abuse of the poor and needy, idolatry and covetousness are the order of the day. God's people need a Deliverer from God's judgment.

**A verse to remember:**
"Bring the whole tithe into the storehouse, that there may be food in my house ... and see if I will not throw open the floodgates of heaven and pour out so much blessing that you will not have room enough" (Mal. 3:10).

---

## SATURDAY Week 39 Malachi's prophecy

☑ Intermarriage rebuked — *Nehemiah 13:23–29*

☑ Priesthood cleansed — *Nehemiah 13:30–31*

☑ The Lord's love for Israel — *Malachi 1:1–5*

☑ The Lord reprimands the priests — *Malachi 1:6–14, 2:1–9*

☑ The people's unfaithfulness — *Malachi 2:10–16*

☑ The Lord will judge His people — *Malachi 2:17, 3:1–5*

☑ The payment of tithes — *Malachi 3:6–12*

☑ God's promise of mercy — *Malachi 3:13–18*
**Greece the world power 333–63 BC**

☑ Coming Day of the Lord — *Malachi 4:1–6*

FOR THOUGHT AND CONTEMPLATION

The last word of the Old Testament is the 'promise of a curse' that would come upon an unfaithful and disobedient people. How different from the last word of the New Testament which shows all sin removed from the universe and the promise of eternal joy and everlasting peace.

---

"Christ redeemed us from the curse of the law by becoming a curse for us, for it is written: 'Cursed is everyone who is hung on a tree.' He redeemed us in order that the blessing given to Abraham might come to the Gentiles through Christ Jesus ..." (Gal. 3:13–14, NIV)

---

## A BIRD'S EYE VIEW OF PSALMS

**Place in the Bible:**
Nineteenth Old Testament book; second book of poetry and wisdom.

**Special features:**
Israel's hymn book brings together a wide variety of hymns, some praising God, others lamenting national sin, some written for public worship and others for private prayer.

**Jesus and the book of Psalms:**
Many Psalms which apparently refer to David can be seen to be further fulfilled in Jesus, the Messiah.

**Teaching:**
The Psalms present God as creator, deliverer, protector, forgiver, provider, guide, the One worthy of praise, thanksgiving and worship.

**A verse to remember:**
"The Lord is my rock, my fortress and my deliverer; my God is my rock, in whom I take refuge" (Psalm 18:2).

# Two announcements

☑ Prefaces to synoptic Gospels — *Matthew 1:1, Mark 1:1, Luke 1:1–4*

☑ Preface to John's Gospel — *John 1:4–5*

Rome the World Power 63 BC–AD 476

☑ Two genealogies of Jesus Christ — *Matthew 1:2–17, Luke 3:23–38*

☑ Birth of John the Baptist announced — *Luke 1:5–25*

☑ Birth of Jesus Christ announced — *Luke 1:26–38*

**FOR THOUGHT AND CONTEMPLATION**

Many Christians skip over the genealogy of Christ because they find it dull and uninteresting. But how wonderfully it underlines the truth that, when Christ came to save, He did not just come *near* to the human race, He came *into* it. The Son of God became the Son of Man, that the sons of men might become the sons of God.

---

"For to us a child is born, to us a son is given, and the government will be on his shoulders. And he will be called Wonderful Counsellor, Mighty God, Everlasting Father, Prince of peace." (Isa. 9:6, NIV)

---

## A BIRD'S EYE VIEW OF LUKE

**Place in the Bible:**
Third New Testament book; third Gospel.
**Written by:**
Luke.
**Special features:**
Dr Luke's observant eye lays special emphasis on certain people and things in his gospel: prayer, joy, the Holy Spirit, the early life of Jesus, children, women and social outcasts.
**Jesus and the Gospel of Luke:**
Luke presents Jesus Christ as the One whose compassion for men and women led Him to provide the solution to mankind's problem of sin and He offers His priceless gift of salvation.
**Teaching:**
Luke, the longest New Testament book, records the fullest life story of Jesus Christ. He states his purpose: "so that you may know the certainty of the things you have been taught" (1:3–4). Luke presents an orderly, meticulously accurate, comprehensive and chronological account of the life, death and resurrection of Jesus. Luke wanted to strengthen the faith of Gentiles and to show that Jesus Christ is the Saviour of every kind of person in the world.
**A verse to remember:**
"'The Son of Man came to seek and to save what was lost'" (Luke 19:10).

---

# The birth of Jesus Christ

☑ Elizabeth's son to Mary — *Luke 1:39–45*

☑ Mary praises God — *Luke 1:46–55*

The birth of John the Baptist 6 BC

☑ Mary stays with Elizabeth — *Luke 1:56*

☑ Birth of John the Baptist — *Luke 1:57–66*

☑ Zechariah's prophecy — *Luke 1:67–79*

☑ John's early years — *Luke 1:80*

☑ The announcement to Joseph — *Matthew 1:18–24*

Birth of Jesus Christ 5 BC

☑ The birth of Jesus — *Luke 2:1–7, Matthew 1:25*

☑ The angels and the shepherds — *Luke 2:8–20*

☑ Circumcision of Jesus — *Luke 2:21*

☑ Presentation in the Temple — *Luke 2:22–38*

**FOR THOUGHT AND CONTEMPLATION**

How slow and unhurried God must have seemed to those who knew the prophecies concerning Christ's first coming. Yet God is always right on time — never a moment too soon, and never a moment too late. He is a punctual God. Keep this thought in mind the next time you are tempted to think the Almighty's schedules are mistimed.

---

"But when the time had fully come, God sent his Son, born of a woman, born under law, to redeem those under law, that we might receive the full rights of sons." (Gal. 4:4–5, NIV)

---

# Jesus' childhood

☑ The wise men — *Matthew 2:1–12*
☑ The flight to Egypt — *Matthew 2:13–18*
☑ From Egypt to Nazareth — *Matthew 2:19–23, Luke 2:39*
☑ Jesus' childhood at Nazareth — *Luke 2:40*

Birth of Paul: AD 10–15 approx

☑ Jesus in the Temple — *Luke 2:41–50*
☑ Jesus' early life — *Luke 2:51–52*
☑ Start of John the Baptist's ministry — *Matthew 3:1–6, Mark 1:2–6, Luke 3:1–6, John 1:6–18*

**FOR THOUGHT AND CONTEMPLATION**

One of the first things children demonstrate when growing up is the truth of the Scripture that says: "Foolishness is bound in the heart of a child" (Prov.,, 22:15). Foolishness appears in all they say and do. How different with Jesus. His wisdom baffled the sages of His day. And why? Because it was the wisdom of God!

---

"The Word became flesh and lived for a while among us. We have seen his glory, the glory of the one and only Son, who came from the Father, full of grace and truth." (Jn. 1:14, NIV)

---

## THE MAIN HIGHLIGHTS OF CHRIST'S LIFE

1. His birth **(Lk. 2:1–7)**
2. The adoration by the shepherds **(Lk. 2:8–20)**
3. The dedication in Jerusalem **(Lk. 2:21–38)**
4. The worship by the wise men **(Matt. 2:1–12)**
5. Flight into Egypt **(Matt. 2:1–12)**
6. Temple visit at age twelve **(Lk. 2:41–50)**
7. His baptism **(Matt. 3:13–17)**
8. His temptation **(Matt. 4:1–11)**
9. Introduction by John the Baptist **(Jn. 1:29)**
10. First temple cleansing **(Jn. 2:13–25)**
11. Conversion of Nicodemus **(Jn. 3:1–21)**
12. The choice of the twelve **(Matt. 10:1–4)**
13. Imprisonment and execution of John **(Matt. 14:1–12)**
14. Peter's great confession **(Matt. 16:13–20)**
15. The transfiguration **(Matt. 17:1–13)**
16. His triumphal entry **(Matt. 21:1–11)**
17. Weeping over Jerusalem **(Matt. 23:37–39; Lk. 19:41)**
18. In the upper room **(Jn. 13—14)**
19. In Gethsemane **(Jn. 18:1–11)**
20. His arrest and trials **(Jn. 18:12—19:15)**
21. The crucifixion **(Jn. 19:16–18)**
22. The resurrection **(Matt. 28:1–7)**
23. The ten appearances
24. The ascension **(Lk. 24:51)**

# The temptation of Jesus

John the Baptist's ministry begins AD 25

☑ John the Baptist's message — *Matthew 3:7–10, luke 3:7–14*

☑ His introduction of Christ — *Matthew 3:11–12, Mark 1:7–8, Luke 3:15–18, John 1:19–28*

☑ The baptism of Jesus — *Matthew 3:13–17, Mark 1:9–11, Luke 3:21–22*

☑ John's declaration — *John 1:29–34*

☑ The temptation in the wilderness — *Matthew 4:1–11, Mark 1:12–13, Luke 4:1–13*

☑ The first three disciples — *John 1:35–42*

☑ Philip and Nathanael — *John 1:43–51*

FOR THOUGHT AND CONTEMPLATION

What a contrast exists between the

temptation of the first Adam and that of Christ, who is called in Scripture the last Adam. The first Adam failed while feasting in a garden, but the second Adam triumphed while fasting in a wilderness. And because He triumphed — so can you!

---

"So it is written: 'The first man Adam became a living being': the last Adam, a life-giving spirit. The spiritual did not come first, but the natural, and after that the spiritual. The first man was of the dust of the earth, the second man from heaven." (1 Cor. 15:45–47, NIV)

---

# Jesus and John

☑ The wedding in Cana — *John 2:1–11*

☑ Jesus in Capernaum — *John 2:12*

☑ Jesus in the Temple — *John 2:13–22*

☑ Jesus' knowledge of human nature — *John 2:23–25*

☑ Jesus and Nicodemus — *John 3:1–21*

☑ Jesus and John — *John 3:22–24*

☑ John's testimony — *John 3:25–36*

☑ The imprisonment of John — *Luke 3:19–20*

☑ Jesus leaves Judea — *Matthew 4:12, John 4:1–3*

☑ Jesus and the woman at the well — *John 4:4–26*

FOR THOUGHT AND CONTEMPLATION

John the Baptist faced a dilemma that, sooner or later, comes to every one of us: who is to be first — me, or Jesus? You know how John decided: it would be Jesus! "He must become greater; I must become less." What decision have you reached about this momentous issue?

---

"I have been crucified with Christ and I no longer live, but Christ lives in me. The life I live in the body, I live by faith in the Son of God, who loved me and gave himself for me." (Gal. 2:20, NIV)

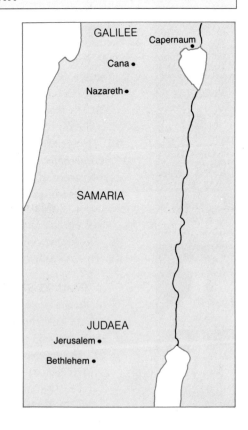

GALILEE   Capernaum

Cana •

Nazareth •

SAMARIA

JUDAEA

Jerusalem •

Bethlehem •

**Jesus' early ministry**

☑ Jesus in Samaria — *John 4:27–42*

☑ Jesus preaches the Gospel — *Matthew 4:17, Mark 1:14–15, Luke 4:14–15, John 4:43–45*

☑ Jesus heals an official's son — *John 4:46–54*

☑ Jesus is rejected at Nazareth — *Luke 4:16–30*

☑ Jesus leaves Nazareth — *Matthew 4:13–16*

☑ Jesus calls four fishermen — *Matthew 4:18–22, Mark 1:16–20, Luke 5:1–11*

☑ Jesus teaches in the synagogue — *Mark 1:21–22, Luke 4:31–32*

☑ The man with an evil spirit — *Mark 1:23–28*

**FOR THOUGHT AND CONTEMPLATION**

Anyone who embarks upon an effective ministry for God will, at some time or other, experience rejection. Jesus did — and so will you. And how you handle that rejection will determine whether your ministry will go backward or forward. Jesus went forward — and in His strength, so can you.

"For we do not have a high priest who is unable to sympathise with our weaknesses, but we have one who has been tempted in every way, just as we are — yet was without sin." (Heb. 4:15, NIV)

---

**Jesus heals many**

☑ The man with an evil spirit — *Luke 4:33–37*

☑ Jesus heals many people — *Matthew 8:14–17, Mark 1:29–34, Luke 4:38–41*

☑ Jesus in Galilee — *Matthew 4:23–25, Mark 1:35–39, Luke 4:42–44*

☑ Jesus heals a leper — *Matthew 8:2–4, Mark 1:40–45, Luke 5:12–16*

☑ He heals a paralysed man — *Matthew 9:1–8, Mark 2:1–12, Luke 5:17–26*

**FOR THOUGHT AND CONTEMPLATION**

Did the healing ministry of Jesus cease when He left this world and returned to heaven? Many think so. What do *you* believe? If you are unsure about this, turn to Hebrews 13:8 and settle the matter once and for all.

"He himself bore our sins in his body on the tree, so that we might die to sins and live for righteousness; by his wounds you have been healed." (1 Pet. 2:24, NIV)

---

**The authority of Jesus**

☑ Jesus calls Matthew — *Matthew 9:9–13, Mark 2:13–17, Luke 5:27–32*

☑ The question about fasting — *Matthew 9:14–17, Mark 2:18–22, Luke 5:33–39*

☑ The healing at the pool — *John 5:1–9*

☑ The Jews' displeasure — *John 5:10–18*

☑ Jesus' response — *John 5:19–23*

☑ He speaks of His authority — *John 5:24–29*

☑ His witnesses — *John 5:30–47*

**FOR THOUGHT AND CONTEMPLATION**

Do you know the difference between 'power' and 'authority'? Imagine a huge transporter coming down the High Street. That's *power*. Then imagine a policeman stepping out, holding up his hand and commanding the huge vehicle to stop. That's *authority*. And Christ gives that same authority to you and me (see Luke 9:1).

"For by him all things were created: things in heaven and on earth, visible and invisible, whether thrones or powers or rulers or authorities; all things were created by him and for him. He is before all things, and in him all things hold together." (Col. 1:16–17, NIV)

# Jesus chooses the Twelve

☑ The question about the Sabbath — *Matthew 12:1–8, Mark 2:23–28, Luke 6:1–5*

☑ The man with a withered hand — *Matthew 12:9–14, Mark 3:1–6, Luke 6:6–11*

☑ Multitudes healed — *Matthew 12:15–21, Mark 3:7–12*

☑ Jesus chooses the twelve apostles — *Mark 3:13–19, Luke 6:12–16*

☑ Jesus teaches and heals — *Luke 6:17–19*

☑ The Sermon on the Mount — *Matthew 5:1–20*

**FOR THOUGHT AND CONTEMPLATION**

God calls no one to a special ministry or service for Him without providing the resources by which that ministry can be accomplished. And remember this — no matter the task ahead of you, it is never as great as the power behind you.

---

"Brothers, think of what you were when you were called. Not many of you were wise by human standards … But God chose the foolish things of the world to shame the wise; God chose the weak things of the world to shame the strong. He chose the lowly things of this world and the despised things … to nullify the things that are." (1 Cor. 1:26–28, NIV)

---

# The Sermon on the Mount

☑ Jesus' teaching about anger, adultery and divorce — *Matthew 5:21–32*

☑ Vows and revenge — *Matthew 5:33–42*

☑ Love for enemies — *Matthew 5:43–48*

☑ Teaching about giving — *Matthew 6:1–4*

☑ Teaching about prayer and fasting — *Matthew 6:5–18*

☑ Riches in heaven — *Matthew 6:19–23*

☑ God and possessions — *Matthew 6:24–34*

☑ Judging others — *Matthew 7:1–6*

☑ Our heavenly Father — *Matthew 7:7–12*

☑ Further teaching — *Matthew 7:13–23*

☑ The wise man and the foolish man — *Matthew 7:24–27*

☑ Jesus' authority — *Matthew 7:28–29*

**FOR THOUGHT AND CONTEMPLATION**

Some Christians are more concerned about beliefs than behaviour, others about behaviour more than beliefs. The Sermon on the Mount emphasises the necessity of both. Can you spot an area in your life where your doctrine may be right but your actions wrong? Then take whatever steps are necessary to turn it around.

---

"But the man who looks intently into the perfect law that gives freedom, and continues to do this, not forgetting what he has heard, but doing it — he will be blessed in what he does." (Jas. 1:25, NIV)

---

## CHRIST PORTRAYED IN THE GOSPELS

| Matthew | Mark | Luke | John |
|---|---|---|---|
| THE MIGHTY KING | THE LOWLY SERVANT | THE IDEAL MAN | THE DIVINE SON |

| Matthew | Mark | Luke | John |
|---|---|---|---|
| Lion-like | Ox-like | Man-like | Eagle-like |
| For the Jews | For the Gentiles | For the World | For the Church |
| Prophetic | Practical | Historical | Spiritual |
| Messianic | Realistic | Catholic | Christian |
| Power | Service | Sympathy | Wisdom |
| Past | Present | Future | Eternity |

## WEDNESDAY Week 41 Jesus' teaching

☑ Jesus' teaching about happiness and sorrow — *Matthew 8:1, Luke 6:20–26*

☑ Treatment of enemies — *Luke 6:27–36*

☑ Do not judge — *Luke 6:37–42*

☑ A tree and its fruit — *Luke 6:43–45*

☑ Wise and foolish builders — *Luke 6:46–49*

☑ Jesus heals the centurion's servant — *Matthew 8:5–13, Luke 7:1–10*

☑ He raises a widow's son — *Luke 7:11–17*

☑ Jesus commends John the Baptist — *Luke 7:18–30*

FOR THOUGHT AND CONTEMPLATION

One of the great laws of the personality is that truth does not become part of a person until they begin acting upon it. Progress from merely assenting to Christ's teachings to fully agreeing with them depends on behaving consistently with them. How good are you at not just listening to His words, but acting on them?

" …Jesus said, If you hold to my teaching, you are really my disciples. Then you will know the truth, and the truth will set you free.'" (Jn. 8:31–32, NIV)

## THURSDAY Week 41 Jesus and Beelzebub

☑ Jesus condemns wickedness — *Matthew 11:16–19, Luke 7:31–35*

☑ The unbelieving towns — *Matthew 11:20–24*

☑ Invitation to rest — *Matthew 11:25–30*

☑ Jesus at Simon's home — *Luke 7:36–50*

☑ The women who accompanied Jesus — *Luke 8:1–3*

☑ Jesus accused of madness — *Mark 3:20–21*

☑ Jesus and Beelzebub — *Matthew 12:22–30, Mark 3:22–27*

☑ The unpardonable sin — *Matthew 12:31–37, Mark 3:28–30*

☑ The folly of seeking a sign — *Matthew 12:38–45*

FOR THOUGHT AND CONTEMPLATION

Just as between Christ and Satan there was no collision or compromise, so it must also be with every one of Christ's followers. If you are for God, then you must be *against* the devil. Check up to see if there are any compromises in your life. And if so, decide right now to do something about them.

"Submit yourselves, then, to God. Resist the devil, and he will flee from you. Come near to God and he will come near to you …" (Jas 4:7–8, NIV)

## FRIDAY Week 41 The parables of Jesus

☑ Jesus' mother and brothers — *Matthew 12:46–50, Mark 3:31–35, Luke 8:19–21*

☑ The parable of the sower — *Matthew 13:1–9, Mark 4:1–9, Luke 8:4–8*

☑ The purpose of the parables — *Matthew 13:10–17, Mark 4:10–12, Luke 8:9–10*

☑ The explanation — *Matthew 13:18–23, Mark 4:13–20, Luke 8:11–15*

☑ A lamp under a bowl — *Mark 4:21–25, Luke 8:16–18*

☑ The growing seed — *Mark 4:26–29*

☑ The parable of the weeds — *Matthew 13:24–30*

FOR THOUGHT AND CONTEMPLATION

In His ministry of teaching, Jesus' goal was never to impress His hearers but to instruct them. How good are you at presenting profound truth with simplicity and directness? Think up a modern parable and then share its truth with someone — today.

" …speaking the truth in love, we will in all things grow up into him who is the Head, that is, Christ." (Eph. 4:15, NIV)

# PARABLES OF JESUS

The purpose of Jesus' parables was to teach in simple, easy-to-understand picture language the message of the kingdom of God. In addition to these, Jesus used epigrams and other memorable sayings, as the Beatitudes and the Sermon on the Mount show. Jesus used parables so frequently that Mark even says, "(Jesus) did not say anything to them without using a parable" (Mark 4:34).

| | Matthew | Mark | Luke |
|---|---|---|---|
| Lamp under a bushel | 5:14–15 | 4:21–22 | 8:16; 11:33 |
| Houses on rock and on sand | 7:24–27 | | 6:47–49 |
| New cloth on an old garment | 9:16 | 2:21 | 5:36 |
| New wine in old wineskins | 9:17 | 2:22 | 5:37–38 |
| Sower | 13:3–8 | 4:3–8 | 8:5–8 |
| The mustard seed | 13:31–32 | 4:30–32 | 13:18–19 |
| Tares | 13:24–30 | | |
| Leaven | 13:33 | | 13:20–21 |
| Hidden treasure | 13:44 | | |
| Pearl of great value | 13:45–46 | | |
| Drag-net | 13:47–48 | | |
| Lost sheep | 18:12–13 | | |
| Unforgiving servant | 18:23–24 | | |
| Workers in the vineyard | 20:1–16 | | |
| Two sons | 21:28–31 | | |
| Wicked tenants | 21:33–41 | 12:1–9 | 20:9–16 |
| Invitation to the wedding-feast | 22:2–14 | | |
| Fig-tree and summer | 24:22–33 | 13:28–29 | 21:29–32 |
| Ten 'bridesmaids' | 25:1–13 | | |
| Talents/pounds | 25:14–30 | | 19:12–27 |
| Sheep and goats | 25:31–36 | | |
| Seedtime to harvest | | 4:26–29 | |
| Creditor and the debtors | | | 7:41–43 |
| Good Samaritan | | | 10:30–37 |
| Friend in need | | | 11:5–8 |
| Rich fool | | | 12:16–21 |
| Alert servants | | | 12:35–40 |
| Faithful steward | | | 12:42–48 |
| Fig-tree without figs | | | 13:6–9 |
| Wedding-feast | | | 14:7–14 |
| Great banquet | | | 14:16–24 |
| Counting the cost | | | 14:28–33 |
| Lost coin | | | 15:8–10 |
| Prodigal son | | | 15:11–32 |
| Dishonest steward | | | 16:1–8 |
| Rich man and Lazarus | | | 16:19–31 |
| The master and his servant | | | 17:7–10 |
| Persistent widow | | | 18:2–5 |
| Pharisee and the tax collector | | | 18:10–14 |

More parables

🖋 Parables of the mustard seed and the yeast — *Matthew 13:31–33, Mark 4:30–32*

☑ Jesus' use of parables — *Matthew 13:34–35, Mark 4:33–34*

☑ Parable of weeds explained — *Matthew 13:36–43*

🖋 Parable of hidden treasure — *Matthew 13:44*

☑ Parable of the pearl — *Matthew 13:45–46*

🖋 Parable of the net — *Matthew 13:47–50*

☑ The householder — *Matthew 13:51–53*

☑ Jesus calms the storm — *Matthew 8:18, 23–27, Mark 4:35–41, Luke 8:22–25*

🖋 Jesus casts out demons — *Matthew 8:28–34, Mark 5:1–20*

FOR THOUGHT AND CONTEMPLATION

Someone has said that Christ's parables are not "bedtime stories to put us to sleep, but bugle calls to wake us up". Has something leapt out from these parables and given you a jolt? Good. Now apply its truth to your life without a moment's delay.

"Do not merely listen to the word, and so deceive yourselves. Do what it says. Anyone who listens to the word but does not do what it says is like a man who looks at his face in a mirror and, after looking at himself, goes away and immediately forgets what he looks like." (Jas. 1:22–24, NIV)

More healings

☑ Jesus casts out demons — *Luke 8:26–39*

☑ The woman who touched Jesus — *Matthew 9:18–22, Mark 5:21–34, Luke 8:40–48*

☑ Jesus raises Jairus' daughter — *Matthew 9:23–26, Mark 5:35–43, Luke 8:49–56*

🖋 Jesus heals two blind men — *Matthew 9:27–31*

☑ A dumb man speaks again — *Matthew 9:32–34*

🖋 Jesus rejected again at Nazareth — *Matthew 13:54–58, Mark 6:1–6*

FOR THOUGHT AND CONTEMPLATION

The Scripture tells us that "faith comes by hearing, and hearing by the word of God" (Romans 10:17). Is there a physical or psychological problem in your life that, despite any help you have received, refuses to budge? Then, with renewed faith, ask Him to make this the day of your deliverance.

"Now faith is being sure of what we hope for and certain of what we do not see." (Heb. 11:1, NIV)

The mission of the twelve

🖋 Jesus sends out the twelve disciples — *Matthew 9:35–38, 10:1–4, Mark 6:7, Luke 9:1–2*

🖋 His instructions to them — *Matthew 10:5–15, Mark 6:8–11, Luke 9:3–5*

☑ The persecution of the disciples — *Matthew 10:16–33*

🖋 The cost and rewards of discipleship — *Matthew 10:34–42, 11:1, Mark 6:12–13, Luke 9:6*

Death of John the Baptist AD 27

🖋 Death of John the Baptist — *Matthew 14:1–12, Mark 6:14–29, Luke 9:7–9*

FOR THOUGHT AND CONTEMPLATION

What a challenge Christ presented to those twelve disciples when He told them to go and do exactly as He had done. But then, as someone has said, "No one has ever tested the resources of God until they come up against that which is humanly impossible."

"I can do everything through him who gives me strength." (Phil. 4:13, NIV)

## A BIRD'S EYE VIEW OF MATTHEW

**Place in the Bible:**
First New Testament book; first Gospel.
**Written by:**
Matthew.
**Special features:**
Five distinct sections record the teaching of Jesus: the Sermon on the Mount (5), the Twelve being sent out (10), parables about the Kingdom (13), teaching about discipleship (18), and the coming kingdom (24—25).
**Jesus and the Gospel of Matthew:**
Matthew announces that the long-promised Messiah has now arrived. Quoting the Old Testament sixty-five times, he shows how Jesus is the Jewish Messiah and traces Jesus' family tree back to David and Abraham. The Lord is presented as the teacher and preacher of the Messianic age, and dies (and rises from the dead) as only the Messiah could.

**Teaching:**
One of Matthew's main aims in his Gospel is to demonstrate that Jesus really is the Jewish Messiah. And since many had expected the Messiah to be the warrior-king to overthrow Roman occupation, Matthew highlights the real nature of the Messiah's kingdom. The kingdom of heaven is central to many of the parables recorded here and from start to finish Matthew presents Jesus as being 'King of the Jews' at his birth (Matt. 2:2) and at his death (Matt. 27:37). The closing words of his Gospel have Jesus giving His Great Commission "to make disciples of all nations" (Matt. 28:19).

Matthew relies on Jesus Himself for the teaching in his Gospel. Out of Matthew's 1,071 verses, 60 per cent are the spoken words of Jesus.
**A verse to remember:**
"You are the Christ, the Son of the living God" (Matt. 16:16).

---

## TUESDAY Week 42 — The feeding of the five thousand

☑ The feeding of the five thousand — *Matthew 14:13–21, Mark 6:30–44, Luke 9:10–17, John 6:1–13*

☑ Jesus leaves the crowd — *Matthew 14:22–23, Mark 6:45–46, John 6:14–15*

☑ Jesus walks on the water — *Matthew 14:24–33, Mark 6:47–52, John 6:16–21*

☑ He heals the sick at Gennesaret — *Matthew 14:34–36, Mark 6:53–56*

FOR THOUGHT AND CONTEMPLATION

"A miracle," said C.S. Lewis, "is God taking the ordinary processes of nature and *speeding them up*." Normally, nature takes several seasons to make bread; the wheat, the grain, the flour, etc. But what nature takes seasons to do, Christ did in seconds. Carry with you into the day the thrilling fact that God is so much greater than the world He has made.

"Jesus looked at them and said, 'With man this is impossible, but with God all things are possible.'" (Matt. 19:26, NIV)

---

## WEDNESDAY Week 42 — The bread of life

☑ The people seek Jesus — *John 6:22–24*

☑ Jesus teaches about spiritual food — *John 6:25–33*

☑ Jesus, the bread of life — *John 6:34–58*

☑ Many disciples desert Jesus — *John 6:59–71*

☑ The hypocrisy of the scribes and Pharisees — *Matthew 15:1–9, Mark 7:1–13*

☑ Things that make a person unclean — *Matthew 15:10–20, Mark 7:14–23*

FOR THOUGHT AND CONTEMPLATION

How true it is that, although thousands follow Christ when He gives them what they want, few are prepared to follow Him when He confronts them with what *He* wants. Check up on your own discipleship today. Are you more concerned with what you want, or what *He* wants?

"If you love me, you will obey what I command." (Jn. 14:15, NIV)

**Peter's momentous confession**

☑ The Syrophoenician woman — *Matthew 15:21–28, Mark 7:24–30*

☑ Jesus heals many — *Matthew 15:29–31, Mark 7:31–37*

☑ Jesus feeds the four thousand — *Matthew 15:32–38, Mark 8:1–9*

☑ The demand for a sign — *Matthew 15:39, 16:1–4, Mark 8:10–12*

☑ The yeast of the Pharisees and Sadducees — *Matthew 16:5–12, Mark 8:13–21*

☑ Jesus heals a blind man — *Mark 8:22–26*

☑ Peter's declaration — *Matthew 16:13–20*

FOR THOUGHT AND CONTEMPLATION

Do you sometimes find yourself doing what Simon Peter did — one moment listening to the voice of God (Matt. 16:16), the next moment listening to the voice of Satan? (Matt. 16:22) Remember, although you may not be able to avoid hearing Satan's voice, you can most certainly decide to ignore him.

"Be self-controlled and alert. Your enemy the devil prowls around like a roaring lion looking for someone to devour. Resist him, standing firm in the faith …" (1 Pet. 5:8–9, NIV)

---

**The transfiguration**

☑ Peter's declaration — *Mark 8:27–30, Luke 9:18–21*

☑ Jesus speaks of His suffering and death — *Matthew 16:21–23, Mark 8:31–33, Luke 9:22*

☑ Jesus speaks about self-denial — *Matthew 16:24–28, Mark 8:34–38, 9:1, Luke 9:23–27*

☑ The transfiguration — *Matthew 17:1–8, Mark 9:2–8, Luke 9:28–36*

☑ Question about Elijah — *Matthew 17:9–13, Mark 9:9–13*

☑ Jesus' ministry of healing and deliverance — *Matthew 17:14–21*

FOR THOUGHT AND CONTEMPLATION

G. Campbell Morgan points out that, according to Luke, Jesus did not go up the mountain to be transfigured — He went up to pray. Prayer was the goal, transfiguration the result. You just cannot predict the outcome of a time of prayer with the Lord. Who knows what will result from your own prayer time today!

"When you pray, go into your room, close the door and pray to your Father, who is unseen. Then your Father, who sees what is done in secret, will reward you." (Matt. 6:6, NIV)

---

**Who's the greatest?**

☑ Jesus' ministry of healing and deliverance — *Mark 9:14–29, Luke 9:37–43*

☑ Jesus speaks again about His death — *Matthew 17:22–23, Mark 9:30–32, Luke 9:44–45*

☑ Payment of the Temple tax — *Matthew 17:24–27*

☑ Who's the greatest? — *Matthew 18:1–5, Mark 9:33–37, Luke 9:46–48*

☑ Causes of sin — *Matthew 18:6–9, Mark 9:42–50*

☑ The parable of the lost sheep — *Matthew 18:10–14*

☑ John is rebuked — *Mark 9:38–41, Luke 9:49–50*

☑ Teaching on forgiveness and prayer — *Matthew 18:15–20*

FOR THOUGHT AND CONTEMPLATION

How do you view spiritual greatness? Being a leader? Lording it over others? That is not greatness; that is smallness. Greatness is the ability to *serve* others, not control them, and that comes only through a right view of God, yourself and others. How much time do you need to spend on improving your 'serve'?

"The greatest among you will be your servant. For whoever exalts himself will be humbled, and whoever humbles himself will be exalted." (Matt. 23:11–12, NIV)

## THE SEVEN 'I AM'S' OF JESUS

There are no parables, as such, in John's Gospel but there is plenty of teaching in the form of allegories and proverbs (John 10:6). John does, however, record that some of Jesus' teaching was in the form of a parable (see John 3:8, 29; 4:35–38; 10:1–5 and 16:21–22). Then John has the famous 'I am's' of Jesus which are figurative descriptions which Jesus used of himself.

"I am the bread of life." (6:35)

"I am the light of the world." (8:12)

"I am the gate." (10:9)

"I am the good shepherd." (10:11)

"I am the resurrection and the life." (11:25)

"I am the way and the truth and the life." (14:6)

"I am the true vine." (15:1)

---

**SUNDAY Week 43**    ## An unforgiving spirit

☑ The parable of the unforgiving servant — *Matthew 18:21–35*

☑ Jesus' unbelieving brothers — *John 7:1–9*

☑ Jesus at the Feast of Tabernacles — *John 7:10–13*

☑ He teaches in the Temple — *John 7:14–31*

☑ Guards sent to arrest Him — *John 7:32–36*

☑ The water of life — *John 7:37–39*

☑ The dispute — *John 7:40–53*

☑ The woman caught in adultery — *John 8:1–11*

☑ The light of the world — *John 8:12–20*

FOR THOUGHT AND CONTEMPLATION

One of the most terrible effects of an unforgiving spirit is that it interferes with one's own spiritual assurance. "He who does not offer forgiveness to others," said someone, "destroys the bridge over which God's forgiveness passes to his own heart." Solemn words. Write them on your heart today.

"Be kind and compassionate to one another, forgiving each other, just as in Christ God forgave you." (Eph. 4:32, NIV)

---

**MONDAY Week 43**    ## The return of the seventy

☑ Jesus and the Jewish authorities — *John 8:21–30*

☑ Spiritual freedom — *John 8:31–38*

☑ Sons of Abraham — *John 8:39–41*

☑ Children of the devil — *John 8:42–47*

☑ The claims of Jesus — *John 8:48–59*

☑ Samaritan opposition — *Luke 9:51–56*

☑ The cost of following Jesus — *Matthew 8:19–22, Luke 9:57–62*

☑ Jesus sends out the seventy — *Luke 10:1–12*

☑ The unbelieving towns — *Luke 10:13–16*

☑ The return of the seventy — *Luke 10:17–20*

☑ Jesus' joy — *Luke 10:21–24*

What is *your* greatest reason for rejoicing? **That your prayers are answered? That devils are subject to you in Jesus' Name? That you are a successful Christian?** Our *greatest* reason for rejoicing is the fact that our names are written in heaven (Luke 10:20). Spend as much time as you can today thanking your heavenly Father for this stupendous fact!

" ...the rest of my fellow-workers, whose names are in the book of life. Rejoice in the Lord always. I will say it again: Rejoice!" (Phil. 4:3–4, NIV)

## TUESDAY Week 43   The Good Shepherd

☑ The parable of the good Samaritan — *Luke 10:25–37*

☑ Jesus visits Martha and Mary — *Luke 10:38–42*

☑ The healing of the man born blind — *John 9:1–41*

☑ The parable of the shepherd — *John 10:1–6*

☑ Jesus, the Good Shepherd — *John 10:7–21*

☑ Jesus at the Feast of Dedication — *John 10:22–38*

☑ Many believe in Him — *John 10:39–42*

FOR THOUGHT AND CONTEMPLATION

The words, "I am the Good Shepherd", are not a figure of speech; they show that Christ is a loving and concerned protector of His children. Are you overcome with worry and despair? Do you find it difficult to get to sleep at night? Then perhaps, instead of counting sheep, you might try talking to the Shepherd!

"The Lord is my shepherd, I shall lack nothing. He makes me lie down in green pastures, he leads me beside quiet waters." (Psa. 23:1–2, NIV)

## WEDNESDAY Week 43   Warnings and encouragements

☑ Jesus' teaching on prayer — *Luke 11:1–13*

☑ His teaching on Satan's kingdom — *Luke 11:14–26*

☑ True happiness — *Luke 11:27–28*

☑ The demand for a miracle — *Luke 11:29–32*

☑ The light of the body — *Luke 11:33–36*

☑ Blind guides — *Luke 11:37–54*

☑ Warning against hypocrisy — *Luke 12:1–3*

☑ God's care — *Luke 12:4–7*

☑ Confession or rejection — *Luke 12:8–12*

☑ The parable of the rich fool — *Luke 12:13–21*

☑ Trust in God — *Luke 12:22–31*

☑ Treasure in heaven — *Luke 12:32–34*

FOR THOUGHT AND CONTEMPLATION

Recent studies show that millions of people suffer from a low sense of worth. Many feel that they are just names on a computer, or numbers on a card. But in God's sight, every human being is of priceless value. Write out Luke 12:7 on a card and read it at least a dozen times today!

"Your eyes saw my unformed body. All the days ordained for me were written in your book before one of them came to be. How precious to me are your thoughts, O God! How vast is the sum of them!" (Psa. 139:16–17, NIV)

## THURSDAY Week 43   The kingdom of God

☑ Watchful servants — *Luke 12:35–40*

☑ Faithful and unfaithful servants — *Luke 12:41–48*

☑ Jesus, the cause of division — *Luke 12:49–53*

☑ Interpreting the times — *Luke 12:54–59*

☑ Repent or perish — *Luke 13:1–5*

☑ The unfruitful fig tree — *Luke 13:6–9*

☑ Jesus heals on the Sabbath — *Luke 13:10–17*

☑ Parables about the kingdom of God — *Luke 13:18–21*

☑ The narrow door — *Luke 13:22–30*

☑ Jesus' love for Jerusalem — *Luke 13:31–35*

☑ Jesus heals a sick man — *Luke 14:1–6*

☑ Humility and hospitality — *Luke 14:7–14*

Has it ever occurred to you, as you read the account of Christ's ministry on earth, that He seemed to have little or no concern for His own personal needs? Perhaps it was because, as Hudson Taylor so eloquently said, "God's work done in God's way will never lack God's supply."

"But seek first his kingdom and his righteousness, and all these things will be given to you as well." (Matt. 6:33, NIV)

## FRIDAY Week 43 — The challenge of discipleship

☑ The parable of the great banquet — *Luke 14:15–24*

☑ The cost of discipleship — *Luke 14:25–35*

☑ The lost sheep — *Luke 15:1–7*

☑ The lost coin — *Luke 15:8–10*

☑ The lost son — *Luke 15:11–32*

☑ The unjust steward — *Luke 16:1–13*

☑ More teaching — *Luke 16:14–18*

☑ The rich man and Lazarus — *Luke 16:19–31*

FOR THOUGHT AND CONTEMPLATION

The Christian Church is desperately in need of a new definition of discipleship. The word has become smudged and discoloured through years of misuse. Read again the meaning of discipleship as presented by Christ in Luke 14:25–35 and ask yourself: Am I truly His disciple?

" ...If anyone obeys his word, God's love is truly made complete in him. This is how we know we are in him: Whoever claims to live in him must walk as Jesus did." (1 Jn 2:5–6, NIV)

## SATURDAY Week 43 — The resurrection and the life

☑ The unprofitable servant — *Luke 17:1–10*

☑ The death of Lazarus — *John 11:1–16*

☑ Jesus the resurrection and the life — *John 11:17–27*

☑ Jesus weeps — *John 11:28–37*

☑ The raising of Lazarus — *John 11:38–44*

☑ The plot against Jesus — *John 11:45–53*

☑ Jesus goes to Ephraim — *John 11:54*

☑ The healing of the ten lepers — *Luke 17:11–19*

☑ The coming of the kingdom of God — *Luke 17:20–37*

FOR THOUGHT AND CONTEMPLATION

Have you ever realised that Jesus did not say, "I am the resurrection and the life" after He rose from the dead, but prior to it? What does this imply? It implies that Jesus was not the Resurrection because He rose from the dead, but He rose from the dead because He was the Resurrection.

"And if the Spirit of him who raised Jesus from the dead is living in you, he who raised Christ from the dead will also give life to your mortal bodies through his Spirit, who lives in you." (Rom. 8:11, NIV)

## SUNDAY Week 44 — Jesus and divorce

☑ The parable of the persistent widow — *Luke 18:1–8*

☑ The parable of the Pharisee and the tax collector — *Luke 18:9–14*

☑ Jesus' teaching about divorce — *Matthew 19:1–12, Mark 10:1–12*

☑ He blesses little children — *Matthew 19:13–15, Mark 10:13–16, Luke 18:15–17*

☑ The rich young ruler — *Matthew 19:16–30, Mark 10:17–31*

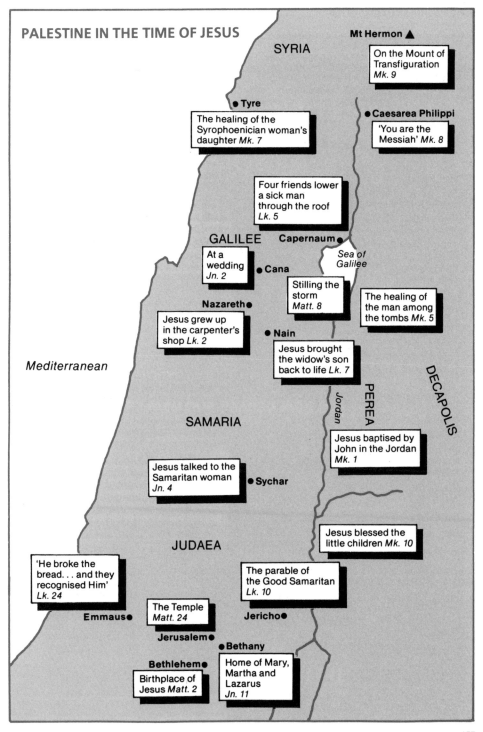

PALESTINE IN THE TIME OF JESUS

SYRIA

Mt Hermon ▲

On the Mount of Transfiguration *Mk. 9*

● Tyre

● Caesarea Philippi

The healing of the Syrophoenician woman's daughter *Mk. 7*

'You are the Messiah' *Mk. 8*

Four friends lower a sick man through the roof *Lk. 5*

GALILEE

Capernaum ●

*Sea of Galilee*

At a wedding *Jn. 2*

● Cana

Stilling the storm *Matt. 8*

The healing of the man among the tombs *Mk. 5*

Nazareth ●

Jesus grew up in the carpenter's shop *Lk. 2*

● Nain

Jesus brought the widow's son back to life *Lk. 7*

*Mediterranean*

SAMARIA

*Jordan*

PEREA

DECAPOLIS

Jesus baptised by John in the Jordan *Mk. 1*

Jesus talked to the Samaritan woman *Jn. 4*

● Sychar

Jesus blessed the little children *Mk. 10*

JUDAEA

'He broke the bread. . . and they recognised Him' *Lk. 24*

The parable of the Good Samaritan *Lk. 10*

The Temple *Matt. 24*

Jericho ●

Emmaus ●

Jerusalem ●

● Bethany

Bethlehem ●

Home of Mary, Martha and Lazarus *Jn. 11*

Birthplace of Jesus *Matt. 2*

157

How do you feel about divorce? God says in the Old Testament that He *hates* it (Mal. 2:16). Around 150,000 divorces per year take place in Britain alone. Spend a few minutes in prayer today asking God what He would have you do to help stop the break-up of Britain's homes and families.

" ...God was reconciling the world to himself in Christ, not counting men's sins against them. And he has committed to us the message of reconciliation." (2 Cor. 5:19, NIV)

## MONDAY Week 44 — The over-ambitious disciples

☑ The rich young ruler — *Luke 18:18–30*

☑ The parable of the workers in the vineyard — *Matthew 20:1–16*

☑ Jesus speaks of the crucifixion — *Matthew 20:17–19, Mark 10:32–34, Luke 18:31–34*

☑ The ambition of James and John — *Matthew 20:20–28, Mark 10:35–45*

☑ The two blind men healed — *Matthew 20:29–34*

☑ Blind Bartimaeus is healed — *Mark 10:46–52, Luke 18:35–43*

FOR THOUGHT AND CONTEMPLATION

How did Jesus deal with problem people in His life, such as His over-ambitious disciples? He turned every problem into a possibility by using it as an opportunity to drive home some new and vital spiritual truth. Put this principle to work in your own life, and it will mean all the difference between success and failure in your relationships

"A man finds joy in giving an apt reply — and how good is a timely word!" (Prov. 15:23, NIV)

## TUESDAY Week 44 — The triumphal entry

☑ The conversion of Zacchaeus — *Luke 19:1–10*

☑ The parable of the gold coins — *Luke 19:11–28*

☑ Jesus arrives at Bethany — *John 11:55–57, 12:1*

☑ The plot against Lazarus — *John 12:9–11*

☑ Jesus is anointed at Bethany — *John 12:2–8*

☑ The triumphant entry into Jerusalem — *Matthew 21:1–11, Mark 11:1–11, Luke 19:29–44, John 12:12–19*

FOR THOUGHT AND CONTEMPLATION

Human nature is such that, on one day, it can receive Christ with palms and rejoicing, and the next day send Him to a cross. Multitudes of people admire Christ, but few become consistent disciples. How about you? Are you just one of Christ's admirers — or a true disciple?

"Dear children, let us not love with words or tongue but with actions and in truth." (1 Jn. 3:18, NIV)

## WEDNESDAY Week 44 — Jesus' authority

☑ Second cleansing of Temple — *Matthew 21:12–17, Mark 11:15–19, Luke 19:45–48*

☑ Cursing of the fig tree — *Matthew 21:18–19, Mark 11:12–14*

☑ The fig tree withers — *Matthew 21:20–22, Mark 11:20–26*

☑ Jesus' authority is challenged — *Matthew 21:23–27, Mark 11:27–33, Luke 20:1–8*

☑ The parable of the two sons — *Matthew 21:28–32*

☑ The parable of the wicked tenants — *Matthew 21:33–46, Mark 12:1–12, Luke 20:9–19*

FOR THOUGHT AND CONTEMPLATION

The authority of Christ is still questioned today — even by Christians! Someone has said there are usually three reactions given to Christ's words — inattention, irritation or instant obedience. Which of these three reactions is characteristic of your response to Christ's words?

"If you love me, you will obey what I command." (Jn 14:15, NIV)

# Jesus silences the opposition

☑ Parable of the wedding feast — *Matthew 22:1–14*

☑ Jesus is questioned: about paying taxes — *Matthew 22:15–22, Mark 12:13–17, Luke 20:20–26*

☑ About the resurrection — *Matthew 22:23–33, Mark 12:18–27, Luke 20:27–38*

☑ About the greatest commandment — *Matthew 22:34–40, Mark 12:28–34, Luke 20:39–40*

☑ Jesus asks a question — *Matthew 22:41–46, Mark 12:35–37, Luke 20:41–44*

FOR THOUGHT AND CONTEMPLATION

One of the things that contributes to inner conflict in our hearts is the fact that, while we are big enough to ask questions, we are often not big enough to understand the answers. Every question will be answered in eternity. If you can hold on to that in the midst of your perplexity, then you will have discovered one of the greatest secrets of effective Christian living.

---

"'For my thoughts are not your thoughts, neither are your ways my ways,' declares the Lord. 'As the heavens are higher than the earth, so are my ways higher than your ways and my thoughts than your thoughts.'" (Isa. 55:8–9, NIV)

---

## A BIRD'S EYE VIEW OF MARK

**Place in the Bible:**
Second New Testament book; second Gospel.
**Written by:**
Mark.
**Special features:**
Mark may be the shortest Gospel but it is the most action-packed one. It leaves the reader almost breathless, with the word "immediately" coming over forty times, as Mark moves in rapid succession from one event to the next, painting his portrait of Jesus.
**Jesus and the Gospel of Mark:**
Mark depicts Jesus Christ as both the Son of God ("The beginning of the gospel about Jesus Christ, the Son of God." 1:1), and (no less than fourteen times) the Son of Man who shows his compassion for people (6:34), and can be deeply moved and troubled (14:33).
**Teaching:**
Mark shows Jesus to be the Servant, who gives his life in teaching, healing and caring for others, who is the suffering Servant who dies on the cross, and who calls His followers to be servants in their Master's service.
**A verse to remember:**
"'The Son of Man did not come to be served, but to serve, and to give his life as a ransom for many'" (Mark 10:45).

---

# Signs of the end

☑ Jesus denounces the scribes and Pharisees — *Matthew 23:1–31, Mark 12:38–40, Luke 20:45–47*

☑ Jesus prophesies judgment — *Matthew 23:32–36*

☑ His lament over Jerusalem — *Matthew 23:37–39*

☑ The widow's mite — *Mark 12:41–44, Luke 21:1–4*

☑ The Temple to be destroyed — *Matthew 24:1–2*

☑ Signs of the end times — *Matthew 24:3–31*

☑ The parable of the fig tree — *Matthew 24:32–35*

☑ The coming of the Son of Man — *Matthew 24:36–51*

FOR THOUGHT AND CONTEMPLATION

We ought not to forget that the whole point and purpose of prophecy is not only to remind us that Christ is coming, but to remind us that we ought to be *ready* to meet Him. Some Christians regard Christ's coming as just another doctrinal fact; others regard it as the hope of their existence. What does this truth do for you?

---

"He who testifies to these things says, 'Yes, I am coming soon.' Amen. Come, Lord Jesus." (Rev. 22:20, NIV)

---

## SATURDAY Week 44 — Watch and pray

- ☑ The destruction of the Temple — *Mark 13:1–2, Luke 21:5–6*
- ☑ Events of the end times — *Mark 13:3–27, Luke 21:7–28*
- ☑ Parable of the fig tree — *Mark 13:28–31, Luke 21:29–33*
- ☑ Warning to be ready — *Mark 13:32–37, Luke 21:34–36*
- ☑ Jesus teaches in the Temple — *Luke 21:37–38*
- ☑ Parable of the wise and foolish virgins — *Matthew 25:1–13*
- ☐ Parable of the talents — *Matthew 25:14–30*

FOR THOUGHT AND CONTEMPLATION

Ready for a challenge? Then take a pen and a sheet of paper and write down the answers to these two questions. How many talents has God given you? What are you doing with them? In thinking about it, don't forget this point — what you don't *use*, you *lose*.

" ...in Christ we who are many form one body, and each member belongs to all the others. We have different gifts, according to the grace given us ..." (Rom. 12:5–6, NIV)

## SUNDAY Week 45 — The corn of wheat

- ☑ The sheep and the goats — *Matthew 25:31–46*
- ☑ The plot against Jesus — *Matthew 26:1–5, Mark 14:1–2, Luke 22:1–2*
- ☑ Mary anoints Jesus — *Matthew 26:6–13, Mark 14:3–9*
- ☑ Judas turns traitor — *Matthew 26:14–16, Mark 14:10–11, Luke 22:3–6*
- ☑ Gentiles desire to see Jesus — *John 12:20–36*
- ☑ The Jews reject Him — *John 12:37–43*
- ☑ Jesus, the Light of the world — *John 12:44–50*
- ☑ Preparation for the Passover — *Matthew 26:17–19, Mark 14:12–16, Luke 22:7–13*

FOR THOUGHT AND CONTEMPLATION

The last few days of Christ's earthly life occupy more space in the Gospels than any other comparable stage of His ministry. If God regards this period as so significant, should not we? Ask God to help you 'enter into His sufferings', as once again you walk the path that leads to Calvary.

"If we endure, we will also reign with him. If we disown him, he will also disown us; if we are faithless, he will remain faithful ..." (2 Tim. 2:12–13, NIV)

## MONDAY Week 45 — The last supper

- ☑ Jesus identifies the betrayer — *Matthew 26:20–25, Mark 14:17–21, John 13:21–30*
- ☑ Jesus' new commandment — *John 13:31–35*
- ☑ He institutes the Lord's Supper — *Matthew 26:26–29, Mark 14:22–25, Luke 22:14–23, 1 Corinthians 11:23–26*
- ☑ The disciples' argument — *Luke 22:24–30*
- ☑ Jesus washes the disciples' feet — *John 13:1–20*
- ☑ He foretells Peter's denial — *Matthew 26:31–35, Mark 14:27–31, Luke 22:31–38, John 13:36–38*

FOR THOUGHT AND CONTEMPLATION

As you see Christ washing His disciples' feet, or taking the bread into His hands and breaking it — what does it say to you? Is it not saying that the greatest lessons in life are taught, not by words, but by actions? Is your witness for Christ merely by words — or is it also by deeds?

"In the same way, faith by itself, if it is not accompanied by action, is dead." (Jas. 2:17, NIV)

## OLD TESTAMENT PEOPLE AND PLACES MENTIONED BY CHRIST

| Old Testament reference | Event | New Testament reference |
|---|---|---|
| *Genesis 1:27; 2:23–24* | Creation of Adam and Eve | *Mark 10:6–8* |
| *Genesis 4:10* | Murder of Abel | *Luke 11:51* |
| *Genesis 6:5–13* | Corruption of Noah's day and flood | *Luke 17:26, 27* |
| *Genesis 18:20; 19:24* | Corruption of Lot's day and the fire | *Luke 17:28, 29* |
| *Genesis 19:26* | Worldliness of Lot's wife | *Luke 17:32* |
| *Exodus 3:1–6* | Moses and the burning bush | *Luke 20:37* |
| *Exodus 16:15* | Moses and the heavenly manna | *John 6:31* |
| *Numbers 21:8* | Moses and the brazen serpent | *John 3:14* |
| *1 Samuel 21:6* | David and the shewbread | *Matthew 12:3, 4* |
| *1 Kings 10:1* | Solomon and the Queen of Sheba | *Matthew 12:42* |
| *1 Kings 17:1, 9* | Elijah, the widow and the famine | *Luke 4:25, 26* |
| *2 Kings 5* | Naaman and his leprosy | *Luke 4:27* |
| *2 Chronicles 24:20, 21* | The murder of Zechariah | *Luke 11:51* |
| *Daniel 9:27; 11:31; 12:11* | Daniel and the abomination of desolation | *Matthew 24:15* |
| *Jonah 1:17* | Jonah and the fish | *Matthew 12:40; 16:4* |
| *Jonah 3:4–10* | The repentance of Nineveh | *Luke 11:30; Matthew 12:41* |

**TUESDAY Week 45** ## Jesus comforts His disciples

☑ Jesus, the Way to the Father — *John 14:1–14*
☑ The promise of the Holy Spirit — *John 14:15–31*
☑ The true vine — *John 15:1–17*
☑ Warning about persecution — *John 15:18–27, 16:1–4*
☐ Jesus teaches about the Comforter — *John 16:5–15*
☑ He speaks about the Father — *John 16:16–28*
☐ The disciples' response — *John 16:29–30*
☑ Jesus promises peace — *John 16:31–33*

**FOR THOUGHT AND CONTEMPLATION**

Have you ever wondered just how the Holy Spirit goes about comforting us in our trials and difficulties? He follows the model laid down for Him by Christ in John 14. Spend a few moments focusing on how Christ comforted His disciples in this matchless chapter — then compare it with the way the Spirit ministers that selfsame comfort in your heart and life.

"Who comforts us in all our troubles, so that we can comfort those in any trouble with the comfort we ourselves have received from God." (2 Cor. 1:4, NIV)

☑ Jesus prays for Himself — *John 17:1–5*

☑ He prays for His disciples — *John 17:6–19*

☑ He prays for the unity of all Christians — *John 17:20–26*

☑ In the garden of Gethsemane — *Matthew 26:30, 36–46, Mark 14:26, 32–42, Luke 22:39–46, John 18:1*

☑ Jesus is betrayed and arrested — *Matthew 26:47–55, Mark 14:43–49, Luke 22:47–53, John 18:2–11*

☑ The disciples desert Him — *Matthew 26:56, Mark 14:50–52*

**FOR THOUGHT AND CONTEMPLATION**

The great preacher Robert McCheyne once said: "If I could hear Christ praying for me in the next room, I would not fear a million enemies." Listen! He *is* praying for you — now. Not in the next room maybe, but before the Throne. Be assured of this — the distance makes no difference!

"Therefore he is able to save completely those who come to God through him, because he always lives to intercede for them." (Heb. 7:25, NIV)

## A BIRD'S EYE VIEW OF JOHN

**Place in the Bible:**
Fourth New Testament book; fourth Gospel.

**Written by:**
John.

**Special features:**
John constantly brings out the meaning of the events in Jesus' life he is describing. John records none of Jesus' parables and carefully chooses from Jesus' numerous miracles seven "signs" which reveal who Jesus Christ really is — the Son of the living God (11:27).

**Jesus and the Gospel of John:**
John shows that Jesus Christ is God in

Jesus's eight "I am" statements.

**Teaching:**
The aim of John's Gospel is given by John in chapter 20:30–31, "that you may believe that Jesus is the Christ, the Son of God, and that by believing you may have life in his name." Throughout his Gospel John highlights the reactions of people to Jesus Christ — they either responded in faith or, in unbelief, rejected Jesus.

**A verse to remember:**
"'For God so loved the world that he gave his one and only Son, that whoever believes in him shall not perish but have eternal life'" (John 3:16).

☑ Jesus before Annas and Caiaphas — *John 18:12–14, 19–23*

☑ His trial before the Sanhedrin — *Matthew 26:57, 59–66, Mark 14:53, 55–64, Luke 22:54, John 18:24*

☑ He is mocked and spat on — *Matthew 26:67–68, Mark 14:65, Luke 22:63–65*

☑ Peter's denial — *Matthew 26:58, 69–75, Mark 14:54, 66–72, Luke 22:55–62, John 18:15–18, 25–27*

☑ Jesus is condemned — *Matthew 27:1–2, Mark 15:1, Luke 22:66–71*

☑ Judas' remorse — *Matthew 27:3–10, Acts 1:18–19*

**FOR THOUGHT AND CONTEMPLATION**

How amazing that the Son of God, equipped as He was with the power to extricate Himself from difficult situations, chose instead to suffer them. And why? Because as William Penn puts it: "No pain, no palm; no thorns, no throne; no gall, no glory; no cross, no crown."

" …'If anyone would come after me, he must deny himself and take up his cross and follow me. For whoever wants to save his life will lose it, but whoever loses his life for me will find it.'" (Matt. 16:24–25, NIV)

## FRIDAY Week 45    His trial before Pilate

☑ Jesus is sent to Pilate — *Matthew 27:11–14, Mark 15:2–5, Luke 23:1–5, John 18:28–38*

☑ Herod questions Jesus — *Luke 23:6–10*

☑ He is sent back to Pilate — *Luke 23:11–12*

☑ Barabbas is released, Jesus is flogged — *Matthew 27:15–26, Mark 15:6–15, Luke 23:13–25, John 18:39–40, 19:1*

☑ Pilate's soldiers mock Jesus — *Matthew 27:27–31, Mark 15:16–19, John 19:2–3*

☑ Pilate seeks to release Jesus — *John 19:4–12*

☑ Pilate's final sentence — *John 19:13–16*

FOR THOUGHT AND CONTEMPLATION

The apostle Paul tells us that when Christ stood before Pontius Pilate, He "made the good confession" (1 Tim. 6:13). What does that mean? This: Christ would not allow the actions of Pilate to determine His. He acted, rather than reacted. He *resolved* to remain silent. He *resolved* to go on loving. When we act rather than react to life, then we do as Jesus did — we 'make a good confession'.

"Whoever acknowledges me before men, I will also acknowledge him before my Father in heaven." (Matt. 10:32, NIV)

## SATURDAY Week 45    The death of Jesus

☑ Jesus' walk to Golgotha — *Matthew 27:32–34, Mark 15:20–23, Luke 23:26–32, John 19:17*

☑ Jesus is crucified — *Matthew 27:35–44, Mark 15:24–32, Luke 23:33–43, John 19:18–27*

☑ Three hours of darkness — *Matthew 27:45–49, Mark 15:33–36, Luke 23:44–45, John 19:28–29*

The Death of Jesus AD29

☑ The death of Jesus — *Matthew 27:50, Mark 15:37, Luke 23:46, John 19:30*

☑ His side is pierced — *John 19:31–37*

☑ Miraculous events at Jesus' death — *Matthew 27:51–56, Mark 15:38–41, Luke 23:47–49*

FOR THOUGHT AND CONTEMPLATION

No more fitting comment can be found for today's reading than the words which appear on the gravestone of an old Welsh preacher:
"Had Christ the death of death to death
Not given death by dying,
The gates of life had never been
To mortals open lying."

"For since death came through a man, the resurrection of the dead comes also through a man. For as in Adam all die, so in Christ all will be made alive." (1 Cor. 15:21–22, NIV)

## SUNDAY Week 46    The Resurrection

☑ Jesus' body laid in the tomb — *Matthew 27:57–61, Mark 15:42–47, Luke 23:50–56, John 19:38–42*

☑ Soldiers put on guard — *Matthew 27:62–66*

☑ The women visit the tomb — *Matthew 28:1–4, Mark 16:1–4, Luke 24:1–2, John 20:1*

☑ The angels' message — *Matthew 28:5–8, Mark 16:5–8, Luke 23:3–8*

☑ Peter and John go to the tomb — *Luke 24:9–12, John 20:2–10*

☑ Jesus appears to Mary Magdalene — *Mark 16:9–11, John 20:11–18*

☑ He appears to other women — *Matthew 28:9–10*

☑ The soldiers are bribed — *Matthew 28:11–15*

FOR THOUGHT AND CONTEMPLATION

Perhaps the most important, yet not widely recognised, fact about Joseph's tomb is that it wasn't a tomb at all; it was a room which the everlasting Christ used for a few nights on His way back to glory. As H.R.L. Sheppard put it: "It was inevitable that Christ should die; it was also inevitable He should rise again. *We could expect nothing less of God.*"

"'Where, O death, is your victory? Where, O death, is your sting?'" (1 Cor. 15:55, NIV)

## Jesus appears to many

☑ On the Emmaus road — *Mark 16:12–13, Luke 24:13–32*

☑ The disciples report to the eleven — *Luke 24:33–35*

☑ Jesus appears to the rest of the disciples —- *1 Corinthians 15:5, Mark 16:14, Luke 24:36–43, John 20:19–25*

☑ He appears to Thomas — *John 20:26–29*

☑ He appears by the Sea of Galilee — *John 21:1–14*

☑ Jesus reinstates Peter — *John 21:15–24*

☑ The Great Commission — *Matthew 28:16–20, Mark 16:15–18, 1 Corinthians 15:6*

☑ Jesus appears to James — *1 Corinthians 15:7*

### FOR THOUGHT AND CONTEMPLATION

Jesus knew full well the temptation that would come to His disciples to think that they had been mistaken about His resurrection, so He appeared to them over a period of forty days — thus building up the evidence and piling up the proof. How characteristic of Jesus to put the interests of others before His own. Is this one of your characteristics too?

"Each of you should look not only to your own interests, but also to the interests of others. Your attitude should be the same as that of Christ Jesus." (Phil. 2:4–5, NIV)

## TEN RESURRECTION APPEARANCES

### FIRST DAY

1. **To Mary Magdalene in the garden** *Mk. 16:9; Jn. 20:11–18*

2. **To the women returning from the tomb** *Mt. 28:9, 10*

3. **To two disciples on the Emmaus Road** *Lk. 24:13–32; Mk. 16:12, 13*

4. **To Peter in Jerusalem** *Lk. 24:34; 1 Cor. 15:5*

5. **To ten of His apostles in the upper room** *Lk. 24:36–43; Jn. 20:19–23*

### REMAINING 40 DAYS

6. **To the eleven in the upper room** *Jn. 20:24–29*

7. **To seven apostles by the Sea of Galilee** *Jn. 21:1–24*

8. **To the eleven and 500 believers on Mount Tabor** *Mt. 28:16–20; 1 Cor. 15:6*

9. **To the eleven and James, Jesus' half-brother, in Jerusalem** *Mk. 16:14–18; Lk. 24:44–49; 1 Cor. 15:7*

10. **To the eleven on the Mount of Olives** *Lk. 24:50–53*

## The Day of Pentecost

☑ The disciples told to wait — *Luke 24:44–49, Acts 1:3–8*

☑ Jesus' ascension — *Mark 16:19–20, Luke 24:50–53, Acts 1:9–12*

☑ The purpose of John's Gospel — *John 21:25, 20:30–31*

☑ Introduction to the Acts — *Acts 1:1–2*

☑ The disciples in the upper room — *Acts 1:13–17, 20–26*

☑ The coming of the Holy Spirit — *Acts 2:1–13*

☑ Peter preaches that Jesus is Christ — *Acts 2:14–36*

☑ The crowd's response — *Acts 2:37–40*

### FOR THOUGHT AND CONTEMPLATION

Suppose there had been no outpouring of the Spirit on the Day of Pentecost, what kind of Christianity would have faced the world? It would have been the kind found in John 20:19. The Day of Pentecost made a dramatic difference to the disciples — it turned them from men of fear to men of fire. Has it made a smiliar difference in you? If not, then pray now that God will give you your own *personal* Pentecost.

"Do not get drunk on wine, which leads to debauchery. Instead, be filled with the Spirit." (Eph. 5:18, NIV)

## A BIRD'S EYE VIEW OF ACTS

**Place in the Bible:**
Fifth New Testament book; first book of history.
**Written by:**
Luke.
**Special features:**
The only book to tell in detail what happened between the ascension of Jesus and the new Christian fellowships.
**Jesus and the book of Acts:**
In the sermons and testimonies in Acts Jesus is presented as the Saviour who is now alive and active through the Holy Spirit after the resurrection. "Salvation is found in no-one else" (4:12).
**Teaching:**
Acts is part two of Luke's gospel, showing how the message of Jesus spread from Jerusalem through the Roman empire until it arrived in Rome itself. There is a strong emphasis on the activity and transforming power of the Holy Spirit.
**A verse to remember:**
"They devoted themselves to the apostles' teaching and to the fellowship, to the breaking of bread and to prayer" (Acts 2:42).

---

**WEDNESDAY Week 46** The power of the early Church

- ☑ Three thousand added to the Church — *Acts 2:41–47*
- ☑ A lame man is healed — *Acts 3:1–11*
- ☑ Peter's second sermon — *Acts 3:12–26*
- ☑ Peter and John imprisoned — *Acts 4:1–4*
- ☑ Their bold testimony — *Acts 4:5–14*
- ☑ They refuse to be silenced — *Acts 4:15–22*
- ☑ The believers unite in prayer — *Acts 4:23–31*
- ☑ The self-sacrifice of the believers — *Acts 4:32–37*
- ☑ Death of Ananias and Sapphira — *Acts 5:1–11*
- ☑ Many signs and wonders — *Acts 5:12–16*

FOR THOUGHT AND CONTEMPLATION

Although the Church of the 20th century is growing by leaps and bounds, there are still too many differences between it and the early Church for us to remain comfortable. For example, in Acts, one sermon brought 3,000 converts. Today we have to preach 3,000 sermons to win one convert. What other differences can you think of? Pray that God will help us close this gap.

"Lord, I have heard of your fame; I stand in awe of your deeds, O Lord. Renew them in our day, in our time make them known ..." (Hab. 3:2, NIV)

---

**THURSDAY Week 46** Stephen, the first martyr

- ☑ The apostles imprisoned but set free — *Acts 5:17–25*
- ☑ They testify to the council — *Acts 5:26–33*
- ☑ The advice of Gamaliel — *Acts 5:34–39*
- ☑ The apostles are released — *Acts 5:40–42*
- ☑ Deacons are appointed — *Acts 6:1–7*
- ☑ Stephen is falsely accused — *Acts 6:8–15*
- ☑ His defence before the council — *Acts 7:1–50*
- ☑ He reproves the Jewish leaders — *Acts 7:51–53*
- Stephen's martyrdom AD 35
- ☑ Stephen's martyrdom — *Acts 7:54–60*

FOR THOUGHT AND CONTEMPLATION

Someone said: "You can't be the salt of the earth without causing someone to smart." Stephen stood up for truth, and lost his life because of it. How important is truth to you? Maybe it's important enough to live by, but is it important enough to die for?

" ...everyone who wants to live a godly life in Christ Jesus will be persecuted." (2 Tim. 3:12, NIV)

# The conversion of Saul

☑ Saul persecutes the Church — *Acts 8:1–4*
☑ Philip's ministry in Samaria — *Acts 8:5–13*
☑ Simon's hypocrisy — *Acts 8:14–25*
☑ Philip and the Ethiopian eunuch — *Acts 8:26–40*
Conversion of Saul AD 37
☑ Saul's conversion — *Acts 9:1–9*
☑ He preaches Christ — *Acts 9:10–22*
☑ His escape — *Acts 9:23–25*
☑ His early experiences — *Galatians 1:17–19*
☑ Barnabas befriends him — *Acts 9:26–29*
☑ He is sent to Tarsus — *Acts 9:30–31*

FOR THOUGHT AND CONTEMPLATION

How were you converted? Was it a dramatic experience like Paul's, or was it simply a quiet conviction that you had passed from death to life? The manner in which we are converted differs, but the results are always the same. Just think — *the spiritual heritage you have in Christ is exactly the same as that of Paul's.*

" ...whoever comes to me I will never drive away." (Jn. 6:37, NIV)

# The first Gentile converts

☑ Aeneas is healed — *Acts 9:32–35*
☑ Dorcas is raised to life — *Acts 9:36–43*
☑ Cornelius sends for Peter — *Acts 10:1–8*
☑ Peter's vision — *Acts 10:9–18*
☑ He goes to Cornelius — *Acts 10:19–33*
☑ Peter preaches the Gospel — *Acts 10:34–43*
☑ Gentiles receive the Holy Spirt and are baptised — *Acts 10:44–48*
☑ The apostles contend with Peter — *Acts 11:1–3*
☑ Peter's defence — *Acts 11:4–18*

FOR THOUGHT AND CONTEMPLATION

What is one of the biggest impediments to the spreading of the Gospel? *Bigotry*! Peter resisted the idea that Gentiles should participate in God's salvation until the Lord well and truly re-orientated him. Any bigotry in you? Then take care — God might have to turn you upside down too!

"If you really keep the royal law found in Scripture, 'Love your neighbour as yourself,' you are doing right. But if you show favouritism, you sin and are convicted by the law as law-breakers." (Jas. 2:8–9, NIV)

# The letter of James

☑ Church established at Antioch — *Acts 11:19–24*
☑ Paul brought to Antioch — *Acts 11:25–26*
☑ Gift sent to Jerusalem — *Acts 11:27–30*
☑ James (John's brother) killed — *Acts 12:1–2*
James' letter written AD 45
☑ The letter of James: Temptations try faith — *James 1:1–15*
☑ God's good gifts — *James 1:16–18*
☑ Doers of the Word — *James 1:19–27*
☑ No respect of persons — *James 2:1–13*
☑ Necessity of good works — *James 2:14–26*
☑ Use of the tongue — *James 3:1–12*
☑ True wisdom — *James 3:13–18*

FOR THOUGHT AND CONTEMPLATION

Perhaps the greatest lesson that comes out of James' writings is his reminder of the power of the tongue. That "little piece of flesh between the jaws", as Martin Luther called it, takes some taming! In fact the Scripture says that no man can tame it. No man perhaps, but with God all things are possible. Have you given God your tongue for taming yet?

"A word aptly spoken is like apples of gold in settings of silver." (Prov. 25:11, NIV)

## A BIRD'S EYE VIEW OF JAMES

**Place in the Bible:**
Twentieth New Testament book; fifteenth letter.
**Written by:**
James, thought to be the brother of Jesus.
**Jesus and the letter of James:**
This letter has fifteen mirror images of Jesus' teaching given in the Sermon on the Mount. Matthew 5:10–12, for example, is reflected in James 1:2, "Consider it pure joy, my brothers, whenever you face trials of many kinds …".
**Teaching:**
James points out that a Christian's belief should be exactly matched by Christian behaviour. James links faith and works together, since works and good deeds done for Christ in His name should always naturally flow out of faith in Christ.
**A verse to remember:**
"What good is it, my brothers, if a man claims to have faith but has no deeds? … faith by itself, if it is not accompanied by action, is dead" (James 2.14–17).

---

## MONDAY Week 47 — Peter's deliverance

☑ Evils that cripple true faith — *James 4:1–17*
☑ Rich unbelievers denounced — *James 5:1–6*
☑ Exhortation to patience — *James 5:7–12*
☑ Encouragement to prayer and confessing of faults — *James 5:13–20*
☑ Peter again imprisoned and freed — *Acts 12:3–17*
☑ Herod's rage — *Acts 12:18–19*
☑ Death of Herod — *Acts 12:20–23*
Paul's first missionary journey AD 45–47
☑ Paul and Barnabas sent out — *Acts 12:24–25, 13:1–3*
☑ They preach in Cyprus — *Acts 13:4–12*

☑ Mark leaves — *Acts 13:13*

FOR THOUGHT AND CONTEMPLATION

What a sad comment it is on human nature, that although the Church prayed for Peter's miraculous deliverance, they seemed unable to believe it when God brought it about. In fact, Peter appeared to have more trouble getting into the prayer meeting than he did in getting out of prison! How ready are you for a miracle?

"Jesus replied, 'What is impossible with men is possible with God.'" (Lk. 18:27, NIV)

---

## TUESDAY Week 47 — Paul's first missionary journey

☑ Paul preaches at Antioch (Pisidia) — *Acts 13:14–41*
☑ The Gentiles receive the message — *Acts 13:42–49*
☑ The Jews drive out Paul and Barnabas — *Acts 13:50–52*
☑ They minister in Iconium and Lystra — *Acts 14:1–18*
☑ Paul is stoned, but revives — *Acts 14:19–20*
☑ They return to Antioch — *Acts 14:21–26*
☑ They report back to the church — *Acts 14:27–28*
☑ The council at Jerusalem — *Acts 15:1–12, Galatians 2:7–10*

FOR THOUGHT AND CONTEMPLATION

What makes a missionary? Crossing the sea? No — seeing the cross! A missionary (a word, incidentally, you'll not find in the Bible) simply means 'someone with a mission'. As you study Paul's missionary strategy, spare a moment to consider your own. If you are a Christian, you are 'someone with a mission'. It may lie across the sea, but, on the other hand, it may lie across the street!

" …Forgetting what is behind and straining towards what is ahead, I press on towards the goal to win the prize for which God has called me heavenwards in Christ Jesus." (Phil. 3:13–14, NIV)

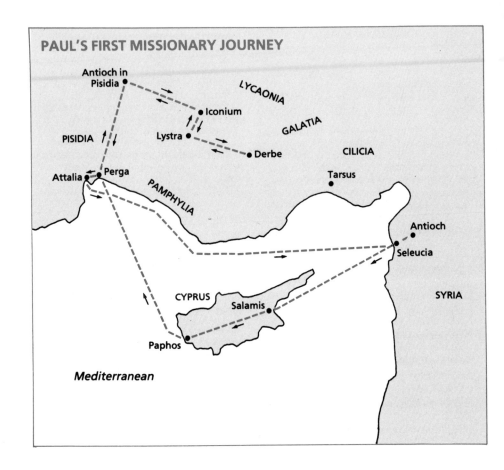

## PAUL'S FIRST MISSIONARY JOURNEY

Antioch in Pisidia
LYCAONIA
Iconium
GALATIA
PISIDIA
Lystra
Derbe
CILICIA
Attalia
Perga
PAMPHYLIA
Tarsus
Antioch
Seleucia
CYPRUS
Salamis
SYRIA
Paphos
Mediterranean

---

## WEDNESDAY Week 47 Paul's second missionary journey

☑ The decision of the Jerusalem council — *Acts 15:13–35*

Second missionary journey AD 50–54

☑ Peter visits Antioch — *Galatians 2:11–14*

☑ Paul and Barnabas separate — *Acts 15:36–41*

☑ Paul goes to Macedonia — *Acts 16:1–15*

☑ He casts out a spirit of divination — *Acts 16:16–21*

☑ Paul and Silas are imprisoned — *Acts 16:22–26*

☑ The Philippian jailer — *Acts 16:27–34*

☑ Paul and Silas freed — *Acts 16:35–40*

☑ They preach at Thessalonica and Berea — *Acts 17:1–13*

☑ Paul goes to Athens — *Acts 17:14–15*

FOR THOUGHT AND CONTEMPLATION

Paul was not only an effective disciple, but an effective *discipler*. He took Silas and discipled him in the methods of the Gospel. Yesterday we asked you to consider your own missionary strategy. Part of that might be to establish some new Christian in the faith. Ask God to show you someone whom you can disciple, then begin to pray for and share with that person as much and as often as you can.

---

"Don't let anyone look down on you because you are young, but set an example for the believers in speech, in life, in love, in faith and in purity." (1 Tim. 4:12, NIV)

## A BIRD'S EYE VIEW OF 1 and 2 THESSALONIANS

Place in the Bible:
Thirteenth and fourteenth New Testament books; eighth and ninth letters.
Written by:
Paul.
Special feature:
The second coming of Christ.
Jesus and the letters of 1 and 2 Thessalonians:
Jesus' return is mentioned over three hundred times in the New Testament, and in 1 Thessalonians 4:17–18 it is meant to encourage Paul's readers.
Teaching:
1 Thessalonians is Paul's letter of encouragement to a group of very new Christians. 2 Thessalonians was written to counter the erroneous ideas of false teachers who appear to have convinced some Thessalonian Christians that the day of the Lord had already arrived. Paul tells them that this is untrue and that certain events will occur prior to Christ's return.
A verse to remember:
"... warn those who are idle, encourage the timid, help the weak, be patient with everyone" (1 Thess. 5.14).

---

**THURSDAY Week 47** Paul teaches in Greece

☑ Paul preaches about the true God — *Acts 17:16–34*

☑ Paul goes to Corinth — *Acts 18:1–11*

☑ Paul before Gallio — *Acts 18:12–17*

☑ The first Thessalonian letter: Their faith, love and patience — *1 Thessalonians 1:1–10*

☑ Paul's integrity — *1 Thessalonians 2:1–12*

☑ Their reception of Paul's message — *1 Thessalonians 2:13–20*

☑ Timothy is sent to encourage them — *1 Thessalonians 3:1–8*

☑ Paul's prayer — *1 Thessalonians 3:9–13*

FOR THOUGHT AND CONTEMPLATION

Someone has described the task of tracing Paul's missionary journeys through the New Testament as "like tracking a bleeding hare across the snow". It seemed that wherever he went, he suffered great persecution and, at times, sustained severe bodily harm. What was the secret of his strong spiritual drive? Turn to 2 Corinthians 5:14 and see. Is this your secret too?

"I have fought the good fight, I have finished the race, I have kept the faith." (2 Tim. 4:7, NIV)

---

**FRIDAY Week 47** The Thessalonian letters

☑ Exhortations to love and purity — *1 Thessalonians 4:1–12*

☑ Comfort concerning those who have died — *1 Thessalonians 4:13–18*

☑ The Lord's return — *1 Thessalonians 5:1–11*

☑ Other instructions and conclusion — *1 Thessalonians 5:12–28*

☑ Second Thessalonian letter: Comfort in persecution — *2 Thessalonians 1:1–12*

☑ The coming of Christ — *2 Thessalonians 2:1–12*

☑ Instruction in conduct — *2 Thessalonians 2:13–17, 3:1–15*

☑ Final prayer — *2 Thessalonians 3:16–18*

☑ End of Paul's second journey — *Acts 18:18–22*

FOR THOUGHT AND CONTEMPLATION

Are you aware that the Christians at Thessalonica were comparatively *new* believers? Yet in the short space of these letters, Paul touches on some of the deepest doctrines of the faith. How sad that so many of today's Christians are still 'spiritual babes', living on 'milk' rather than 'meat'. Is it time *you* grew up?

"When I was a child, I talked like a child, I thought like a child, I reasoned like a child. When I became a man, I put childish ways behind me." (1 Cor. 13:11, NIV)

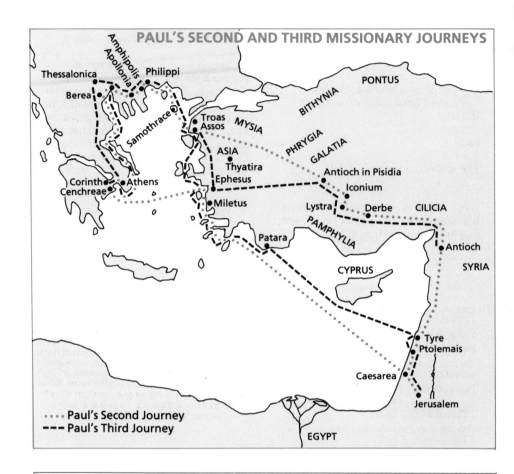

## PAUL'S SECOND AND THIRD MISSIONARY JOURNEYS

Amphipolis
Apollonia
Thessalonica
Philippi
PONTUS
Berea
BITHYNIA
Troas
Samothrace
Assos
MYSIA
ASIA
PHRYGIA
GALATIA
Thyatira
Antioch in Pisidia
Corinth
Athens
Ephesus
Iconium
Cenchreae
Miletus
Lystra
Derbe
CILICIA
PAMPHYLIA
Patara
Antioch
CYPRUS
SYRIA
Tyre
Ptolemais
Caesarea
Jerusalem
•••• Paul's Second Journey
--- Paul's Third Journey
EGYPT

---

**Paul's third missionary journey**

Third missionary journey AD 54–58

☑ Antioch to Ephesus — *Acts 18:23–28*
☑ Paul teaches at Ephesus — *Acts 19:1–12*
☑ Jewish exorcists disgraced — *Acts 19:13–20*
☑ Demetrius stirs up trouble — *Acts 19:21–32*
☑ The city clerk calms the crowd — *Acts 19:33–41*
☑ First letter to the Corinthians: Paul's greeting — *1 Corinthians 1:1–9*
☑ Divisions in the church — *1 Corinthians 1:10–16*
☑ The power of the Gospel — *1 Corinthians 1:17–31*
☑ God's wisdom revealed by the Spirit — *1 Corinthians 2:1–16*

FOR THOUGHT AND CONTEMPLATION

Wherever Paul went, he left behind him men and women upon whose lives he had made a tremendous spiritual impact. You may not be able to make as much impact as Paul, but you ought to be able to make *some* impact. Someone once wrote: "The world doesn't need a definition of religion so much as a demonstration of it." How much impact are you making upon the people you meet day by day?

---

"My message and my preaching were not with wise and persuasive words, but with a demonstration of the Spirit's power." (1 Cor. 2:4, NIV)

## A BIRD'S EYE VIEW OF 1 CORINTHIANS

**Place in the Bible:**
Seventh New Testament book; second letter.
**Written by:**
Paul.
**Jesus and the letter of 1 Corinthians:**
Jesus is seen as being relevant to all areas of a Christian's life, for He "has become for us wisdom from God — that is, our righteousness, holiness and redemption" (1 Cor. 1:30).
**Teaching:**
Paul gives advice on divisions between Christians; incest; Christians taking each other to court; Christian freedom being abused; worship services getting out of control; getting married or staying single; food which had been consecrated to idols; women wearing veils; spiritual gifts; and what the resurrection from the dead should mean for Christ's followers.
**A verse to remember:**
"Do you not know that your body is a temple of the Holy Spirit, who is in you, whom you have received from God? You are not your own; you were bought at a price. Therefore honour God with your body" (1 Cor. 6:19–20).

---

**SUNDAY Week 48** ## Straight talking

☑ Christian service evaluated — *1 Corinthians 3:1–15*

☑ The temple of God — *1 Corinthians 3:16–17*

☑ All things are ours — *1 Corinthians 3:18–23*

☑ Paul's apostleship — *1 Corinthians 4:1–13*

☑ Paul as a father in Christ — *1 Corinthians 4:14–21*

☑ The Corinthians rebuked concerning incest — *1 Corinthians 5:1–8*

☑ Discipline of sinning believers — *1 Corinthians 5:9–13*

☑ Lawsuits rebuked — *1 Corinthians 6:1–8*

☑ The sacredness of the body — *1 Corinthians 6:9–20*

FOR THOUGHT AND CONTEMPLATION

The ministry of the great apostle Paul was not only winning, but winnowing. He knew no church could grow when its members persisted in their sinful ways — hence his scathing challenges and rebukes. Do any of Paul's words hit home with you? Then do something about it— *now.*

---

"Therefore, if anyone is in Christ, he is a new creation; the old has gone, the new has come!" (2 Cor. 5:17, NIV)

---

**MONDAY Week 48** ## Paul answers questions

☑ Questions about marriage — *1 Corinthians 7:1–16*

☑ Advice to remain in the same state — *1 Corinthians 7:17–31*

☑ Advantages of singleness — *1 Corinthians 7:32–40*

☑ Concerning meat offered to idols — *1 Corinthians 8:1–6*

☑ Do not cause a brother to sin — *1 Corinthians 8:7–13*

☑ Paul's rights as an apostle — *1 Corinthians 9:1–14*

☑ He waives them — *1 Corinthians 9:15–23*

☑ His unfading crown — *1 Corinthians 9:24–27*

FOR THOUGHT AND CONTEMPLATION

If you had the privilege of asking Paul a question bearing on some aspect of the Christian life, what would it be? Paul may not be here to answer your enquiry, but keep in mind that every problem relating to Christian life and experience *is answered somewhere in the Word of God.* The better you know your Bible, the more readily you will discover the answers.

---

"Do your best to present yourself to God as one approved, a workman who does not need to be ashamed and who correctly handles the word of truth." (2 Tim. 2:15, NIV)

# Paul instructs the church

☑ Jewish heritage reviewed — *1 Corinthians 10:1–14*

☑ No compromise in relation to the Lord's Supper — *1 Corinthians 10:15–22*

☑ Doing all to God's glory — *1 Corinthians 10:23–33*

☑ Paul corrects some abuses — *1 Corinthians 11:1–16*

☑ Right and wrong celebration of the Lord's Supper — *1 Corinthians 11:17–22, 27–34*

☑ Use of spiritual gifts — *1 Corinthians 12:1–11*

☑ Comparison with the human body — *1 Corinthians 12:12–31*

**FOR THOUGHT AND CONTEMPLATION**

**Although we are indebted to Paul for clear** teaching on many issues, one of the greatest debts we owe him is for his instructions on the threefold aspect of Holy Communion. Someone has defined those three aspects in these words — *retrospect, introspect, and prospect.* Can you discover them?

---

" …Jesus took bread, gave thanks and broke it, and gave it to his disciples, saying, 'Take and eat; this is my body.' Then he took the cup, gave thanks and offered it to them, saying, 'Drink from it, all of you. This is my blood of the new covenant, which is poured out for many …'" (Matt. 26:26–28, NIV)

---

# Love — the greatest gift

☑ The centrality of love — *1 Corinthians 13:1–13*

☑ Prophecy to be desired — *1 Corinthians 14:1–11*

☑ Prophecy builds up the church — *1 Corinthians 14:12–25*

☑ Orderly worship — *1 Corinthians 14:26–40*

☑ Paul proves the resurrection — *1 Corinthians 15:1–4, 8–28*

☑ Objections answered — *1 Corinthians 15:29–49*

☑ From mortal to immortal — *1 Corinthians 15:50–54*

☑ The believer's triumph — *1 Corinthians 15:55–58*

**FOR THOUGHT AND CONTEMPLATION**

Most definitions of love focus on exciting or romantic feelings. But although love may *contain* feeling, genuine love is really an action of the will. Charles Finney described it like this: "Love is the bringing about of the highest good in the life of another individual." Examine 1 Corinthians 13 again, and see whether the emphasis is on feelings or the will!

---

"Whoever does not love does not know God, because God is love." (1 Jn.4:8, NIV)

---

# Paul shares his heart

☑ The collection for the poor — *1 Corinthians 16:1–12*

☑ Conclusion — *1 Corinthians 16:13–24*

☑ Paul goes to Macedonia — *1 Timothy 1:3, Acts 20:1*

☑ Second Corinthian letter: God's comfort in trials — *2 Corinthians 1:1–14*

☑ Paul's reasons for not coming — *2 Corinthians 1:15–24*

☑ The repentant offender to be restored — *2 Corinthians 2:1–11*

☑ Paul's triumphant ministry — *2 Corinthians 2:12–17*

☑ The glorious Gospel — *2 Corinthians 3:1–18*

**FOR THOUGHT AND CONTEMPLATION**

**How do you respond to criticism — with a** grudge or with grace? In 2 Corinthians, Paul tells how his character and conduct were under attack. He was charged with fickleness, pride, boasting, weakness, uncouth speech, meanness, dishonesty and unsoundness of mind. How does he respond? Read 2 Corinthians 2:14 once again and you'll see. Is this how you come out when under attack?

---

"Blessed are you when people insult you, persecute you and falsely say all kinds of evil against you because of me. Rejoice and be glad, because great is your reward in heaven …" (Matt. 5:11–12, NIV)

## A BIRD'S EYE VIEW OF
## 1 and 2 TIMOTHY, TITUS

Place in the Bible:
Fifteenth to seventeenth New Testament books; tenth to twelfth letters.
Written by:
Paul.
Jesus and the letters of 1 Timothy, 2 Timothy and Titus:
1 Timothy reminds us that Jesus is the go-between between God and man (1 Tim. 2:5–6). 2 Timothy 1:10 says Jesus came to earth to destroy death and to bring life. Titus gives a breathtaking statement about Jesus' activity in our lives: "Jesus Christ ... gave himself for us to redeem us from all wickedness and to purify for himself a people that are his very own, eager to do what is good" (Titus 2:13–14).
Teaching:
Paul gives instructions to Titus and Timothy about how they are to exercise oversight in their Christian fellowships.
A verse to remember:
"... he saved us, not because of righteous things we had done, but because of his mercy." (Titus 3:5)

---

**FRIDAY Week 48** ## The Christian as a steward

☑ Paul's sufferings and reward — *2 Corinthians 4:1–18*

☑ The apostle's hope — *2 Corinthians 5:1–15*

☑ The new creation — *2 Corinthians 5:16–21*

☑ The proof of Paul's ministry — *2 Corinthians 6:1–10*

☑ Separation from unbelievers required — *2 Corinthians 6:11–18, 7:1*

☑ Paul's heart revealed — *2 Corinthians 7:2–16*

☑ An example of giving — *2 Corinthians 8:1–10*

☑ Encouragement to give — *2 Corinthians 8:11–15*

FOR THOUGHT AND CONTEMPLATION

Some Christians give like Moses' rock — only when they are struck. Some give like a sponge — only when they are squeezed. But others give like the flowers — because they delight to give. What kind of giver are you?

"Each man should give what he has decided in his heart to give, not reluctantly or under compulsion, for God loves a cheerful giver." (2 Cor. 9:7, NIV)

---

## A BIRD'S EYE VIEW OF
## 2 CORINTHIANS

Place in the Bible:
Eighth New Testament book; third letter.
Written by:
Paul.
Jesus and the letter of 2 Corinthians:
In this letter Jesus Christ is presented as the Christian's Lord, "For we do not preach ourselves, but Jesus Christ as Lord, and ourselves as your servants for Jesus' sake" (2 Cor. 4:5).

Teaching:
Paul concentrates on two topics: suffering and glory. Seven times (1:8–11; 2:12–17; 4:16–18; 6:3–10; 7:5–8; 11:1–10; 11:21–29) Paul reiterates how the privilege of Christian leadership brings pain and misunderstanding in its wake. God's glory, which Moses knew, should be the experience of all Christians according to chapters 3—5.
A verse to remember:
"Therefore, if anyone is in Christ, he is a new creation; the old has gone, the new has come!" (2 Cor. 5:17).

---

**SATURDAY Week 48** ## Paul's thorn in the flesh

☑ Paul sends Titus — *2 Corinthians 8:16–24, 9:1–5*

☑ Results of generosity — *2 Corinthians 9:6–15*

☑ Paul defends his authority — *2 Corinthians 10:1–18*

☑ Paul's godly jealousy — *2 Corinthians 11:1–15*

☑ His boasting — *2 Corinthians 11:16–29*

☑ He glories in his weaknesses — *2 Corinthians 11:30–33*

☑ His visions of the Lord — *2 Corinthians 12:1–5*

☑ The thorn in the flesh — *2 Corinthians 12:6–10*

173

A good deal of debate has gone on down the centuries in relation to what exactly Paul's thorn in the flesh was. Some say it was weak eyesight; others that it was recurring malaria, or even a speech impediment. One wag said: "Paul had a thorn in the flesh, and we know little about it. If we had a thorn in the flesh, we would make sure everyone knew *everything* about it." True of you?

"These have come so that your faith — of greater worth than gold, which perishes even though refined by fire — may be proved genuine and may result in praise, glory and honour when Jesus Christ is revealed." (1 Pet. 1:7, NIV)

---

### SUNDAY Week 49 — Law and grace

☑ Paul's effective service — *2 Corinthians 12:11–18*

☑ His honest dealing — *2 Corinthians 12:19–21*

☑ Conclusion — *2 Corinthians 13:11–14*

☑ Paul travels to Corinth — *Acts 20:2–3*

☑ The Galatian letter: Paul's gospel from God — *Galatians 1:1–16, 20–24*

☑ His visit to Jerusalem — *Galatians 2:1–6*

☑ Justification by faith — *Galatians 2:15–21*

☑ Bondage under the law — *Galatians 3:1–18*

☑ The law brings us to Christ — *Galatians 3:19–29*

FOR THOUGHT AND CONTEMPLATION

There is a popular idea abroad today that we are only free when we have no restraints placed upon us: no laws, no authority, no responsibility. Galatians shows, as someone put it, that "freedom is not the right to do what we want, but the power to do what we ought".

" ...through Christ Jesus the law of the Spirit of life set me free from the law of sin and death." (Rom. 8:2, NIV)

---

### A BIRD'S EYE VIEW OF GALATIANS

**Place in the Bible:**
Ninth New Testament book; fourth letter.
**Written by:**
Paul.
**Jesus and the letter of Galatians:**
The transforming power of Jesus' cross delivers Christ's followers from the curse of the law: "Christ redeemed us from the curse of the law by becoming a curse for us, for it is written: 'Cursed is everyone who is hung on a tree.'" (Gal. 3:13).

**Teaching:**
Paul expresses his dismay that a group of Christians should revert to their legalistic way of living instead of continuing to live their Christian lives depending solely on Christ. Justification by faith, not by works of the law, is the urgent message of this book.
**A verse to remember:**
"I have been crucified with Christ and I no longer live, but Christ lives in me. The life I live in the body, I live by faith in the Son of God, who loved me and gave himself for me" (Gal. 2:20).

---

### MONDAY Week 49 — Paul's three great confessions

☑ Folly of legal observances — *Galatians 4:1–20*

☑ The bondwoman and the free woman — *Galatians 4:21–31*

☑ Freedom in Christ — *Galatians 5:1–15*

☑ The Spirit and the flesh — *Galatians 5:16–26*

☑ Various exhortations — *Galatians 6:1–10*

☑ Conclusion — *Galatians 6:11–18*

☑ Letter to the Romans: Introduction and prayer — *Romans 1:1–12*

☑ The power of the Gospel — *Romans 1:13–17*

☑ Man's universal sin — *Romans 1:18–32*

FOR THOUGHT AND CONTEMPLATION

Preachers are often at pains to point out that in Romans 1, Paul shares three great confessions concerning the Gospel of Christ: (1) I am a debtor (v. 14); (2) I am ready (v. 15); (3) I am not ashamed (v. 16). Reflect on these three statements for a few minutes and ask yourself: "Is this *my* attitude toward Christ's glorious Gospel?"

"I am not ashamed of the gospel, because it is the power of God for the salvation of everyone who believes; first for the Jew, then for the Gentile." (Rom. 1:16, NIV)

# Justification by faith

☑ All men to be judged by their deeds — *Romans 2:1–16*

☑ Circumcision alone is insufficient — *Romans 2:17–29*

☑ The advantages of being a Jew — *Romans 3:1–8*

☑ All mankind are sinners — *Romans 3:9–20*

☑ Justification by faith — *Romans 3:21–31*

☑ Abraham as an illustration — *Romans 4:1–25*

☑ Results of justification — *Romans 5:1–11*

☑ Adam and Christ contrasted — *Romans 5:12–21*

FOR THOUGHT AND CONTEMPLATION

Justification by faith is one of the greatest truths in the whole of Scripture. It means God accepts us *just-as-if* we had never sinned. Do you understand it? Give yourself this test. List all your Christian activities, then ask yourself: "Am I doing these things in order to be saved, or because I am saved?" If the answer is, "In order to be saved," then you need to think again.

---

"For all … are justified freely by his grace through the redemption that came by Christ Jesus." (Rom. 3:23–24, NIV)

---

## A BIRD'S EYE VIEW OF ROMANS

**Place in the Bible:**
Sixth New Testament book; first letter.
**Written by:**
Paul.
**Jesus and the letter of Romans:**
Jesus's death and resurrection are the basis for a Christian's salvation, according to Romans chapter 3:23–25, "all … are justified freely by his grace through the redemption that came by Christ Jesus. God presented him as a sacrifice of atonement, through faith in his blood."

**Teaching:**
Paul writes that everyone is condemned by God's perfect standard and that the only way a Jew or non-Jew can ever be accepted by God is through faith in Christ. Paul showed how the good news transformed peoples' relationship with God, and also with each other. How Christians are to live their spiritual lives is explained in chapters 6—8.
**A verse to remember:**
"I am not ashamed of the gospel, because it is the power of God for the salvation of everyone who believes: first for the Jew, then for the Gentile" (Rom 1:16).

---

WEDNESDAY Week 49 # Out of '7' into '8'

☑ Death to sin through baptism — *Romans 6:1–14*

☑ Servants of righteousness — *Romans 6:15–23*

☑ Believers united to Christ — *Romans 7:1–6*

☑ The purpose of the law — *Romans 7:7–13*

☑ The conflict between the old and new natures — *Romans 7:14–25*

☑ Freedom from condemnation — *Romans 8:1–9*

☑ The privileges of the child of God — *Romans 8:10–17*

☑ Future glory — *Romans 8:18–27*

☑ More than conquerors — *Romans 8:28–39*

FOR THOUGHT AND CONTEMPLATION

Christians sometimes ask each other: "Have you stepped out of '7' into '8' yet?" They refer, of course, to Romans chapters 7 and 8. In chapter 7, Paul is in deep bondage: in chapter 8, he is gloriously free. What accounts for the difference? *The Holy Spirit.* Has this experience happened to you? If not, ask God to do something for you — today.

---

"So if the Son sets you free, you will be free indeed." (Jn. 8:36, NIV)

---

Israel's future restoration

☑ Paul's concern for the Jews — *Romans 9:1–13*
☑ God's sovereignty — *Romans 9:14–29*
☑ Israel's present failure — *Romans 9:30–33*
☑ Paul's prayer for Israel — *Romans 10:1–4*
☑ The righteousness of faith — *Romans 10:5–11*
☑ Jew and Gentile equally in need — *Romans 10:12–21*
☑ Israel not finally rejected — *Romans 11:1–11*
☑ They will be grafted back — *Romans 11:12–21*
☑ Gentiles cautioned against pride — *Romans 11:22–32*
☑ Praise of God's wisdom and goodness — *Romans 11:33–36*

FOR THOUGHT AND CONTEMPLATION

**Ready for a searching test? Then here goes. In the three chapters you have read today, Paul shows his great knowledge of the Old Testament Scriptures by quoting from ten different books. How many can you identify? 1–4: good! 5–7: very good! 8–10: fantastic!**

"For prophecy never had its origin in the will of man, but men spoke from God as they were carried along by the Holy Spirit." (2 Pet. 1:21, NIV)

Practical applications

☑ Call for dedication — *Romans 12:1–2*
☑ Faithful use of spiritual gifts — *Romans 12:3–8*
☑ The transformed life — *Romans 12:9–21*
☑ Obedience to authorities — *Romans 13:1–7*
☑ Love as the fulfilment of the law — *Romans 13:8–14*
☑ Warning against judging — *Romans 14:1–13*
☑ Do not offend a brother — *Romans 14:14–23*
☑ Maintaining unity — *Romans 15:1–14*
☑ Paul's future plans — *Romans 15:15–29*
☑ His request for prayer — *Romans 15:30–33*

FOR THOUGHT AND CONTEMPLATION

**In the first eleven chapters of Romans, Paul has discussed the key doctrines of the Christian faith. Now, however, he moves from doctrine to duty — a necessary consequence. What we believe *must* affect the way we behave. If it doesn't, then it is not 'sound doctrine'.**

"All Scripture is God-breathed and is useful for teaching, rebuking, correcting and training in righteousness, so that the man of God may be thoroughly equipped for every good work." (2 Tim. 3:16–17, NIV)

Paul goes to Jerusalem

☑ Personal greetings — *Romans 16:1–16*
☑ Warning against those who cause divisions — *Romans 16:17–20*
☑ Further greetings and conclusion — *Romans 16:21–27*
☑ Paul at Troas — *Acts 20:4–12*
☑ Paul meets the Ephesian elders — *Acts 20:13–17*
☑ His farewell address — *Acts 20:18–38*
☑ From Miletus to Caesarea — *Acts 21:1–9*
☑ Agabus' prophecy — *Acts 21:10–12*
Paul goes to Jerusalem AD 58
☑ Paul travels to Jerusalem — *Acts 21:13–19*
☑ He takes a vow — *Acts 21:20–26*

FOR THOUGHT AND CONTEMPLATION

**Did Paul disobey the Holy Spirit in going to Jerusalem? Acts 21:4 certainly seems to suggest so. How careful we must be that our enthusiasm to work for God does not lead us to go ahead of the guidance of God. God's will must take precedence over God's work.**

"Instead, you ought to say, 'If it is the Lord's will, we will live and do this or that.'" (Jas. 4:15, NIV)

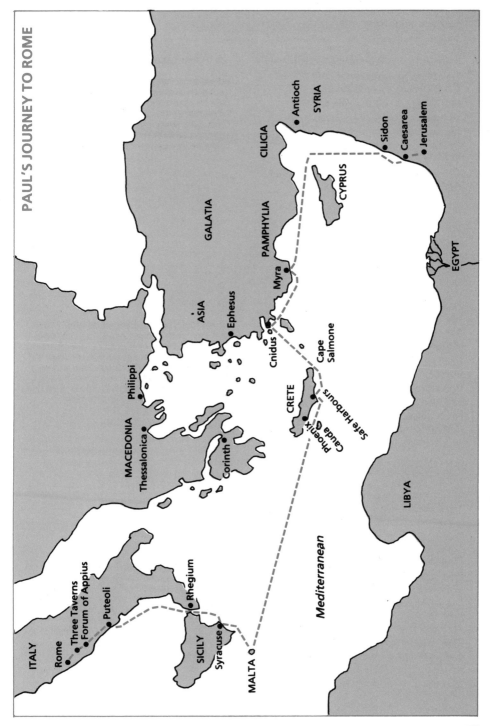

# Paul before the Jews

☑ Paul is seized in the Temple — *Acts 21:27–40*
☑ His defence before the Jews — *Acts 22:1–21*
☑ The Jews' rage — *Acts 22:22–25*
☑ Paul is released — *Acts 22:26–30*
☑ Paul speaks before the council — *Acts 23:1–5*
☑ Dissension between the Pharisees and Sadducees — *Acts 23:6–10*
☑ The Lord's promise — *Acts 23:11*
☑ The Jews' plot is discovered — *Acts 23:12–22*
☑ Paul sent to Caesarea — *Acts 23:23–35*

**FOR THOUGHT AND CONTEMPLATION**

Whether or not we believe Paul was mistaken in going to Jerusalem, it is certain that his arrest there was due to his clear emphasis on the superiority of the Christian faith over every other religion. If you were arrested on that selfsame charge, would there be enough evidence to convict you?

"Jews demand miraculous signs and Greeks look for wisdom, but we preach Christ crucified: a stumbling block to Jews and foolishness to Gentiles." (1 Cor. 1:22–23, NIV)

---

# Paul before the Romans

☑ Tertullus accuses Paul — *Acts 24:1–9*
☑ Paul's defence before Felix — *Acts 24:10–21*
☑ Paul kept prisoner at Caesarea — *Acts 24:22–27*
☑ Paul before Festus — *Acts 25:1–9*
☑ He appeals to Caesar — *Acts 25:10–12*
☑ Festus confers with Agrippa — *Acts 25:13–27*
☑ Paul before Agrippa — *Acts 26:1–23*
☑ He persuades Festus and Agrippa of his innocence — *Acts 26:24–32*

**FOR THOUGHT AND CONTEMPLATION**

When faced with a difficult decision, Felix took the path of least resistance. For two years he let Paul's case drag on — all because it was politically inexpedient to release him. Are you facing a difficult decision at the moment? Then here's some good advice — decide *first* to do what God wants, and then all other decisions will fall into line.

"Trust in the Lord with all your heart and lean not on your own understanding; in all your ways acknowledge him, and he will make your paths straight." (Prov. 3:5–6, NIV)

---

# Paul's journey to Rome

☑ Paul sails towards Rome — *Acts 27:1–11*
☑ They are caught in a storm — *Acts 27:12–20*
☑ Paul takes command — *Acts 27:21–38*
☑ They escape safely to land — *Acts 27:39–44*
☑ The natives receive them kindly — *Acts 28:1–10*
Journey to Rome AD 60–61
☑ They travel on to Rome — *Acts 28:11–16*
☑ Letter to Philemon: Greetings — *Philemon 1:1–7*
☑ His request on behalf of Onesimus — *Philemon 1:8–22*
☑ Conclusion — *Philemon 1:23–25*

**FOR THOUGHT AND CONTEMPLATION**

Paul's short letter to Philemon is an excellent illustration of what some people call 'lathering before you shave'. This means emphasising a person's good points before you confront them with their bad points. See how Paul commends before he commands. Now make a decision today that, from now on, you will do the same.

"Be devoted to one another in brotherly love. Honour one another above yourselves." (Rom. 12:10, NIV)

## A BIRD'S EYE VIEW OF PHILEMON

**Place in the Bible:**
Eighteenth New Testament book; thirteenth letter.
**Written by:**
Paul.
**Special feature:**
The only personal letter of Paul's in the New Testament.
**Jesus and the letter to Philemon:**
The whole letter can be seen as an analogy of the forgiveness a believer discovers in Christ.
**Teaching:**
Paul reminds Philemon of the mercy and grace he has received from Christ and pleads with him to show similar kindness to his runaway slave.

**A verse to remember:**
"He is very dear to me but even dearer to you, both as a man and as a brother in the Lord. So ... welcome him as you would welcome me" (Philemon 16–17).

---

## WEDNESDAY Week 50 Paul writes to the Colossians

☑ Paul's prayer for the Colossians — *Colossians 1:1–14*

☑ The pre-eminence of Christ — *Colossians 1:15–23*

☑ Paul's labour of love — *Colossians 1:24–29, 2:1–3*

☑ His joy in them — *Colossians 2:4–7*

☑ Warning against erroneous beliefs — *Colossians 2:8–23*

☑ The believer's walk — *Colossians 3:1–25, 4:1–6*

☐ Closing greetings and instructions — *Colossians 4:7–18*

**FOR THOUGHT AND CONTEMPLATION**

One of the most important phrases in the Bible is the one found in Colossians 1:27: "Christ in you, the hope of glory." One great preacher, while meditating on these words one day, put his conclusions in this way: "Life with Christ is an endless hope: without Him, it is a hopeless end."

---

"I have been crucified with Christ and I no longer live, but Christ lives in me. The life I live in the body, I live by faith in the Son of God, who loved me and gave himself for me." (Gal. 2:20, NIV)

---

## A BIRD'S EYE VIEW OF COLOSSIANS

**Place in the Bible:**
Twelfth New Testament book; seventh letter.
**Written by:**
Paul.
**Jesus and the letter of Colossians:**
His is the all sufficient Saviour according to 1:19–20, "For God was pleased to have all his fulness dwell in him, and through him to reconcile to himself all things ... by making peace through his blood, shed on the cross."
**Teaching:**
Christ is supreme and provides complete salvation. The desire to hang on to Jewish ideas about food laws, festivals and circumcision, and to worship angels should evaporate at the sight of Christ.

**A verse to remember:**
"We proclaim him, admonishing and teaching everyone with all wisdom, so that we may present everyone perfect in Christ" (Col. 1:28).

---

## THURSDAY Week 50 The letter to the Ephesians

☐ The believer's position in Christ — *Ephesians 1:1–14*

☑ Paul's prayer for wisdom and revelation — *Ephesians 1:15–23*

☑ The riches of God's grace — *Ephesians 2:1–10*

☑ Jews and Gentiles one in Christ — *Ephesians 2:11–22*

☑ The mystery of the Church — *Ephesians 3:1–12*

☑ Paul's second prayer — *Ephesians 3:13:21*

☑ Ministries in the Church — *Ephesians 4:1–16*

☑ The walk of the believer — *Ephesians 4:17–32*

Are you feeling a little jaded or under the weather today? Then here's a guaranteed cure. Count the blessings and privileges you have in Christ as outlined in Ephesians 1:3–14. We'll be surprised if you don't break out into a paean of praise. In the Greek this whole section (yes, from verse 3 to verse 14) is one long continuous sentence. It's seemingly endless — just like God's blessings!

---

"Blessed be the Lord, who daily bears us up; God is our salvation." (Psa. 68:19, RSV)

---

## A BIRD'S EYE VIEW OF EPHESIANS

**Place in the Bible:**
Tenth New Testament book; fifth letter.
**Written by:**
Paul.
**Jesus and the letter of Ephesians:**
Paul's phrase "in Christ", or its equivalent, appears over thirty times in Ephesians. What Christ's followers are can be seen from what they are "in Christ".
**Teaching:**
Paul wants to help Christ's followers to become more conscious of their relationship to God "in Christ" and to go to Christ for spiritual strength. So in chapter 1 he outlines the privileges open to all Christians: redemption, power, grace, adoption and heavenly citizenship. The last three chapters give over thirty directions about how they should behave as followers of Christ.

**A verse to remember:**
"Live a life worthy of the calling you have received. Be completely humble and gentle; be patient, bearing with one another in love" (Eph. 4:1–2).

---

FRIDAY Week 50 — ## The exaltation of Christ

☑ Life in the Spirit — *Ephesians 5:1–21*
☑ Application to particular relationships — *Ephesians 5:22–33, 6:1–9*
☑ The armour of God — *Ephesians 6:10–18*
☑ Conclusion — *Ephesians 6:19–24*
☑ Letter to the Philippians: Paul's thanksgiving and prayer — *Philippians 1:1–11*
☑ He encourages them — *Philippians 1:12–30*
☑ Christ the believer's example — *Philippians 2:1–18*
☑ Paul's future plans — *Philippians 2:19–30*

### FOR THOUGHT AND CONTEMPLATION

The letter to the Philippians was written in a prison cell, but no one would ever know it. One preacher says of this letter: "Philippians with one accord, tells of rejoicing in the Lord." Paul had learned to triumph over all his circumstances. Have you?

---

"I am not saying this because I am in need, for I have learned to be content whatever the circumstances." (Phil. 4:11, NIV)

---

## A BIRD'S EYE VIEW OF PHILIPPIANS

**Place in the Bible:**
Eleventh New Testament book; sixth letter.
**Written by:**
Paul.
**Special features:**
The characteristic feature of this letter is the great emphasis on joy.
**Jesus and the letter of Philippians:**
Paul explains how Jesus gives His power in chapter 4:13, "I can do everything through him who gives me strength".
**Teaching:**
In addition to the theme of joy Paul teaches how believers are to be like Christ, especially in His humility, and so solve their problem of disunity. Paul tells his readers ten times how they are to "think" or view life: "Your attitude should be the same as that of Christ Jesus" (Phil. 2:5).
**A verse to remember:**
"For to me, to live is Christ and to die is gain" (Phil. 1:21).

# Paul in Rome

☑ Paul's earnest desire — *Philippians 3:1–21*
☑ Exhortation to stand firm — *Philippians 4:1–9*
☑ Paul's contentment — *Philippians 4:10–19*
☑ Conclusion — *Philippians 4:20–23*
☑ Paul's conference with the Jews — *Acts 28:17–29*
☑ Paul stays in Rome — *Acts 28:30–31*

Paul released from prison AD 64

☑ First letter to Timothy: Greeting — *1 Timothy 1:1–2*
☑ The purpose of the law — *1 Timothy 1:4–11*
☑ Paul's call — *1 Timothy 1:12–17*
☑ His charge to Timothy — *1 Timothy 1:18–20*

FOR THOUGHT AND CONTEMPLATION

One Christian wrote out Philippians 4:8 in big bold letters and hung it by his television set. "Whatsoever things are true ... honest ... just ... pure ... lovely ... of good report ... think on *these* things." He said it cut down his viewing by 50%. Worth emulating?

"Do not conform any longer to the pattern of this world, but be transformed by the renewing of your mind. Then you will be able to test and approve what God's will is — his good, pleasing and perfect will." (Rom. 12:2, NIV)

## FIRST ADAM — LAST ADAM

| First Adam | | Last Adam |
|---|---|---|
| He brought sin and death into the world | The nature of the act | He brought righteousness and life into the world |
| In the Garden of Eden | The place of the act | On the cross of Calvary |
| Disobedience *(Gen. 3:6)* | The reason for the act | Obedience *(Lk. 22:42)* |
| Condemnation<br>1. Immediate judgment upon himself.<br>2. Imputed judgment upon his posterity.<br>3. Eternal judgment upon all. | The results from the act | Justification<br>1. Immediate justification.<br>2. Imputed righteousness.<br>3. Eternal life. |
| The **law** served to demonstrate the **seriousness** of his act | Relationship of the act to law and grace | **Grace** served to demonstrate the **"much more"** of his act *(Rom. 5:9, 10, 15, 17, 20)* |
| It abounded | The scope of the act | It abounded much more |

# Paul instructs Timothy

☑ Guidance for the church — *1 Timothy 2:1–15*
☑ Qualifications of elders and deacons — *1 Timothy 3:1–16*
☑ Timothy to be an example — *1 Timothy 4:1–16*
☑ The work of a minister — *1 Timothy 5:1–16*
☑ Elders to be respected — *1 Timothy 5:17–25*
☑ Value of godliness with contentment — *1 Timothy 6:1–10*
☑ Paul's charge to Timothy — *1 Timothy 6:11–19*
☑ Conclusion — *1 Timothy 6:20–21*

FOR THOUGHT AND CONTEMPLATION

'Good manners' are a missing ingredient, not only in contemporary society, but also in many of today's Christian communities. Do you know how to "behave in the household of God"? (1 Tim. 3:15) Absorb Paul's teaching in this letter, and never again will you be at a loss to know how to behave in the Master's House.

" ...everything should be done in a fitting and orderly way." (1 Cor. 14:40, NIV)

Order in the Church

☑ Letter to Titus: Selection of elders — *Titus 1:1–16*

☑ Pattern for Christian living — *Titus 2:1–15, 3:1–7*

☑ Importance of good works — *Titus 3:8–11*

☑ Final directions — *Titus 3:12–15*

☑ Peter's first letter: The Christian's security — *1 Peter 1:1–12*

☑ Exhortation to holiness and love — *1 Peter 1:13–25*

☑ A chosen people — *1 Peter 2:1–10*

☑ Patience in suffering — *1 Peter 2:11–20*

☑ Christ's example — *1 Peter 2:21–25*

FOR THOUGHT AND CONTEMPLATION

Read carefully Paul's letter to Titus. It contains some timely words of advice for every Christian, irrespective of their age, sex or level of maturity. Have you spotted a deficiency in your own life, or that of your church, while reading these passages today? Then ask God just what you should do to bring things into harmony with His purposes.

" ...each one should retain the place in life that the Lord assigned to him and to which God has called him." (1 Cor. 7:17, NIV)

---

Christ our example

☑ The life of peace — *1 Peter 3:1–13*

☑ Keeping a good conscience — *1 Peter 3:14–22*

☑ The righteous life — *1 Peter 4:1–11*

☑ Rejoicing in sufferings — *1 Peter 4:12–19*

☑ Exhortation to be strong — *1 Peter 5:1–9*

☑ Concluding prayer — *1 Peter 5:10–14*

☑ Letter to the Hebrews: Christ greater than angels — *Hebrews 1:1–14*

☑ He took on man's nature — *Hebrews 2:1–9*

☑ His sufferings and victory — *Hebrews 2:10–18*

FOR THOUGHT AND CONTEMPLATION

Are you experiencing some pressure and suffering at the moment? Then make sure you are suffering for doing what is *right*, not for what is *wrong*. Remember to imitate Christ who, "when He was reviled, reviled not again" — then you will be sure of an eternal reward.

"But how is it to your credit if you receive a beating for doing wrong and endure it? But if you suffer for doing good and you endure it, this is commendable before God." (1 Pet. 2:20, NIV)

---

## A BIRD'S EYE VIEW OF 1 and 2 PETER

**Place in the Bible:**
Twenty-first and twenty-second New Testament books; sixteenth and seventeenth letters.

**Written by:**
Peter.

**Jesus and the letters of 1 and 2 Peter:**
Suffering for Christ and Christ's own suffering are brought together in 1 Peter 4:12–13. Peter recalls Jesus' transfiguration (2 Peter 1:17–18) and writes about his future coming in glory (3:10–13).

**Teaching:**
In 1 Peter some Christians were already facing persecution for their faith, while others were about to be persecuted and so Peter writes to bring a message of Christian hope, and to comfort them. 2 Peter counters a different problem — an attack from within — false teachers.

**A verse to remember:**
"... no prophecy of Scripture came about by the prophet's own interpretation. For prophecy never had its origin in the will of man, but men spoke from God as they were carried along by the Holy Spirit" (2 Pet. 1:20–21).

**Christ's pre-eminence**

☑ Christ greater than Moses — *Hebrews 3:1–6*
☑ Warning against unbelief — *Hebrews 3:7–13*
☑ Necessity for faith — *Hebrews 3:14–19*
☑ Our Sabbath rest — *Hebrews 4:1–13*
☑ Christ our High Priest — *Hebrews 4:14–16, 5:1–14*
☑ Exhortation to go on to maturity — *Hebrews 6:1–12*
☑ God's unchangeableness — *Hebrews 6:13–20*
☑ Melchizedek a type of Christ — *Hebrews 7:1–28*

FOR THOUGHT AND CONTEMPLATION
The truth of Christ's pre-eminence must be applied, not only to the laws and personalities of the Old Testament, but equally to the many aspects of our own daily lives. Do you, for example, see Christ as superior to your wife, your husband, your bank account, your job and your career? Remember, if you do not crown Him Lord of all, you do not crown Him Lord at all!

---

"For by him all things were created: things in heaven and on earth, visible and invisible ... all things were created by him and for him, He is before all things, and in him all things hold together." (Col. 1:16–17, NIV)

---

## A BIRD'S EYE VIEW OF HEBREWS

**Place in the Bible:**
Nineteenth New Testament book; fourteenth letter.
**Written by:**
Author unknown.
**Jesus and the letter of Hebrews:**
In Hebrews Jesus is portrayed as our Great High Priest.
**Teaching:**
Followers of Christ should press on until they become mature Christians. Jesus is better than angels, Moses and the whole Old Testament priesthood because Christ's sacrifice was totally effective in dealing with sin. So the readers are told to stop hankering after Jewish practices and beliefs. They are to keep their eyes fixed on Christ.

**A verse to remember:**
"Unlike the other high priests, he does not need to offer sacrifices day after day, first for his own sins, and then for the sins of the people. He sacrificed for their sins once for all when he offered himself" (Heb. 7:27).

---

**The new covenant**

☑ The true High Priest — *Hebrews 8:1–5*
☑ The new covenant is superior — *Hebrews 8:6–13*
☑ Description of the tabernacle — *Hebrews 9:1–10*
☑ Its fulfilment in Christ — *Hebrews 9:11–22*
☑ Christ's sufficient sacrifice — *Hebrews 9:23–28, 10:1–18*
☑ True worship — *Hebrews 10:19–25*
☑ Rejection of Christ fatal — *Hebrews 10:26–31*
☑ The believer's reward — *Hebrews 10:32–39*
☑ Examples of faith — *Hebrews 11:1·10*

FOR THOUGHT AND CONTEMPLATION

It is important to keep in mind that every Bible doctrine is designed to affect our behaviour. Because Christ is a *better* High Priest ... because He has provided a *better* way ... because He initiates a *better* covenant ... we must respond to that truth with *better* obedience. Make up your mind that, with God's help, you will be a *better* Christian today than you were yesterday.

---

"For those God foreknew he also predestined to be conformed to the likeness of his Son, that he might be the firstborn among many brothers." (Rom. 8:29, NIV)

---

# The superiority of faith

☐ The faith of the patriarchs — *Hebrews 11:11–22*

☑ Moses and other Old Testament examples — *Hebrews 11:23–40*

☑ Exhortation to persevere — *Hebrews 12:1–11*

☑ Following peace and holiness — *Hebrews 12:12–17*

☑ Superiority of New Testament dispensation — *Hebrews 12:18–29*

☑ Various exhortations — *Hebrews 13:1–19*

☑ Conclusion — *Hebrews 13:20–25*

☑ Peter's second letter: Adding to our faith — *2 Peter 1:1–11*

**FOR THOUGHT AND CONTEMPLATION**

What is your favourite definition of faith? A little boy, when asked to define faith, said: "Faith is believing what you know isn't true"! The best definitions, of course, are always Scriptural ones. According to Hebrews, faith is "the evidence of things not seen". "Seeing is believing" is the world's motto. "Not seeing is believing" is the Christian's motto. And why? Because "faith is the evidence of things *not seen.*"

" ...everyone born of God overcomes the world. This is the victory that has overcome the world, even our faith." (1 Jn. 5:4, NIV)

## A BIRD'S EYE VIEW OF JUDE

**Place in the Bible:**
Twenty-sixth New Testament book; twenty-first letter.

**Written by:**
Jude.

**Special features:**
Jude draws illustrations from The book of Enoch (vv. 14–15) and The Assumption of Moses (v. 9) which are not in the Bible. Jude does not put them on the same level as Scripture, but realised his readers would be familiar with them.

**Teaching:**
Ungodly men were threatening to poison the church with immoral ideas and denial of the Gospel. Jude calls his readers to stand firm and persevere in the faith.

**A verse to remember:**
"To him who is able to keep you from falling and to present you before his glorious presence without fault and with great joy — to the only God our Saviour be glory, majesty, power and authority, through Jesus Christ ..." (Jude 24–25).

---

# Peter's ladder of virtues

☑ Peter confirms the truth of the Gospel — *2 Peter 1:12–21*

☑ Signs of the coming apostasy — *2 Peter 2:1–22*

☑ Apostasy in the end times — *2 Peter 3:1·10*

☑ Exhortation to godly living — *2 Peter 3:11–18*

☑ Letter of Jude: History of apostasy — *Jude 1:1–7*

☑ Apostate teachers described — *Jude 1:8–19*

☑ Encouragement to believers — *Jude 1:20–23*

☑ Doxology — *Jude 1:24–25*

**FOR THOUGHT AND CONTEMPLATION**

You must have heard at least one sermon on the famous passage found in 2 Peter 1:5–11. Preachers often refer to it as "Peter's ladder of virtues". Go over it again at your leisure some time today, and ask yourself the question: "Which rung am I on?"

"Finally, brothers, whatever is true, whatever is noble, whatever is right, whatever is pure, whatever is lovely, whatever is admirable — if anything is excellent or praiseworthy — think about such things." (Phil. 4:8, NIV)

# Second letter to Timothy

☑ Paul encourages Timothy — *2 Timothy 1:1–18*

☑ The good soldier of Christ — *2 Timothy 2:1–13*

☑ The Lord's faithful servant — *2 Timothy 2:14–26*

☑ Apostasy in the last days — *2 Timothy 3:1–13*

☑ The defence of the good soldier — *2 Timothy 3:14–17, 4:1–8*

☑ Paul deserted by many — *2 Timothy 4:9–18*

☑ Final greetings — *2 Timothy 4:19–22*

Martyrdom of Peter and Paul AD 67–68

☑ First letter of John: Its purpose — *1 John 1:1–4*

☑ Dealing with sin — *1 John 1:5–10*

**FOR THOUGHT AND CONTEMPLATION**

The second letter to Timothy is really Paul's last will and testament to his spiritual son. What a wealth of wisdom it contains. Pause for a moment, and reflect on what you would write if you had to pass on to a spiritual son or daughter the things you have learned in the Christian life. If you can, write down your conclusions.

"And this is love: that we walk in obedience to his commands. As you have heard from the beginning, his command is that you walk in love." (2 Jn. 1:6, NIV)

## A BIRD'S EYE VIEW OF 1 JOHN

**Place in the Bible:**
Twenty-third New Testament book; eighteenth letter.
**Written by:**
John.
**Jesus and the letter of 1 John:**
John pictures Jesus as the One who purifies believers from sin: "But if we walk in the light, as he is in the light, we have fellowship with one another, and the blood of Jesus, his Son, purifies us from all sin" (1 John 1:7).

**Teaching:**
John wrote this letter to help Christians know for certain that they were indeed followers of Christ: "I write these things to you who believe ... so that you may know that you have eternal life" (5:13). Christ's followers have the Holy Spirit resident in them and should be characterised by a special quality of love for fellow Christians.

**A verse to remember:**
"This is how we know what love is: Jesus laid down his life for us. And we ought to lay down our lives for our brothers" (1 John 3:16).

---

# Love and obedience

Writings of John AD 95–100

☑ Obedience required — *1 John 2:1–14*

☑ Warning against worldliness and unbelief — *1 John 2:15–23*

☑ Abiding in Him — *1 John 2:24–28*

☑ God's love for us — *1 John 2:29, 3:1–2*

☑ Righteousness and sin — *1 John 3:3–10*

☑ Love in action — *1 John 3:11–24*

☑ Overcoming the world — *1 John 4:1–6*

☑ Love is of God — *1 John 4:7–21*

☑ Our victory — *1 John 5:1–12*

☑ Our confidence and security — *1 John 5:13–21*

**FOR THOUGHT AND CONTEMPLATION**

"Love," says Thomas Fuller, a great Christian philosopher, "delights not only to ascend, but also to descend." How true. This is precisely what happened at the first Christmas — Love came *down*. Let that thought simmer in your mind throughout today.

"For God so loved the world that he gave his one and only Son, that whoever believes in him shall not perish but have eternal life." (Jn 3:16, NIV)

## A BIRD'S EYE VIEW OF 2 and 3 JOHN

**Place in the Bible:**
Twenty-fourth and twenty-fifth New Testament books; nineteenth and twentieth letters.
**Written by:**
John.
**Jesus and the letter of 2 John:**
Deceivers who do not "acknowledge Jesus Christ as coming in the flesh" (v. 7) are to be avoided. The key to a relationship with God is continuing in the teaching of Christ. (v. 9).

**Teaching:**
2 John concentrates on how Christians should not have fellowship with false teachers who are enemies of the Christian Gospel. 3 John stresses the need to show hospitality to true Christian brothers and criticises one church leader (Diotrephes) for his malicious gossip and unwelcoming attitude to visiting believers.
**A verse to remember:**
"Anyone who runs ahead and does not continue in the teaching of Christ does not have God; whoever continues in the teaching has both the Father and the Son" (2 John 9).

---

TUESDAY Week 52    # Messages to the seven churches

☑ Second letter of John: Walking in the truth —
*2 John 1:1–13*

☑ Third letter of John: Gaius commended —
*3 John 1:1–8*

☑ Concerning Diotrephes and Demetrius —
*3 John 1:9–14*

☑ The book of Revelation: Introduction —
*Revelation 1:1–8*

☑ John's vision — *Revelation 1:9–20*

☑ Message to the church in Ephesus —
*Revelation 2:1–7*

☑ In Smyrna — *Revelation 2:8–11*

☑ In Pergamos — *Revelation 2:12–17*

☑ In Thyatira — *Revelation 2:18–29*

**FOR THOUGHT AND CONTEMPLATION**

What does Christ expect of His Church? The answer lies in His words to the seven churches of Asia. His message to each church is characterised by one important word. *Love*, for example, is the key word for the church at Ephesus. Now find the others.

---

" ...to present her to himself as a radiant church, without stain or wrinkle or any other blemish, but holy and blameless." (Eph. 5:27, NIV)

---

## A BIRD'S EYE VIEW OF REVELATION

**Place in the Bible:**
Twenty-seventh New Testament book; first book of prophecy.
**Written by:**
John.
**Jesus and the prophecy of Revelation:**
This book's opening verse states that it is "the revelation of Jesus Christ" and the whole book is about Jesus Christ and his glory, concluding with the words, "'Yes, I am coming soon.' Amen. Come, Lord Jesus. The grace of the Lord Jesus be with God's people. Amen" (Rev. 22:20–21).

**Teaching:**
John relates a series of visions to show that the only One who has authority to judge the world and to reign over it in righteousness is the risen Lord Jesus Christ (Rev. 19:16).

**A verse to remember:**
"Now the dwelling of God is with men, and he will live with them. They will be his people, and God himself will be with them and be their God. He will wipe every tear from their eyes. There will be no more death or mourning or crying or pain, for the old order of things has passed away" (Rev. 21:3–4).

The way to worship

☑ Message to the church in Sardis — *Revelation 3:1–6*
☑ In Philadelphia — *Revelation 3:7–13*
☑ In Laodicea — *Revelation 3:14–22*
☑ The throne of God — *Revelation 4:1–11*
☑ The sealed book — *Revelation 5:1–8*
☑ Worship of the Lamb — *Revelation 5:9–14*
☑ The six seals opened — *Revelation 6:1–17*
☑ The sealing of the 144,000 — *Revelation 7:1–8*

FOR THOUGHT AND CONTEMPLATION

"Worship," said A.W. Tozer, "is the missing jewel in the Church." It is certainly not the missing jewel in heaven. The 24 elders casting down their crowns is a form of worship. What are you willing to cast down before Him in worship today?

"God is spirit, and his worshippers must worship in spirit and in truth." (Jn. 4:24, NIV)

---

The seven trumpet judgments

☑ The multitude in heaven — *Revelation 7:9–17*
☑ The seventh seal is opened — *Revelation 8:1–6*
☑ The first four trumpets — *Revelation 8:7–13*
☑ The fifth and sixth trumpets — *Revelation 9:1–21*
☑ The angel with the little book — *Revelation 10:1–11*
☑ The Temple measured — *Revelation 11:1–2*
☑ The two witnesses — *Revelation 11:3–13*
☑ The seventh trumpet — *Revelation 11:14–19*

FOR THOUGHT AND CONTEMPLATION

If God did not institute a final day of judgment, then the universe would remain unbalanced. Judgment will surely come. If you are a Christian, then rejoice — because for you the judgment has passed. In Christ there is no more condemnation.

"Therefore, there is now no condemnation for those who are in Christ Jesus, because through Christ Jesus the law of the Spirit of life set me free from the law of sin and death." (Rom. 8:1–2, NIV)

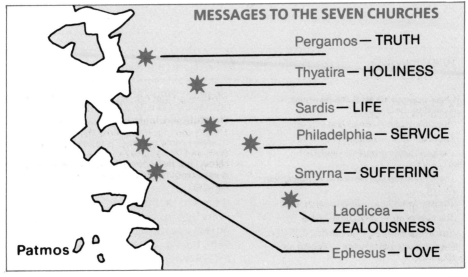

MESSAGES TO THE SEVEN CHURCHES

Pergamos — TRUTH

Thyatira — HOLINESS

Sardis — LIFE

Philadelphia — SERVICE

Smyrna — SUFFERING

Laodicea — ZEALOUSNESS

Ephesus — LOVE

Patmos

The Church and her enemies

☑ The woman, the child and the dragon —
*Revelation 12:1–8*

☑ Satan cast down to the earth — *Revelation 12:9–17*

☑ The two beasts — *Revelation 13:1–15*

☑ The mark of the beast — *Revelation 13:16–18*

☑ The followers of the Lamb — *Revelation 14:1–5*

☑ The three angels — *Revelation 14:6–13*

☑ Vision of Christ with a sickle — *Revelation 14:14–20*

☑ The song of Moses — *Revelation 15:1–4*

☑ The seven golden vials — *Revelation 15:5–8*

**FOR THOUGHT AND CONTEMPLATION**

There have been many enemies of the Church, but there is a day coming when they will be swept away for ever. Make no mistake about it — truth and righteousness will ultimately triumph.

"Then the end will come, when he hands over the kingdom to God the Father after he has destroyed all dominion, authority and power. For he must reign until he has put all his enemies under his feet." (1 Cor. 15:24–25, NIV)

---

The fall of Babylon

☑ The seven plagues — *Revelation 16:1–21*

☑ Vision of the woman sitting on the beast — *Revelation 17:1–6*

☑ Its interpretation — *Revelation 17:7–18*

☑ Destruction of Babylon — *Revelation 18:1–8*

☑ Lament for Babylon — *Revelation 18:9–19*

☑ The church to rejoice over her fall — *Revelation 18:20–24*

☑ Praise given to God — *Revelation 19:1–5*

☑ The marriage supper of the Lamb — *Revelation 19:6–10*

**FOR THOUGHT AND CONTEMPLATION**

"The Bible," someone said, "is like a tale of two cities — Babylon is one, and Jerusalem the other." Babylon represents sin, Jerusalem represents righteousness. How reassuring to learn that there will be a new Jerusalem, but not a new Babylon. Hallelujah — sin is to be removed — *forever*.

"But you have come to Mount Zion, to the heavenly Jerusalem, the city of the living God. You have come to thousands upon thousands of angels in joyful assembly, to the church of the first-born, whose names are written in heaven ..." (Heb. 12:22–23, NIV)

---

The new heaven and new earth

☑ Christ destroys the beast and his armies — *Revelation 19:11–21*

☑ The millennium — *Revelation 20:1–6*

☑ The final battle — *Revelation 20:7–10*

☑ The great white throne — *Revelation 20:11–15*

☑ The new heaven and new earth — *Revelation 21:1–8*

☑ The new Jerusalem — *Revelation 21:9–27*

☑ The river of life — *Revelation 22:1–5*

☑ Free invitation to all — *Revelation 22:6–19*

☑ Final promise and blessing — *Revelation 22:20–21*

**FOR THOUGHT AND CONTEMPLATION**

The Bible ends with the glorious hope of Christ's coming. Notice how the affirmation, "Surely I come quickly," is followed by a swift and immediate response — "Even so, come, Lord Jesus." How swift and immediate is your response to the thought of Christ's coming?

" ...'Amen! Praise and glory and wisdom and thanks and honour and power and strength be to our God for ever and ever. Amen!'" (Rev. 7:12, NIV)